State of Darkness

US Complicity in Genocides Since 1945

David Model

authorHOUSE®

AuthorHouse™
1663 Liberty Drive, Suite 200
Bloomington, IN 47403
www.authorhouse.com
Phone: 1-800-839-8640

First published by AuthorHouse 4/29/2008

ISBN: 978-1-4343-7516-2 (sc)

Printed in the United States of America
Bloomington, Indiana

This book is printed on acid-free paper.

<u>DEDICATION</u>

Children's oblivious frolicking in the street,
The cubicles in the market replete with wares,
Vendors beseeching people in the crowded square,
Customers foraging for bargained provisions,
The smell of food permeating the air,
Clothes and trinkets crowding the shelves,
None of which portends their unforeseen fate.

A faint drone above whispers its omen,
Children's eyes frozen in fear,
Recognizing the approaching scourge above,
The drone announcing its fateful mission.
Screams and wailing replace idle banter,
Debris from the cubicles litter the laneway,
Holes become monuments to those who vanished,
The innocence of children violated again.

Wanton destruction's unremitting journey,
Leaving unanswered questions in its path,
As to why such vile deeds are accepted by so many.
The seeds of social progress so desperately needed,
Having failed to germinate into a communal flower,
Deprived of sunlight by the immaturity of man,
Resulting in the fleeting death of children,
Whose only sin was their place of birth.

By David Model

ACKNOWLEDGEMENTS

I am deeply indebted to my wife, Nancy Sperling, for all her hard work in editing the text and for being my harshest critic in order to encourage me to do my best work. Her patience and understanding were vital to the success of this project.

As well, I would also like to thank my colleagues at Seneca College for the insights derived from our many discussions on the issues covered in this book.

Finally, I am very appreciative of the support of Lisa Metcalf at AuthorHouse whose friendly and intelligent contribution made the whole publishing process that much easier.

CONTENTS

1 HIROSHIMA AND NAGASAKI: A millionth of a second.   1

2 GUATEMALA: Smoke and mirrors.   12

3 VIETNAM: Destroying a nation to save it.   35

4 CAMBODIA: Double jeopardy.   56

5 LAOS: Innocent bystander.   77

6 INDONESIA: Our son of a bitch.   91

7 EAST TIMOR: Where have all the villages gone?   110

8 IRAQ – 1990: Riches to rags.   124

9 IRAQ: SANCTIONS: Death by a thousand cuts.   144

10 IRAQ—2003: Bloodied and bowed.   164

INTRODUCTION

Most adults in North America can recite the pedagogical couplet, "In 1492 Columbus sailed the ocean blue," and remember Christopher Columbus as the explorer who discovered the New World. "Columbus Day" is a commemoration of his bold achievements in traveling to the New World, cementing his stature in history as one of the great explorers. Notwithstanding this testimonial to his greatness, there are 2,787,000 (U.S. Census Bureau, 2004-2005) Americans who vehemently oppose the celebration of someone whom they consider to be the moral equivalent of Hitler. The real and savage legacy of Columbus was that he was the forerunner of a succession of mass murders who all but eliminated the native population in the Western Hemisphere, including a 97.5 percent reduction in the American native population by the end of the nineteenth century.

In 1493, Columbus returned to the new world with an invasion force of seventeen ships to conquer the local inhabitants and steal their wealth. Upon arrival, he declared himself governor and viceroy of the Caribbean islands and settled on the island of Española, now known as Haiti and the Dominican Republic.

Any obstacle posed by the native Taino population, who already occupied the land in the Caribbean, was quickly overcome through displacement, enslavement, and extermination. They were forced to abandon their well-cultivated fields to work as slave laborers for their conquerors. As well, all Taino natives over the age of fourteen were required to give a hawk's bell of gold to the Spaniards every three months or both their hands were cut off. Extermination assumed many shocking forms, including burning at the stake, hacking children into pieces for dog food, hanging, or roasting on spits.

When Columbus first arrived in the Caribbean, there were about eight million native inhabitants, but when he departed in 1500, his savagery and brutality had reduced their numbers to 100,000 (*A Little Matter of Genocide*, Ward Churchill). He had virtually annihilated the entire Taino population in the Caribbean, setting a model for future explorers who were also encumbered by a local native population.

In 1585, following Columbus, the first British permanent colonists, led by Sir Walter Raleigh, settled on territory now known as North Carolina. Despite the fact that the natives were very hospitable and not only fed the colonists but taught them to farm, Sir Walter Raleigh, with a fresh supply of recruits from the next British supply ship, murdered the entire native population. This brutal act was a precursor of the treatment to be inflicted on the natives throughout America.

The history of Thanksgiving echoes the same sort of gratitude shown by Sir Walter Raleigh. When colonists arrived at the Plymouth colony in 1620, they were rescued by the local inhabitants, who shared their food and showed them how to farm. Their reward was extermination.

Several myths persist about the fate of the natives in America with the intent of minimizing the extent of the slaughter, including underestimating the original population, obfuscating or suppressing data, and attributing their death to disease inadvertently introduced by the European settlers. In an exhaustive study, Ward Churchill, in *A Little Matter of Genocide,* definitively dispels these myths and elucidates the real causes of the disappearance of between twelve and fifteen million natives (*A Little Matter of Genocide,* Ward Churchill).

Many diabolical methods were exploited by the colonists to expunge such a large population of aboriginal people. Jesuits and then Franciscan missionaries subjected the natives, who were rounded up by the military, to slave labor without providing them with adequate nutrition, thus causing their death. Many died during the "trail of tears" marches after the 1830 Indian Removal Act sanctioned the relocation of Indians to lands west of the Mississippi by forcing them to march as much as 300 miles without provisions and adequate food. One of the more popular methods of annihilating the natives who occupied the land so coveted by the colonists was to destroy their means of survival. Destruction of their canoes and fishing gear along with burning their agricultural land and villages deprived the aboriginal peoples of the means to feed and house themselves and to maintain their health.

Thwarting the natives' ability to survive was a major contributing factor in the so-called "Indian Wars," which began soon after the arrival of the first settlers and ended in the 1890 Wounded Knee Massacre. In fact, the designation "Indian Wars" is very misleading because it creates the impression, popularized in the popular culture, that Indians were warlike, savage, and aggressive. One excellent example occurred at Wounded Knee, where the Seventh Cavalry captured about 350 Lakota Sioux and massacred 300.

Another method of annihilation was biological warfare, which was an efficient method for destroying an entire village. By distributing blankets from military smallpox hospitals masked as gifts to the natives, contamination of the entire village was guaranteed.

By 1900, survivors of the pogrom of Native Americans were forced to live on 2.5 percent of their former land where it was virtually impossible to grow crops. Even after their virtual eradication and their isolation on arid, remote lands, they were subject to a policy of assimilation in order to destroy any vestiges of their culture, customs, language, and identity. Native children were kidnapped at an early age and placed in boarding schools where they were forbidden to practice their traditions or speak their language in an effort to completely wipe out any trace of these "savages."

The treatment of the indigenous people by American colonists and later the American government was clearly a crime against humanity that seems to transcend all others. Mass murder does not capture the enormity of a crime that seeks to exterminate an entire people or to prevent their existence.

Twenty-five years after Wounded Knee, a massacre of an entire national group erupted in Turkey. The Armenian minority in Ottoman Turkey had been subjected to periodic abuse at the hands of staunchly nationalistic Turks. In 1915, during World War I, the Turks drove the Armenians from their homes and proceeded to massacre between 800,000 and one million people.

Shocked by the Turkish massacre of the Armenian population,

the subsequent failure of the Turkish leaders to suffer any consequences for their crime, and the protection sovereignty afforded the perpetrators, Raphael Lemkin, a Polish Jew and international lawyer, launched a crusade to create a new international convention for crimes against humanity in which an entire group was targeted.

His ongoing interest in the subject of mass killing was based on his fear that such crimes could arise again and on his conviction that a new international law was called for to prevent and punish crimes of a similar nature. In pursuit of this goal, he spoke out at an international crime conference in 1933 in Madrid where he summoned the international community to unite for the purpose of framing a new law.

Lemkin was now on an impassioned mission to convince the world that it was necessary to adopt a new international law prohibiting massacres similar to the one suffered by the Armenians. His crusade and its support reached a crossroads when the atrocities committed by the Third Reich were uncovered. Their crime of planning and carrying out the attempted extermination of entire groups, in particular the Jews, simply because they belonged to that group, exceeded in barbarism and savagery other crimes against humanity. The commission of such crimes meant that a whole people, their culture, and customs would simply disappear from existence.

While the Nazi military juggernaut rolled across Europe, Winston Churchill spoke of the extermination of "whole districts" and referred to the crime as "a crime without a name." Lemkin realized that he needed to search for a word that was truly unique, and after giving it much thought, combined the Greek derivative *geno* meaning "race" or "tribe" with the Latin derivative *cide* meaning "killing" and formed the word *genocide*.

Genocide clearly applied to Hitler's slaughter of six million Jews and five million Poles, Communists, Gypsies, and homosexuals. The hideous enormity of the killing induced American and European leaders to become more open to loosening the definition of sovereignty, which had been one of the major obstacles to creating an international law that violated territorial integrity. When Lemkin became encouraged that his ideas pertaining to a law on genocide would be better received, he fought in the capitals of Europe and in Washington for a resolution on genocide in the embryonic General Assembly of the United Nations. On December 11, 1946, the General Assembly introduced Resolution 96 (1), *The Crime of Genocide*, which begins:

> Genocide is a denial of the right of existence of entire human groups…such denial of the right of existence shocks the conscience of mankind, results in great losses to humanity in the form of cultural and other contributions represented by these human groups and is contrary to moral law and to the spirit and aims of the United Nations.

It then affirms that:

> Genocide is a crime under international law which the civilized world condemns and for the commission of which principals and accomplices—whether private individuals, public officials and statesmen, and whether the crime is committed on religious, racial, or political or any other grounds—are punishable.

The resolution called for the creation of a committee to draft the new law. Lemkin attended almost every session of the legal committee of the United Nations and lobbied anyone whom he could corner about the moral imperative of passing a law prohibiting genocide. On December 9, 1948, the committee approved a draft and submitted it to the General Assembly for a vote in which fifty-five delegates voted yes and none voted no. Article II and III of the text reads as follows:

> Article II: In the present Convention, genocide means any of the following acts committed with intent to destroy, in whole or in part, a national, ethnical, racial, or religious group, as such:
>
> 1. Killing members of the group;
>
> 2. Causing serious bodily or mental harm to members of the group;

3. Deliberately inflicting on the group conditions of life calculated to bring about its physical destruction in whole or in part;

4. Imposing measures intended to prevent births within the group;

5. Forcibly transferring children of the group to another group.

Article III: The following acts should be punishable:

1. Genocide;

2. Conspiracy to commit genocide;

3. Direct and public incitement to commit genocide;

4. Attempt to commit genocide;

5. Complicity in genocide.

Though the convention had passed the General Assembly, twenty nations had to ratify it domestically before it became law. Full ratification entails a nation enacting "implementing legislation" that criminalizes genocide in the ratifying country. On October 16, 1950, the twentieth nation ratified the Genocide Convention.

Surprisingly, the United States did not ratify the convention for another thirty-eight years. One of the impediments to ratification in the United States was the wording of the text in the convention in which certain key terms were not clearly defined, such as in the phrase "in whole or in part," which opened the door to many interpretations. Southern senators warned that the Genocide Convention could be invoked on the basis of "in whole and in part" to charge lynch mobs in the South for their treatment of blacks and to overturn Jim Crow laws.

On the question of the meaning of "in part," the American Bar Association (ABA), the convention's most powerful critic, supported the southern senators' apprehension that a few armed citizens causing harm to a people of a racial minority would face charges of committing genocide. In addition, the ABA was fearful about more federal interference in state's rights, which violated the Tenth Amendment. There were opponents who feared an investigation into the eradication of Native Americans in the nineteenth century. Samantha Power identifies the underlying problem as, "American opposition was rooted in a traditional hostility toward any infringement on U.S. sovereignty" (*A Problem from Hell: America and the Age of Genocide,* Samantha Power, p. 69).

Ratification of the Genocide Convention languished in a state of inertia until William Proxmire, the senator from Wisconsin, perplexed by the Senate's paralysis on this issue, stood up in the Senate in 1967 and delivered his maiden speech on genocide. Proxmire's unflagging and relentless campaign of daily speeches in the Senate injected new blood into the ratification project; however, ratification of the Genocide Convention seemed to lack the urgency and flamboyancy to attract a sufficient number of strong supporters. One positive step toward ratification occurred when the ABA dropped its opposition in 1976.

Ratification inched closer to realization on every occasion when the Soviet Union accused the United States of human rights violations and threw the absence of ratification of the Genocide Convention in America's face. The final catalyst resulted from an error in judgment on the part of President Reagan. The White House had planned a visit to West Germany's Bitburg cemetery where the President intended to lay a wreath to commemorate the end of World War II, overlooking the fact that forty-nine Nazi Waffen SS officials were buried at that site. At the same time, Reagan had refused invitations to visit Holocaust memorials. Many U.S. Senators, the Jewish lobby, and other Jewish organizations expressed their shocked outrage at the naively insensitive decision. Reagan's defense of his decision didn't appease his opponents, and his popularity suffered accordingly. On May 5, 1985, when he visited Bitburg, there were demonstrations in Boston, Miami, New Haven, Newark, Atlanta, West Hartford, and Milwaukee. Having dug himself into a deep hole, President Reagan ratified the Genocide Convention with the intention of restoring people's faith in him.

Another major obstacle to ratification was fear that the United States or its officials could be judged by an international court, as it had been when Nicaragua won its case after filing charges in 1984 against the mining of its harbors. The Senate demanded that ratification included an "opt-out" clause that granted the president the right to decide when consent would be granted to the court's jurisdiction. In other words, the United States included the power to decide when the International Court of Justice had jurisdiction in any case involving the United States. "Opt-out" provisions in U.S. law are covered under legal provisions called Reservations, Understandings, and Declarations or RUDs, which state that, "with reference to Article IX of the Convention, before any dispute to which the United States is a party may be submitted to the jurisdiction of the International Court of Justice, the specific consent of the United States is required in each case."

The "opt-out" clause automatically triggered the doctrine of reciprocity, which would prohibit the United States from ever laying genocide charges against any other nation or its leaders. If the U.S. filed genocide charges against another country, that country would be allowed to invoke the reciprocity doctrine and incorporate the "opt-out" clause into its own implementing legislation, which would be honored by the courts.

Finally, on February 11, 1986, the U.S Senate adopted a resolution to draw up ratifying legislation. Full ratification would incorporate the Genocide Convention into American federal law adjusted for any changes written into the implementing legislation. In October 1988, the Senate approved the Genocide Convention and named it the "Proxmire Act," honoring William Proxmire in recognition of his dedication to achieving ratification.

The United States discovered during the ratification process that some of the terms in the Genocide Convention were vague, resulting in different interpretations of the convention, exemplified by the diverse analysis of many scholars on the subject. Two of the terms open to different interpretations are "in whole or in part" and "intent." As well, the meaning of "complicity" must be clearly defined and the definition of "group" must be clarified.

If "in whole or in part" was intended to mean "almost all," then the obligation of ratifying states to suppress any further genocide kicks in too late to save many of the victims. If it was intended to mean very few, the door would then be open to abuse, as countries would exploit the definition to use force against the alleged offending state. Lemkin's original intention was that the level of destruction should be sufficiently substantial to imperil the existence of the group. Lemkin defined genocide to be "…a coordinated plan of different actions aimed at the destruction of the essential foundations of the life of national groups with the aim of annihilating the groups themselves." The key for Lemkin was the *intention* to destroy the whole group rather than actual destruction of the entire group. In a paper written for the Preparatory Commission of the International Criminal Court, Amnesty International interprets "in part" to mean: "It is sufficient to impose criminal responsibility for genocide if the accused aimed to destroy a large number of the group in a particular community." Amnesty International's interpretation broadens the scope of crimes of genocide by removing the requirement that the defendants intended to destroy the whole group and replaced it with the need to show that they only intended to destroy "a large number of the group." The International Criminal Tribunal for the former Yugoslavia broadened the scope even further by concluding that "…the killing of all members of part of a group located within a small geographical area…would qualify as genocide if carried out with the intent to destroy the part of the group as such located in this small geographical area." There is no consensus on the meaning of "in part," and only precedents set by courts trying cases of genocide will sharpen its focus.

As well, proving "intent" is problematic. One of the dangers of establishing "intent" is that any action to thwart further acts of genocide must be postponed until "intent" is clearly proven. Intent can be proven by examining orders or statements of suspects or by a "coordinated systematic pattern of coordinated acts." In a report to the United Nations, Benjamin Whitaker argued that "…a court should be able to infer necessary intent from sufficient evidence, and that in certain cases this would include actions or omissions of such a degree of criminal negligence or recklessness that the defendant must reasonably be assumed to have been aware of the consequences of his conduct" (*The UN Report on Genocide 1985*, Benjamin Whitaker). According to Whitaker, if a defendant could reasonably have predicted that his actions or lack thereof would have resulted in genocide notwithstanding any deliberate attempt to commit it, it is reasonable to assume that he knew he was committing genocide, and that constitutes "intent." Robert Gellately and Ben Kiernan agree with Whitaker's interpretation of "intent" and argue that:

> In this legal definition genocidal intent also implies acts of destruction that are not the specific goal but are predictable outcomes or by-products of a policy, which may have been avoided by a change in that policy. Deliberate pursuits of any policy in the knowledge that it would lead to the destruction of a human group thus constitutes genocidal intent.

(*The Specter of Genocide: Mass Murder in Historical Perspective*, Edited by Robert Gellately and Ben Kiernan, p. 15)

In addition to the ambiguity of terms, the issue of which targeted groups should be included in the convention triggered heated debates over whether groups such as political, cultural, economic, and sexual groups needed the protection of a law prohibiting and punishing genocide.

No issue was subjected to more debate than the decision as to whether to include political groups. There were a number of opponents to incorporating political groups into the convention. These opponents included several Latin American countries that feared the inclusion of "political groups" because it would limit their ability to suppress insurgencies; the Soviet Union, who feared that Stalin would be charged with exterminating minorities throughout Central Asia; and the United States, who feared violations of their sovereignty by an international criminal court. The issue of "political groups" was resolved when an agreement was struck between the United States and the Soviet Union whereby the United States would agree to drop political groups from the classification of groups in the convention in exchange for the removal of any reference to an international criminal court. Lemkin's support for the removal of "political groups" was based on his apprehension that too many states would otherwise oppose the convention.

"To destroy, in whole or in part, a national, ethnic, racial or religious group" does not explicitly include destruction of a group's culture, although United Nations Resolution 96 (see above) states that genocide "results in great losses to humanity in the form of cultural and other contributions." Since the loss of culture can occur without physically destroying the group through the abolition of language, restrictions on tradition, practices, and customs, and attacks on intellectuals, artists, musicians, and authors, the distinctiveness of the group is lost through cultural destruction as well as physical destruction. If a group disappears because of destruction of their culture, culture is implied as a group by the Genocide Convention. As well, the United Nations Declaration of Human Rights, which took effect on December 10, 1948, states in Article 27, Paragraph 1, "Everyone has the right to freely participate in the cultural life of the community, to enjoy the arts and to share in scientific advancement and its benefits." Furthermore, the United Nations International Covenant on Economic, Social and Cultural Rights, which took effect on January 3, 1976, states in Article 15, Paragraph 1 that, "the States Parties to the present Covenant recognize the right of everyone:...To take part in cultural life." Most importantly, according to the International Criminal Tribunal for the Former Yugoslavia, acts of cultural genocide were referred to as the "very foundation of the group" and held that the Serbian destruction of Muslim libraries and mosques and attacks on cultural leaders established genocidal intent against Muslims in the former Yugoslavia. Therefore, "destruction" will apply to the loss of culture as well as the loss of life.

Another important term that needs clarification is the term "complicity." The meaning of "complicity" in international law is defined more specifically than the meaning according to the dictionary. The Merriam-Webster dictionary defines complicity as "association or participating in or as if in a wrongful act."

The Nuremberg Principles don't explicitly define "complicity," but Article 6 states that

> Leaders, organizers, instigators, accomplices participating in the formulation or execution of a common plan or conspiracy to commit any of the foregoing crimes are responsible for all acts performed by any persons in execution of such a plan.

Christopher Kutz, professor of legal philosophy, defines those who are complicit in international law as those who are:

> Marginally effective participants in a collective harm [who] are accountable for the victim's suffering, not because the individual differences they make, but because their intentional participation in a collective endeavour directly links them to the consequences of that endeavour. The notion of participation rather than causation is at the heart of both complicity and collective action.

According to this interpretation, the question is not how much an individual contributed to the consequences of a harmful act as much as the fact that they intentionally participated in an endeavour with harmful consequences.

There are legal precedents to shed further light on the question of complicity, such as Milosevic's trial at the Hague Tribunal. Cecile Aptel, a policy coordinator for the prosecution in Milosevic's case, argued that it is not necessary to prove intent but only necessary to prove that Milosevic knew that the Bosnian Serbs had genocidal intent.

Several important principles emanate from these definitions. One is that in order for a party to be complicit, they must have knowledge of the genocidal intent of the perpetrators. Second, complicity is not related to the extent of their contribution to the consequences of genocide, only to the fact that they had knowledge of the genocide. Furthermore, complicity does not require that there was intent on the part of the complicit individual(s) but only that there was knowledge of the genocidal intent of the perpetrators.

Complicity for the purposes of the analysis in this book shall mean:

1. Intentional participation in an act of genocide;

2. Participation will include organizing, planning, supplying arms, advice, training, intelligence, any direct military support such as planes, ships, ground troops, or any form of construction necessary for the commission of genocide;

3. Knowledge of the genocidal intent of the perpetrators;

4. Genocidal intent is not required for those charged with complicity.

Despite the disagreements over the interpretation of the convention, a number of cases have been brought before various courts to prosecute cases of genocide against responsible officials in those countries. Special ad hoc tribunals have been established to hold trials for those accused of genocide, including the International Criminal Tribunal for the Former Yugoslavia where Serbian leaders were prosecuted for alleged genocide against groups in Bosnia and Kosovo, and the International Criminal Tribunal for Rwanda where extreme Hutus were prosecuted for genocide against the Tutsis and moderate Hutus.

These ad hoc tribunals were necessary due to the lack of progress on the part of the United Nations in creating a permanent court. An international court dedicated to prosecuting genocide and other crimes against humanity was first proposed in 1948 when the General Assembly adopted Resolution 260, which indicated that the offense of genocide "shall be tried by a competent tribunal of the State in the territory of which the act was committed or by such international penal tribunal as may have jurisdiction..." and invited the International Law Commission (ILC) "to study the desirability and possibility of establishing an international judicial organ for the trial of persons charged with genocide…" From 1949 to 1954, the ILC prepared several draft statutes for such a court, but disagreements forestalled further progress. In 1994, the ILC completed its work on the draft statute, which was adopted by the United Nations in 1998 and enforced on July 1, 2002, after the sixtieth ratification by member nations. The ILC is not an organ of the United Nations but an independent organization with an independent budget.

The ILC consists of 103 member states as of November 1, 2006, but Lemkin's dream was not fully realized when the United States refused to become a member. The U.S. refusal to join is not a mystery given that the United States is by far the most powerful military power in the world with the largest economy. The ever-expanding empire has used its military and economic power to expand its hegemony to the far corners of the planet to ensure military dominance, to enrich its multinational corporations, to secure access to vital resources, and to force its economic system onto noncompliant nations.

For example, the United States used its military power to secure control of Iraqi oil; to overthrow the democratically elected government of Jacobo Arbenz in Guatemala in 1954 in order to preserve the holdings of the United Fruit Company; to invade Panama in 1989 to maintain control over the Panama Canal; to undermine the government of Daniel Ortega during the 1980s due to his refusal to become compliant; to assassinate Patrice Lumumba in 1960 because he declared his neutrality during the Cold War; to assassinate Salvador Allende in 1973 because he threatened American multinationals with nationalization; to support Suharto's massacre of his opponents in 1965 to create a bulwark against the expansion of communism; and to overthrow the democratically elected Mossadegh in Iran in 1953 to protect British and American oil multinationals.

Many atrocities were committed in the process of forcing these nations to serve the strategic and economic interests of the United States. Some of these atrocities qualify as genocide under the UN Convention. Notwithstanding the absence of any actual intent to commit genocide, the consequences of American actions could have been clearly predicted by any reasonable person and, therefore, qualify as genocide. According to many scholars on the subject of genocide, motivation is not to be confused with intent. If the known consequences of a set of policies result in genocide, "intent" is then said to exist.

In order to determine which atrocities qualify as genocide, I will apply the UN Convention to possible cases of American genocide and will also incorporate any interpretations of ambiguous terms that have been advocated by leading scholars in the field or are based on decisions of the courts. There have not been sufficient precedents established by the courts at this time to base interpretations on precedents alone.

I will adhere strictly to the convention and will only consider the slaughter of national, ethnic, religious, cultural, or racial groups as acts of genocide.

"In whole or in part" will mean one of the following:

1. A level of destruction that is sufficiently substantial to imperil the existence of the group (Lemkin's original intention)

2. "The accused aimed to destroy a large part of the group in a particular community;" (Reporter for the Preparatory Commission of the International Criminal Court)

3. "…the killing of all members of the group located within a small geographical area" (International Criminal court for the Former Yugoslavia)

"Intent" occurs when:

1. "Intent" can be proven by examining orders, statements, or a systematic pattern of coordinated acts

2. "Actions or omissions of such criminal negligence or recklessness that the defendant must reasonably be assumed to have been aware of the consequences

of his conduct" (Benjamin Whitaker's report to the UN)

3. "Acts of destruction that are not the specific goal but are predictable outcomes or by-products of a policy, which may have been avoided by a change in that policy" (Robert Gellately and Ben Kiernan)

The remaining clauses in the convention will be interpreted in the strictest possible sense without allowing any leeway for nuance of meaning.

Applying the convention can sometimes be problematic; however, in the case of the bombing of Hiroshima and Nagasaki in 1945, none of the ambiguities of the Genocide Convention become an impediment to concluding that the United States committed genocide.

The next case is somewhat more complex. American atrocities against Guatemala involved overthrowing Jacobo Arbenz in 1954, a democratically elected leader, because he put the interests of his own people ahead of the interests of American multinationals. He was replaced with a series of brutal dictators who were able to remain in power with U.S. assistance. The Guatemalan people were then subjected to repression and savagery at the hands of these tyrants who murdered 300,000 Mayans. America shares complicity in this genocide.

An example of the direct use of American military power took place between 1954 and 1973 in Vietnam where American forces were responsible for over three million deaths as well as massive destruction of the countryside. The United States is guilty of genocide in Vietnam.

Cambodia is a difficult case. The United States bombed the countryside, killing 600,000 people. This directly contributed to the rise of the Khmer Rouge in 1975, who killed another two million people during the four years they were in power. The United States is guilty of both genocide for the bombing of Cambodia and complicity in the genocide perpetrated by the Khmer Rouge.

Laos was also a victim of genocide perpetrated by the Americans. An American-supported government excluded the Pathet Lao, a group who had fought the French for the independence of Laos. Subsequently, the Pathet Lao formed an insurgency group to overthrow the government in Vientiane and received support from North Vietnamese troops who were protecting the Ho Chi Minh Trail. The United States bombed the countryside indiscriminately to destroy the Pathet Lao and the section of the trail running through Laos. American actions constituted genocide.

A typical example of American intervention occurred in Indonesia where General Suharto overthrew President Sukarno in 1965 with the assistance of the United States. With American military aid, General Suharto was able to maintain himself in power until 1998, during which time he murdered 600,000 opponents and committed genocide in East Timor. The United States is complicit in the genocides committed by Suharto.

The United States was clearly complicit in genocide in East Timor. They armed Indonesia and gave them the green light for the invasion, during the course of which, one-third of the population was murdered.

Saddam Hussein was maneuvered into invading Kuwait by the United States, giving Washington the opportunity to declare war against Iraq. The U.S. and its partners bombed Iraq back into the pre-industrial age, destroying the infrastructure and killing over 100,000 people. The United States is unequivocally guilty of genocide in Iraq.

Iraqis were victims of sanctions imposed by the United Nations but controlled by the United States. Due to the sanctions, which were effective from 1990 and 2002, Iraqis were denied medical equipment, drugs, and equipment to repair essential utilities. The sanctions were responsible for the death of a million people, half of whom were children. The sanctions accelerated the process of genocide, and America is guilty of genocide for imposing the sanctions.

In 2003, the United States again bombed Iraq and then imposed a military occupation on a country that had already endured colossal suffering. Conditions today are worse than they were before the bombing in 2003. Furthermore, Iraq has been plunged into an internecine, sectarian war by the military occupation. America has even further destroyed this once prosperous country and is again guilty of genocide.

I will prove in the following chapters beyond a reasonable doubt that all the above atrocities qualify as acts of genocide by assessing each case according to the terms of the Genocide Convention and the criteria discussed in the introduction.

Ignoring the international judicial system, the United States has committed international crimes with impunity because no other power or coalition of powers has been capable of forcing the American government to give up its leaders for trial or to enforce any penalties imposed by the courts. Impunity has endowed the United States with a license to project force wherever American interests were at stake. In total, these acts of genocide represent the barbarous, unconscionable destruction of life and property of a hegemonic superpower with an unrelenting, implacable blueprint for amassing power and wealth to enrich its multinational corporations.

HIROSHIMA AND NAGASAKI: A MILLIONTH OF A SECOND.

In a mere millionth of a second, the Japanese cities of Hiroshima and Nagasaki were leveled to the ground on August 6 and 9, 1945, respectively, causing all of their citizens near ground zero to be vaporized. In total, 135,000 people perished instantly. Incredibly, President Truman claimed that dropping the two atom bombs saved millions of lives and staved off the exigency of invading mainland Japan with ground forces.

In reality, the decision to use the bomb deliberately overlooked the fact that Japan was already defeated and had lost the capacity and the will to prolong the war any further. In addition, Japan was desperately trying to surrender.

In fact, the tragic dropping of two atomic weapons was not the end of World War II but the beginning of the Cold War. The Truman administration was cognizant of the fact that the Soviet Union would challenge the United States for world domination after World War II, and President Truman was determined, by flaunting the enormous power of the new weapon, to demonstrate to the USSR that they should exercise restraint when attempting to expand their sphere of influence after World War II.

Truman's determination to use the bomb as a warning precluded any interest in accepting a Japanese surrender. Long before Hiroshima was bombed, the Japanese were desperately offering to surrender through a number of embassies in allied countries including the Soviet Union, Switzerland, and Portugal. American leaders were aware of Japanese peace feelers from diplomatic intercepts (the Japanese code had been broken before the war) and could have ended the war without the unnecessary loss of life in Hiroshima and Nagasaki.

Additionally, military leaders did not conduct a legitimate investigation into the number of lives that might be saved by dropping two atomic bombs, and surprisingly, most of the top military leaders believed that using the atomic bomb was unnecessary and mistaken.

Using nuclear weapons was also a barbaric mistake inasmuch as they were dropped on nonmilitary targets and constituted crimes against humanity. In this chapter, it will be proven that these crimes against humanity constituted genocide.

When Truman made the decision to use two nuclear weapons, Japan was already defeated. She had lost most of her Pacific empire to the Americans in brutal battles where their defensive perimeter in the Pacific Ocean continually shrank as American forces inched closer to mainland Japan through fierce battles in the Solomon, Marshall, and Mariana Islands. The Philippines fell next, after which the two key islands, Iwo Jima and Okinawa, close to the Japanese mainland, were taken by American ground forces in savage battles where the American Marines sustained immense losses. The United States had now prepared the way for bombing of Japan with conventional weapons.

Even before Okinawa, U.S. submarines were mercilessly destroying unprotected merchant vessels by the middle of 1943, forcing the Japanese to use escort protection for their merchant ships. Submarine attacks continued, and by the end of 1944, the United States had sunk half of Japan's merchant fleet. The loss of merchant vessels had severely diminished Japan's supply of natural resources, food, and oil, and by the summer of 1945, American submarines had a chokehold on the traffic of merchant vessels serving Japan. The lack of incoming supplies was beginning to cause starvation among the Japanese people.

In addition to the damage inflicted by American submarines, American bombers were unleashing a tempest of bombs on Japanese cities and industries. On June 14, 1944, American planes bombed the huge steel and iron complex in Yawata on the island of Kyushu followed by a series of bombing attacks on aircraft industries in Tokyo and in a number of other Japanese cities.

In February 1945, further bombing missions struck at Kobe,

2

Japan's sixth-largest city with incendiary bombs, destroying five of twelve factories and a shipyard. A second attack with incendiary bombs struck Tokyo and destroyed 28,000 structures (homes, factories, etc.) followed by another raid on Tokyo where sixteen square miles of the city was incinerated and 267,000 buildings were destroyed. More than 83,000 people were killed and another 41,000 were injured.

By the end of February 1945, Japan's cities had been severely damaged, the industrial base virtually destroyed, the navy and air force rendered virtually useless, and the people of Japan were suffering from a lack of food. The U.S. military command was now faced with the decision as to whether to continue to fight, demand surrender, or use the new bomb.

Well before the United States was discussing its options about ending the war, the Tojo government in Japan was replaced by the Koiso government in 1944. There was a new cabinet who, along with the emperor, were in favor of bringing hostilities to an end. Koiso covertly urged the Soviet Union to assist him in securing a mediated peace, but the Soviets did not want the war to end before they had conquered more Japanese territory for postwar strategic reasons.

Truman was aware (Potsdam Papers) of Japanese peace feelers to other embassies, which had been intercepted by American intelligence. For example, on August 11, 1944, American intelligence had intercepted messages to the Japanese Embassy in Moscow ascertaining whether Russia was willing to assist in bringing about peace. On May 7, 1945, Portugal transmitted a peace feeler directly to Truman reporting that "...the Japanese are ready to cease hostilities, provided they are allowed to retain possession of their home lands."

Notwithstanding the fact that the Japanese were no longer capable of prolonging the war much further, in April 1945, the Joint Chiefs of Staff ordered their field commanders to prepare for the invasion of mainland Japan. They presented their plan to President Truman with an unsubstantiated rough estimate of the number of American lives that would be lost in such an invasion.

The loss of American lives in an invasion of the mainland was the major argument for using the new atomic weapon; however, many high-ranking officers in the U.S. military disagreed with the estimate of the number of lives that would have been lost and thus were strongly opposed to the use of the new weapon. The Chairman of the Joint Chiefs of Staff, Fleet Admiral William D. Leay, recognized that "…the use of this barbarous weapon at Hiroshima and Nagasaki was of no material assistance in our war against Japan" (*Was Hiroshima Necessary to End the War*, Gar? Alperovitz). On September 20, 1945, Major General Curtis E. LeMay made it clear that "the atomic bomb had nothing to do with the end of the war at all" (*The Decision to Use the Bomb*, Gar Alperovitz). According to Admiral William Halsey, Commander of the Third Fleet, "The first atomic bomb was an unnecessary experiment…It was a mistake ever to drop it." General Dwight Eisenhower commented that "I voiced…my grave misgivings…on the basis of my belief that Japan was already defeated and that dropping the bomb was completely unnecessary."

The opinions of the military commanders were irrelevant anyway because Truman didn't consult them about his options for ending the war, preferring to predicate his decision to a large extent on the advice of Secretary of State J. Byrnes. He was Truman's closest advisor and strongly supported the use of the bomb. Byrnes exercised enormous influence on the important Interim Committee, appointed by Truman on April 25, 1945, to evaluate all options on how to end the war. The Interim Committee recommended that "…the Secretary of War should be advised that…the present view of the Committee was that the bomb should be used…on a war plant surrounded by workers' homes."

Further, it should be noted that the committee only called for the bombing of a primarily military target, but Truman bombed two cities in which there was an absence of military targets, an important fact that he hid from the American people. In a speech on August 9, 1945, Truman lied by claiming that "the world will note that the first atomic bomb was dropped on Hiroshima, a military base. That was because we wished in this first attack to avoid, insofar as possible, the killing of civilians" (Public Papers of the Presidents of the United States). This is further evidence that Truman was not just interested in ending the war but that he felt compelled to stage a massive demonstration of the power of the atom bomb.

As well as suggesting a target, the committee recommended the preservation of the institution of emperor. Such a guarantee would have facilitated Japan's decision to surrender given the historical and symbolic nature of this institution. American demands for an unconditional surrender precluded a promise to preserve the institution of emperor. It is tragically ironic that despite Japan's eventual unconditional surrender, Truman did not insist on the elimination of the institution of emperor. This decision of President Truman indicated that he might have withheld any guarantees about the emperor in order to delay surrender until he could use the bomb.

With the committee's recommendation and the plan for the invasion of Japan in his back pocket, Truman agreed to meet with Churchill and Stalin (the Big Three) in Potsdam on July 17, 1945, where the most crucial question facing the three leaders was how to end the war with Japan.

Prior to the Potsdam meeting, many military leaders (H. Stimson, Secretary of War; Admiral Halsey, Secretary of the Navy; G. Marshall, Army Chief of Staff; Admiral King, Commander in Chief of the U.S. fleet; and Henry Arnold, Commander of the Armed Forces) urged President Truman to clarify the surrender terms to reassure the Japanese leadership that the institution of emperor would be retained. According to the minutes of a meeting at the White House on June 18, 1945:

> Admiral Leary said that he could not agree with those who said to him that unless we obtain the unconditional [no guarantees for retention of the Emperor] surrender of the Japanese that we will have lost the war. He feared no menace from Japan in the foreseeable future, even if we were unsuccessful in forcing unconditional surrender.

(*The Decision to Use the Bomb*, Gar Alperovitz)

5

Astonishingly, Truman did not relent and demanded unconditional surrender.

The timing of the Potsdam meeting was further confirmation that Truman's real agenda was to use the bomb before the war came to an end. Winston Churchill, aware of the need to proceed quickly, requested that the Potsdam Conference be held as soon as possible. Truman replied that it would be difficult for him to leave Washington before the end of the fiscal year, which occurred on June 30. Churchill's frustration was evident when he responded that "I would have suggested the middle of June but for your preference for your fiscal year because I feel that every minute counts." In a follow-up response he reiterated, "In this case I consider that we should try to bring the meeting off sometime in June, and I hope your fiscal year will not delay it..."

Truman's primary motivation for postponing the conference was based on the fact that the new bomb had not yet been successfully tested. The meeting of the Big Three finally took place on July 17, 1945. The timing of the meeting, one day after the first successful test of the bomb, exposed Truman's hidden agenda to postpone the Potsdam meeting until the new weapon's capability was demonstrated to the USSR.

The result of the Potsdam Conference was the Potsdam Declaration, which included, "There must be eliminated for all time the authority and influence of those who deceived and misled the people of Japan into embarking on world conquest" and "We call upon the Government of Japan to proclaim the now unconditional surrender of all the Japanese armed forces..." Absent in these statements are any guarantees about maintaining the institution of emperor, which provoked a response of "withhold comment" until further analysis of the declaration. The Japanese response was ambiguous but lacked any disavowal of the declaration.

Despite the provisional Japanese response, Truman was still considering the use of the bomb. Given the context in which President Truman would be making the decision about ending the war, there was little room for doubt about which choice he would make. The

Interim Committee had recommended using the bomb, Truman's closest advisor strongly favored the bomb, and Truman was intensely apprehensive about Soviet expansionism.

Truman's decision to destroy 135,000 innocent human beings in a single instant for the sake of warning the USSR about the consequences of its postwar agenda ranks as one of the great evil deeds in history. There was no justification, rationale, or excuse for his unconscionable decision. Between the two bombings, the Japanese frantically tried to contact the Soviets for a clarification of their position. A meeting of the six Japanese officials was called for August 9, 1945, to discuss surrender, but on the same day Nagasaki disappeared from the map. Brutally stripped of any other options, Japan surrendered.

Before judging whether dropping the bombs on Hiroshima and Nagasaki were acts of genocide, it is important to first determine whether these acts are in violation of international law. The central issue is to assess at what point a legitimate military action crosses over the line into war crimes. According to Howard Zinn, "…the debate centers on the military utility and moral proportionality of the policy." Given that the Japanese military machine was no longer effective, defense industries had been destroyed, major cities in Japan had been fire-bombed, the United States embargo was depriving the Japanese of vital supplies, and the Japanese made serious efforts to surrender, there can be no legitimate argument for making the case that the bombs were of "military utility." In addition, the cities targeted were not of military significance and could not possibly serve a useful military purpose. It would be impossible to defend the case for "moral proportionality" at this point in the war. Ruthlessly murdering 135,000 innocent civilians can never be defended on moral grounds, because there were international laws at the time prohibiting the killing of civilians. Article XXV of the Hague conventions warns that "The attack or bombardment, by whatever means, of towns, villages, dwellings, or buildings which are undefended are prohibited." Further, a League of Nations resolution, unanimously approved on September 30, 1938, affirms that "the intentional bombing of civilian populations is illegal." As well, it lacked moral proportionality because of the massive destruction of two

Japanese cities and civilians and the readiness of Japan to surrender before the bombs were dropped.

In addition to the League of Nations, the United Nations later adopted a resolution in 1961 declaring that:

> The use of nuclear weapons and thermo-nuclear weapons is contrary to the spirit, letter and aims of the United Nations and, as such, a direct violation of the Charter of the United Nations. The use of nuclear and thermo-nuclear weapons would exceed even the scope of war and cause indiscriminate suffering and destruction to mankind and civilization and, as such, is contrary to the rules of international law and to the laws of humanity.

(UN Resolution 1649 [XVI], 1961)

It is important to note that the United Nations does not distinguish between military targets and civilian targets but condemns all use of nuclear weapons. Therefore, the bombing of Hiroshima and Nagasaki would have been illegal under this resolution as of 1961.

The International Committee of the Red Cross (ICRC) affirmed the position of the UN on the question of nuclear weapons on June 27, 2002, when it proclaimed that "the ICRC finds it difficult to envisage how the use of nuclear weapons could be compatible with the principles and rules of international humanitarian law."

The most authoritative judicial decision on the legality of the use of nuclear weapons was an advisory opinion rendered by the International Court of Justice (World Court). As a result of Resolution 49/75K of the General Assembly, the United Nations called on the World Court on December 19, 1994, to examine the following question: "Is the threat or use of nuclear weapons in any circumstances permitted under international law?" Although an advisory opinion lacks any legal force, it is an authoritative statement of the law. On July 8, 1996, the court issued an advisory opinion which found that "a threat or use of force by means of nuclear weapons that is contrary to Article 2, paragraph 4 [All members shall refrain...from the threat or use of force against the territorial integrity...of any state] of the United Nations Charter... is unlawful." Retroactively applying this advisory opinion to the bombing of Hiroshima and Nagasaki solidifies the conclusion that the United States violated international law.

Clearly, there is definitive proof that the use of nuclear weapons violates international humanitarian law with some qualifications as set out in the World Court advisory. Moreover, Protocol I, Chapter II, Article 51 [right of individual or collective self-defense] of the Geneva conventions states that "the civilian population and individual civilians shall enjoy protection against dangers arising from military operations." Thus, not only is the use of nuclear weapons itself illegal, but the targeting of two cities populated exclusively by civilians is a violation of international law.

Not only are these bombings in violation of international law, but they reach the apogee of crimes against humanity, namely genocide. There is solid evidence that the bombings of Hiroshima and Nagasaki meet the criteria of "group," "intent," and "in whole or in part" in the Genocide Convention.

The "group" in this case consists of part of a national group, namely Japanese citizens, who were located in the two particular communities of Hiroshima and Nagasaki and hence meet the criteria of group as set out in the introduction. It is not necessary to intend to destroy the entire national group, but rather it is sufficient to destroy "part" of a national group that is located in a particular community.

It can also be proven that the proportion of the "whole" population represented by Hiroshima and Nagasaki is sufficient to qualify as genocide based on precedent.

One of the precedents involves the massacre of 800 Palestinian civilians in the Sabra and Shatila refugee camps in Lebanon. Israeli General Ariel Sharon was complicit in the massacre, which has been defined by both the General Assembly of the UN and the UN Human Rights Commission as genocide. The General Assembly of the United Nations condemned the massacre at Sabra and Shatila in Resolution A/RES/37/123(A-F), December 16, 1982, which "resolves that the massacre was an act of genocide."

The UN Humans Rights Commission adopted a resolution in its forty-first session that "strongly condemns anew Israeli's responsibility for the large-scale massacre in the Sabra and Shatila refugee camps, which constituted an act of genocide..."

Another precedent involves the massacre in Srebrenica by a Serbian officer, Radislav Krstic. Srebrenica is a small town that lies at the border of Bosnia and Serbia. Its 25 percent Serbian population doomed this small community to be a hot spot where many battles might be fought. Srebrenica was on the border of Serbia, and thus it was exposed to attacks by Serbian forces next door and Serb forces in Bosnia. To protect the Muslims, the United Nations declared it a safe area in 1993 and had hoped to send lightly armed peacekeepers to protect six areas of heavy Muslim concentration. When the United States refused to send troops to protect Srebrenica, European countries that already had some troops there were reluctant to send additional troops. With only a light contingent of UN troops, the Serbs launched their assault in July 1995. The superior Serb forces were able to capture the enclave with minimum resistance. Women, children, and the elderly were transported out of the enclave, while 10,000 to 15,000 military-aged men were captured. To prevent any further Muslim attacks on Serbian population centers, the Serbs killed thousands of those who remained. There is an ongoing controversy over the number of Muslims who were killed ranging from 2,000 to 7,000.

Krstic led the Serbian forces who were responsible for the capture of Srebrenica and as the leader was captured and charged with genocide. On August 2, 2001, he was convicted by the International Criminal Court for the Former Yugoslavia, an ad hoc court which morphed into permacy since the ratification of the International Criminal Court in 2002. The presiding judge Almiro Rodrigues announced the decision of the court:

> By deciding to kill all the men of Srebrenica of fighting age,
> a decision was taken to make it impossible for the Bosnian
> Muslim people of Srebrenica to survive...You are guilty
> of having agreed to the plan to conduct mass executions

of all the men of fighting age. You are therefore guilty of genocide.

(*A Problem from Hell: America and the Age of Genocide*, Samantha Power)

Krstic appealed his case to the Appeals Chamber of the International Criminal Court. According to a summary of the Appeals Chamber ruling prepared by the judges of the court, Radislav Krstic is "...guilty of aiding and abetting genocide." Furthermore, it stated that:

> In this case, the factual circumstances, as found by the trial chamber, permit the inference that the killing of the Bosnian Muslim men was done with genocidal intent. The scale of the killing...is a sufficient factual basis for the finding of specific genocidal intent.

The scale of the massacre in both these cases confirms that the scale of the massacres of Hiroshima and Nagasaki meet the criteria of "in whole or in part." As well, the "intent" of the two bombings in Japan is indisputable. Both Truman and American military leaders knew beyond a shadow of a doubt that a massive number of people would be killed in the two cities bombed.

It is now clear that the bombing of Hiroshima and Nagasaki meet the criteria of the Genocide Convention and thus qualify as acts of genocide. If the bombing of Hiroshima had been a military necessity, it would have qualified as a violation of the Geneva Conventions for targeting civilians. The evidence conclusively confirms that there was no military necessity. It is inconceivable that the United States would have to wreak such ruthless destruction and horror on 100,000 innocent civilians at the same time as Japan was sending out peace feelers. The bombing of Nagasaki is a reminder of the profound lack of conscience and remorse to which the mind can plummet. Having already demonstrated to Japan the pure futility of prolonging the war, Truman chose to pursue his agenda of warning the Soviets over the horrific brutal death of 35,000 more Japanese. These two bombings undeniably capture the true meaning of genocide.

GUATEMALA: SMOKE AND MIRRORS.

Ten years after Guatemala elected its first democratic government in 1944, an American-organized coup led to a succession of dictators who killed over 200,000 people. In the 100 years preceding 1944, Guatemala was led by autocratic rulers. Following the revolution in 1944, Guatemalans were finally living under a democratically elected leader and a new constitution. In 1951, Jacobo Arbenz was elected president of Guatemala on an agenda of land reform, industrialization, amelioration of living standards, and a program of outreach to the Mayan population. He was also a nationalist who aspired to create a capitalistic society with a heart while refusing to capitulate to the American demands to abandon land reform and other social programs.

In 1954, leaders of countries in Latin America faced two options: either accept their role as a member of the American empire or expect their term as leader to be considerably shortened. The United States was very apprehensive about developing countries setting an example of a socially just society in contrast to the American model, which tended to distribute wealth to the dominant elite. If those same countries choose to be independent of American imperatives or threatened the corporate interests of U.S. companies, Washington inevitably reacted by engineering the overthrow of the recalcitrant leader and replacing him with someone who was more compliant.

After unsuccessfully pressuring Arbenz to comply with American interests, the Government of Dwight Eisenhower, through the CIA, devised a scheme to convince Arbenz that he was under attack by a formidable insurgency, hoping that he would surrender. After he surrendered in 1954, he was replaced with an American hand-picked dictator, Castillo Armas, who reversed all of Arbenz's policies and embarked on a program of repression and bloodshed. The United States supported Armas and all the dictators who succeeded him despite their massacre of over 200,000 Mayans.

The United States was directly complicit in the death of the Mayans through their strong support for these dictators who ruled Guatemala for almost 50 years. As these dictators were guilty of genocide, so were the American administrations that supported them.

The Guatemalan democracy appeared after 100 years of aristocratic leaders who were supported by the landowners and emerging middle class. Landowners represented 2.2 percent of the population but owned 70 percent of the land. Compounding the problem of inequity in land distribution was the fact that one-half of the land lay fallow and only one-third of the land was arable.

The landed aristocracy and the middle class benefited from governmental, social, and economic policies, while the lower classes were marginalized. Mayan tribes were the largest group in the lower classes, comprising almost 70 percent of the total population of Guatemala. Ongoing expropriation of their land forced them to become dependent on the landowners who increasingly turned to export crops such as bananas to the United States. When the land became dedicated to a few crops for export, the inevitable result was the need to import food at higher prices.

The outcome of these conditions was deepening poverty and malnutrition among the Mayan people who lived on less than one dollar per year and had a life expectancy of forty. They lived in huts in mountain villages where they attempted to grow enough crops to survive, but only when they had sufficient time between jobs on the large farms.

The largest landowner was the United Fruit Company, an American multinational, which had become the largest banana producer in the world. The United Fruit Company was originally the Boston Fruit Company and was founded by Minor C. Keith, whose original project was to build railways in Central America.

United Fruit Company's president persuaded other landowners to support Jorge Ubico for president in 1931. After Ubico was elected, the company was then granted additional land and a ninety-nine-year lease on all its landholdings, giving United Fruit half the land in Guatemala. The company was also relieved of the burden of paying virtually any taxes, import duties, and export duties and was allowed to greatly undervalue the worth of its land for taxation purposes. Such largesse was necessary to satisfy Ubico's main constituency, the landowners and the multinationals, for which he created conditions that allowed them to operate cheaply and peacefully.

The loss of revenues from taxation on the United Fruit Company deprived the government of a source of revenue that could have been used to improve the lives of the lower classes. In addition, falling coffee and banana prices doomed the economy to stagnation, resulting in more unemployment and poverty. The growing poverty and unemployment combined with the deprivation of land provoked a backlash.

Ubico characterized the growing insurgents as communists and claimed that they were a threat to stability and order. He ordered guards to stand on each corner in towns and cities and to provide additional security for the presidential palace. To deter any further action by the insurgents, he instilled terror among the people by arbitrarily arresting them, followed by torture and execution.

As the insurgency mounted and the students at the University of San Carlos called a strike in 1944, Ubico resigned at the request of the United States. The army's general staff put together a triumvirate whose purpose was to convene the National Assembly in order to elect a new president. The general staff pressured the elected officials to vote for General Frederico Ponce Vaides. Ponce, a puppet of Ubico, implemented oppressive measures and abandoned any pretense of a democracy, provoking resentment against yet another undemocratic and brutal dictator. Opposition groups organized to overthrow the government.

On October 19, 1944, a contingent of army officers led by Jacobo Arbenz and Major Francisco Javier Araña along with students and the Guatemala National Guard rebelled against Ponce, forcing him to seek asylum in the Mexican embassy.

The insurgents called for an election to be held on December 19, 1944. The day that Juan José Arévalo won the election by a landslide is referred to by Guatemalans as the October Revolution.

His government ushered in a period of moderate economic, social, and agrarian reform. He passed a labor code in 1948, which protected workers from arbitrary treatment by management and prohibited any kind of discrimination in the workplace. Arévalo understood the desperate need for social reform to address the abject poverty of the majority of the population. As well, he created the Commission of Social Security to extend benefits to those in need and set up the Guatemalan Institute for Social Security, which was financed by workers, employers, and the state. To improve healthcare, he augmented the Ministry of Public Health and Assistance, placed nurses in White Cross clinics, initiated vaccination programs, and installed water-filtering systems in rural areas. Over seven million dollars was spent on educational projects, which included the creation of the National Literacy Committee, the building of schools, and additional pay for teachers. Agrarian reform was desperately needed to redistribute land fairly to the landless peasants, to increase the efficiency of farming, and to free up a sufficient number of farmers who were needed in the growing industrial sector. Land redistribution was implemented with the Law of Expropriation, which confiscated lands owned by the large landowners with compensation based on taxes filed with the government.

None of these reforms aroused any suspicion or concerns in the United States given that anticommunism in the late 1940s had not reached the level of hysteria witnessed in the 1950s. The reforms were moderate, and no alarm bells were set off in Washington when Arévalo expropriated land. On the other hand, the landowners in Guatemala saw the land reform policy as the first step in the abolition of private property.

American fears about the direction of the Guatemalan government escalated following the election of Jacobo Arbenz in 1951. Expanding land reform programs introduced by Arévalo and improving conditions for the Mayans were some of the policies on his agenda. In his inaugural address he said that he wanted:

> To transform Guatemala from a dependent nation with a
> semi-colonial economy into a country that is economically
> independent; to transform Guatemala from a backward
> country with a semi-feudal economy into a modern capitalist
> country; to proceed in a way that will ensure the greatest
> possible improvement in the living standard of the great
> masses of the people.

(*Guatemala, United States Assistance, and the Logic of Cold War
Dependency*, Alan McPherson)

These reforms, in addition to the presence of a small number of
communists in his administration, began to elicit fear in Washington.
Despite the fact that three of Arbenz's closet advisors were members
of the Labor Party, Partido Guatemalteco Trabajadores (PGT), there
was no evidence that Guatemala had any ties with international
communism, and the military remained fiercely anticommunist.

Nevertheless, Truman ordered the FBI to send agents to
Guatemala to search for radical influences and to assess the politics of
both major and minor people in the government. The FBI forwarded
a number of reports to Washington in which the agents provided an
analysis of the extent of communist infiltration. The objectivity of
these reports was completely undermined by the fact that the sources
of information were people who worked for Ubico.

Eisenhower, who followed Truman, was much more aggressive
in his policies toward Guatemala. Notwithstanding the FBI report, the
absence of any substantial evidence of Guatemalan ties to communism
posed a problem to the Eisenhower administration, who disapproved
of the reforms of Arbenz, and in particular the land reforms. They were
searching for a rationale to remove Arbenz from power and replace him
with somebody more malleable. A State Department memorandum
warned that "the Secretary [Dulles] said that we must realize that it
will be impossible to produce evidence clearly linking the Guatemalan
Government to Moscow; that the decision must be a political one and

based on our conviction that such a tie must exist" (Memorandum of Conversation by the Secretary of State, May 11, 1954).

Taking action against Arbenz was treated as an imperative by the Eisenhower Administration mainly because of the land reform policies implemented in Guatemala. Decree 900, passed unanimously by the Guatemalan Congress on June 17, 1952, planned for the redistribution of fallow, unimproved, or leased land. The legislation created the National Agricultural Bank to provide credit to those farmers who needed it.

Available UFCO land proved very tempting for redistribution. UFCO allowed 85-percent of their land to lay fallow while only growing bananas on 15 percent of it. Decree 900 targeted only unused land belonging to UFCO and offered compensation based on the tax value of the land that had been filed with the government. The plan for agricultural reform was based on a study conducted by the previous administration that had drawn on the advice of experts from all over Latin America.

The predicament for Arbenz over the issue of UFCO was one of double jeopardy. On the one hand, the U.S. government was committed to protecting its corporate interests, and on the other hand, there were very close ties between UFCO and the Eisenhower Administration. Following are some of the connections:

- Secretary of State John Foster Dulles had been a partner with the law firm that represented UFCO;

- Former UFCO President Thomas Dudley was the brother of Eisenhower's first Assistant Secretary of State for Central America;

- Allen Dulles, Director of the CIA, did litigation for UFC;

- John Cabot, Assistant Secretary of State for inter-American Affairs, held a substantial amount of stock in UFCO;

- Anne Whitman, Eisenhower's personal secretary, was the ex-wife of a UFCO director and vice-president;

- Walter Bedell Smith, Under-Secretary of State was a director of UFCO.

By the time Arbenz had implemented his new land reform program, Washington was completely convinced that the Soviet Union had successfully infiltrated the Arbenz Administration and was preparing to take over the reigns of government as a stepping-stone to infiltrating other countries in the hemisphere.

As a first step to reversing many of the new reforms and to expunge the growing cancer of communism in Guatemala, Eisenhower appointed John Peurifoy, a new tough Ambassador to Guatemala. After meeting with Arbenz on December 16, 1953, at the Embassy, he communicated the following message to people in the State Department:

> [Arbenz] began by saying [that the] problem here is one between the United Fruit Company and his government. He spoke at length and bitterly on [the] Fruit Company's history since 1904, complaining especially that now his government has a $70 million budget to meet and collects only $150,000 in taxes...I interrupted here to say I thought we should put first things first, that as long as Communists exerted their present influence in [the] Guatemalan government I did not see any real hope of better relations...I came away definitely convinced that if the President is not a Communist he will surely do until one comes along and that normal approaches will not work in Guatemala.

(*Foreign Relations of the United States*, 1952–1954)

Peurifoy commented that normal approaches were not working, heralding the imminent overthrow of Jacobo Arbenz. The planning had already begun and involved the highest levels of the White House, CIA, and State Department, who were all obsessed with preventing any of the details of the operation from becoming public knowledge.

To maintain the utmost secrecy, documents were classified as top secret, the CIA burned many of its papers, and anyone brought into the project was sworn to secrecy.

Furthermore, to legitimize the campaign, President Eisenhower instructed his brother Milton to travel to South and Central America on a fact-finding mission to sell the importance of Latin American solidarity to the American people. Despite the fact that he never visited Guatemala, Milton Eisenhower curiously reported that there was communist infiltration there.

As well as legitimacy, a legal façade was created to mandate the overthrow of Arbenz. The strategy was to persuade the Organization of American States (OAS) to support it. John Foster Dulles, Secretary of State, used bribes and threats to coerce the delegates at the tenth Inter-American Conference in Caracas, Venezuela, to support a resolution titled "Declaration of Solidarity for the Preservation of the Political Integrity of the American states against International Communism." The Resolution passed.

PBSUCCESS became the code name of the plot with its headquarters in Opa Locka, Florida, on the outskirts of Miami. The estimated cost of the operation was roughly seven million dollars, utilizing 100 CIA agents. Approximately thirty planes to be flown by American pilots were stationed in Nicaragua, Honduras, and the Canal Zone.

The offensive began on June 18, 1954. Without the direct use of U.S. forces, Operation PBSUCCESS was forced to rely on smoke and mirrors to overthrow Arbenz. Guatemala had the strongest army in Central America, and only a massive infusion of money and troops to support Castillo Armas, the person chosen by the United States to lead the new government, could have provided any assurance of victory. Given the clandestine nature of the operation, such overt assistance was out of the question.

To win the coup without any real military power meant creating the illusion of a powerful invading force led by Armas. Americans were counting on a fragment of Arbenz's forces deserting him after learning that the war would be lost, impelling Arbenz to resign.

To make the illusion plausible, Washington provided Armas with money to hire mercenaries and established training camps in Nicaragua and Honduras. The strategy was to manufacture the myth that an army of liberation was marching to Guatemala City and that Armas's victory was a fait accompli. In an effort to convince wealthy urban Guatemalans, many of whom were army officers, that Arbenz was doomed to failure, the CIA broadcast antirevolutionary programs from Honduras and Nicaragua. The broadcasters claimed that Armas was fully prepared to overthrow Arbenz and was accompanied by legions of exiled Guatemalans whom he had recruited.

The CIA had recruited expert pilots who were using outdated planes, not identifiable as CIA planes, to fly sorties over Guatemala and drop bombs on key targets in Guatemala City to convince the citizens that a major siege was underway.

CIA communications experts jammed local radio stations in order to prevent accurate information from reaching the capital as well as broadcasting their own news. They reported huge Armas victories in the countryside and the relentless march of Armas troops toward the capital.

However, the CIA was nervous that if Arbenz ordered his air force to intercept the CIA bombers, U.S. chicanery would be exposed. To solve this problem, the CIA began broadcasting the exploits of alleged heroic Soviet aviators who had defected to the West in the hope that one or more Guatemalan pilots would defect. The plan succeeded, as one pilot did defect. The CIA then plied him with alcohol to persuade him to make an appeal to his fellow pilots to follow his example. Fearing further defections, Arbenz grounded his air force, thus depriving himself of the means to uncover the plot.

As a final resort, Foreign Minister Toriello implored the United Nations to intervene in order to resolve the crisis. Arbenz's hope that the UN would send a team of investigators to Guatemala to evaluate the problem met with resistance from Henry Cabot Lodge, U.S. Ambassador to the UN, who attempted to delay a meeting of the Security Council until after Arbenz's defeat. To win the vote, Washington had to convince Britain and France, who supported Guatemala's resolution, to at least to abstain. With pressure from the United States on both these countries, the Guatemalan Resolution was defeated, and consequently Arbenz resigned.

After the resignation, the CIA promulgated the lie that the people of Guatemala had formed an insurgency to overthrow the harsh dictator, Arbenz. Eisenhower reported that "the major factor in the successful outcome was the disaffection of the Guatemalan armed forces and the population as a whole with the tyrannical regime of Arbenz" (*Mandate for Change: The White House Years, 1953–1956*, Dwight D. Eisenhower).

Following the plan, Castillo Armas was installed as the new leader. Thus began a reign of terror under Armas as well as under all the dictators who followed. Armas began by targeting all possible opposition to his regime and either jailed or executed them. He set up a committee with the power to declare anyone a communist, after which thousands were arbitrarily arrested and then tortured or murdered.

To further tighten his grip on power, he disenfranchised three-quarters of Guatemalan voters and outlawed all political parties, unions, and peasant organizations. To silence dissidents, he shut down opposition newspapers and burned "subversive" books. In 1956, he implemented a new constitution and declared himself president for four more years.

Without any opposition, there was no resistance to declaring all expropriation of land invalid by passing decree, which forced peasants to vacate their newly acquired land. As well, they formed the National Committee of Defense against Communism, which was in fact a death squad.

However, after a taste of the suppression, brutality, and deprivation of living under dictators for six more years, an insurgency was all but inevitable. The insurgency coalesced around several officers in the Guatemalan army who had unsuccessfully attempted a coup against General Miguel Ydígoras Fuentes, the dictator, in 1960. They resented the use of Guatemalan territory to train the Bay of Pigs invaders but failed in their bid to overthrow Fuentes when the United States assisted his army. Following the aborted coup, some of its leaders fled to the hills where they organized an insurgency.

At first, the insurgents' attacks were based on practical concerns as they robbed a bank to obtain money and attacked an army outpost for guns. By 1961, students demanded democracy, social justice, and the ideals of the October Revolution and thus joined the protest. Students joined the protest in 1961 when the Association of Economic Students organized a demonstration to show solidarity with the Cuban revolution. State security forces opened fire on the protesters, killing three and wounding many more.

When Ydígoras held fraudulent elections in December 1961 and declared a state of siege to suppress ongoing student-led protests, student leaders walked into Congress chambers and laid a wreath of flowers, which in part read, "Legality, democracy, and liberty are incompatible with dictatorship." They signed it the "Association of University Students." Massive demonstrations proliferated over the next few days, which mushroomed into a strike of university and secondary school students. Using sticks, stones, and Molotov cocktails, students managed to halt the advance of security forces. Peasant and workers also joined the protest. Finally, after a series of violent confrontations, police and security forces quashed the rebellion, but they could not extinguish the spirit of the protesters. In February 1963, a number of different groups including students, the Patriotic Workers Youth, ex-military officers, and peasants formed a guerrilla army called the Rebel Armed Forces (FAR).

Throughout the balance of the 1960s, the guerrillas were unable to overthrow the government. This was primarily due to sustained military aid from the U.S. government and the presence of American military advisors who advised Guatemalan military leaders on how to operate an effective counter-insurgency campaign and create death squads.

The counter-insurgency received an enormous boost in the 1966 fraudulent presidential elections when Julio Cesar Mendez Montenegro won and decided to leave counter-insurgency activities to American experts. U.S. Colonel John D. Webber was sent to Guatemala to expand training for 5,000 Guatemalan troops as well as to bring in U.S. Jeeps, trucks, communication equipment, and helicopters. Additionally, the United States supplied fighter planes to be used for attacking the guerrillas in the mountains. When the United States supplied the Guatemalan armed forces with armored vehicles, grenade launchers, training and radio equipment, and helicopters in 1961, John Gordon, the American Ambassador to Guatemala, defended the shipment by claiming, "But liberty must be defended wherever it is threatened and that liberty is now being threatened in Guatemala."

To further terrorize the insurgents and potential recruits, death squads were created in 1966, whose membership included part of the army, police, and government officials. Among the death squad's activities were arbitrary arrest, torture, imprisonment, abduction, and summary executions. The United States provided equipment and instructions on torture techniques, and American Green Berets taught their Guatemalan recruits various methods of interrogation as well as participating in death squad activities themselves.

American equipment, training, and advisors transformed the Guatemalan forces into an efficient killing machine. In an unclassified Department of State document, the Deputy Chief of Mission in the American Embassy in Guatemala, Viron Vaky, sent the following report to the State Department expressing concerns that:

> The official squads are guilty of atrocities. Interrogations are brutal, torture is used and bodies are mutilated…This leads to an aspect that I personally find the most disturbing of all—that we have not been honest with ourselves. We have condoned counter-terror; we may even in effect have encouraged or blessed it.

The Vaky report obliterated any claim by the American Government that it was unaware of the atrocities perpetrated against the people of Guatemala.

Other reliable sources have carefully documented the extent of the human rights violations such as the "Historical Clarification Commission" (CEH), created by the UN in June 1994 to, "clarify with all objectivity, equity and impartiality the human rights violations and acts of violence that have caused the Guatemalan population to suffer, connected with the armed conflict." The CEH Report also reported that:

> Some of the human rights violations were committed by means of covert operations. The military had clandestine units called "commandos" or "special squads" whose supplies, vehicles, arms, funding and operational instructions were provided by the regular structures of the army, especially military intelligence…Death squads were also used… Their objective was to eliminate alleged members, allies or collaborators of the "subversives."

(*Historical Clarification Commission*, Christian Tomuschat, Otila Lux de Cotí, Alfredo Balsells Tojo, June 1994)

One group of victims singled out for special attention was the Mayan population, who it was believed were collaborating with the insurgency and providing it with many of its recruits. According the CEH:

> The Army's perception of Mayan communities as natural allies of the guerrillas contributed to increasing and aggravating human rights violations perpetrated against them, demonstrating an aggressive racist component of extreme cruelty that led to the extermination en masse, of defenseless Mayan communities purportedly linked to the guerrillas—including children, women and the elderly— through methods whose cruelty has enraged the moral conscience of the civilized world.

(Ibid.)

In 1966, during a sweep of guerrilla strongholds, massive army bombing massacred thousands of persons, mainly unarmed peasants, in the regions where the guerrillas based their operations. The onslaught persisted until 1972 when the government announced the military defeat of the guerrillas. Throughout this period, death squads relentlessly sought out possible enemies of the state to be interrogated, tortured, and murdered.

While the counter-insurgency campaign was succeeding in weakening the guerrilla base in the countryside and in the mountains, student activism flourished, particularly after the union of students with the clandestine Guatemalan Workers' Party (PGT) who embarked on a campaign of building a mass movement.

It took a major earthquake in 1976 to unite the various factions opposing the continual succession of dictators when organized students, union members, urban slum-dwellers, and peasant villagers joined together in one large protest movement. This new organization of insurgents began to grow and become more aggressive.

The government's response to the renewed popular movement was a fierce killing spree targeting mainly peasants, workers, and residents of poor urban neighborhoods. Frequently, government officials would march in broad daylight into an urban center to assassinate suspected insurgents to send a clear message to those who opposed the government.

The brutality of the murderous regime in Guatemala was well known to Washington, as confirmed by a declassified State Department report, which noted that "Guatemala is a violent society. The conscious acceptance and use of violence as an instrument of politics contribute to the extraordinary levels of murder, kidnapping and disappearance" (*Guatemala's Disappeared*, Department of State).

Despite the atrocities perpetrated by the government of Guatemala, American military assistance to Guatemala continued unabated. The assistance continued until President Carter implemented an arms embargo against Guatemala in March 1977.

Following Carter, President Reagan was much less concerned about human rights. Notwithstanding U.S. knowledge of the human rights record of the Guatemalan government, Reagan endeavored to lift the embargo and in the interim shipped 3.2 million dollars of trucks and Jeeps by removing them from the list of equipment covered by the embargo. The embargo was lifted in 1983.

The severity of the atrocities was reported by the Inter-American Commission on Human Rights in its 1981 report in which it documented that:

> The Inter-American Commission of Human Rights (IACHR) has been following the human rights situation in Guatemala with real concern for several years. This concern is due to the generalized violence that country is undergoing, from which—to use the words of the IACHR itself—the "agents of the Guatemalan Government or persons who have had the approval of tolerance of that government" have not been excluded.

A massacre occurred at Cocob in Mayan territory where, according to an unclassified CIA cable, "the social population appeared to fully support leftist guerrillas…the soldiers were forced to fire at anything that moved…the Guatemalan authorities admitted that many 'civilians' were killed in Cocob, many of whom were non-combatants." This strategy is reminiscent of the "search and destroy" missions in Vietnam during which American forces sought out villages suspected of supporting the Viet Cong and then destroyed them, their food supply, and frequently all of its inhabitants. The Historical Clarification Commission reported that:

> The CEH is able to confirm that between 1981 and 1983 the Army identified groups of the Mayan population as an internal enemy, considering them to be an actual or potential support base for the guerrillas, with respect to material sustenance, a source of recruits and a place to hide their members.

(*Historical Clarification Commission*, Christian Tomuschat, Otilia Lux de Cotí, Alfredo, Balsells Tojo)

A declassified CIA document confirms the search and destroy objective of counter-insurgency forces. According to a CIA document, February 2, 1982:

> In mid-February 1982, the Guatemalan army reinforced its existing force in the central [native territory]. The command officers of the units involved have been instructed to destroy all towns and villages which are cooperating with the guerrilla army of the poor (EGP) and eliminate all sources of resistance.

In 1982, the CIA and White House supported Rios Montt in a coup d'etat. The CIA and the Pentagon were also included in his inner circle, and six of Montt's top generals were educated at the School of the Americas (now referred to as Western Hemispheric Institution for Security Cooperation), a notorious school for dictators and their military personnel, located at Fort Benning, Georgia. Montt suspended the constitution, convened secret military tribunals, and embarked on a crackdown involving abduction, torture, and assassinations.

Montt unleashed a scorched earth policy called "rifles and beans" against the natives in an attempt to eliminate the guerrillas' base of support in the villages. Those who cooperated were the recipients of beans, while those who didn't were the recipients of bullets. The result was the destruction of 600 villages and the death of more than 19,000 people. In addition, the offensive against Mayan villages resulted in the flight of somewhere between 500,000 and 1,000,000 refugees. The Council of Hemispheric Affairs (COHA), a nonprofit independent research and information organization whose purpose is to promote the common interests of the hemisphere, reported that:

> International attention is again focused on Guatemala as one of the world's gross violators of human rights... Between 1979–1985, Guatemala's armed forces carried out an orchestrated campaign against opponents of a series of military dictatorships, murdering more than 70,000 civilians, most of them members of the indigenous community.

(*News and Analysis*–1988, Council of Hemispheric Affairs)

Reagan's support of Montt not only included calling him a "man of great personal integrity" but also a supply of weapons such as $2 million in helicopter spare parts, $6.3 million in other military supplies, and $300,000 for military training. Dictators who succeeded Montt were also the recipient of generous donations of aid. The COHA reports that:

> Congress has fully supported the Reagan Administration's policy toward Guatemala. In FY1988, it gave over $134.9 million in non-military aid, and has allocated $136 million for FY1989. Moreover, Guatemala received over $9.4 million in "non-lethal" military aid in 1988, and Capitol Hill has allocated an additional $9 million for 1989.

(*News and Analysis–1988*, Council of Hemispheric Affairs)

After Reagan left office in 1988, the army's campaign of counter-insurgency and death squads did not subside nor did American support for the Guatemalan military. According to the COHA:

> Several thousand human rights deaths ago...Vinicio Cerezo Arevalo took office in early 1986 as only the second elected civilian president in Guatemala since a 1954 C.I.A.-plotted coup terminated the then-ruling constitutional government of Jacobo Arbenz. At the time of his inauguration, Cerezo claimed that his primary goal was to peaceably transfer the presidency to another "freely elected" civilian in 1991. The significance of even this modest aspiration vanished in the closing moments of his shattered presidency, in a nation whose government now rivals El Salvador as being corrupt to its marrow, as well as being indifferent to the violence engaged in by the nation's military and associated right-wing death squads.

(*News and Analysis*–1991, Council on Hemispheric Affairs)

U.S. military aid was forced to go underground in 1990 under the administration of President G.H. Bush when public outrage at U.S support of a country with a terrible human rights record made it necessary for the government to cut off public funding. The CIA secretly compensated for the loss of assistance with millions of dollars. Annual payments of $5 million to $7 million continued into the Clinton administration.

Despite the ongoing hostilities, presidential and public pressure prompted the Catholic Church to act as a mediator in search of an agreement that ultimately achieved fruition in 1993 with a package of constitutional reforms approved by a popular referendum on January 30, 1994.

Following the passage of the constitution, a peace process brokered by the United Nations began to produce results as the government and insurgency forces signed a number of agreements, including one on human rights, resettlement of displaced persons, and indigenous rights. The peace process culminated in the signing of peace accords, formally ending the thirty-six-year brutal reign of terror.

Five years later, in 2002, violations of human rights began to rise again, targeting primarily those demanding implementation of the peace accords or justice for the atrocities of the past. According to Amnesty International:

> Since President Óscar Berger came into office in January 2004, thousands of rural families in Guatemala have been evicted from their homes. During many evictions, security forces used excessive force, resulting in beatings and other ill-treatment, the destruction of homes and property, and in some cases, killing.

(*Guatemala: Human Rights Concerns*, Amnesty International)

As of 2006, the indigenous people of Guatemala are still being denied their basic human rights. The government systematically fails to recognize their ancestral lands and ignores their property rights in order to exploit natural resources.

Moreover, economic conditions in Guatemala are extremely poor, with 80 percent of the people living in poverty and social development indicators such as infant mortality, illiteracy, and chronic malnutrition among the worst in the hemisphere.

Well before 2006, the displacement and massacre of Mayans had reached genocidal proportions. They were targeted both by the Guatemalan army and death squads who brutally murdered over 200,000 aboriginals. The intent was not only to destroy the guerrilla base but also to destroy an ethnic group. According to the Historical Clarification Commission:

> In consequence, the CEH concludes that agents of the State of Guatemala, within the framework of counterinsurgency operations carried out between 1981 and 1983, committed acts of genocide against groups of Mayan people which lived in the four regions analyzed. This conclusion is based on the evidence that, in light of the Convention on the Prevention and Punishment of the Crime of Genocide, the killing of members of Mayan groups occurred (Article II.a), serious bodily or mental harm was inflicted (Article II.b) and the group was deliberately subjected to living conditions calculated to bring about its physical destruction in whole or in part (Article II.c). The conclusion was also based on the evidence that all these acts were committed "with intent to destroy, in whole or in part" groups identified by their common ethnicity, by reason thereof, whatever the cause, motive, or final objective of these acts may have been.

(Article II, first paragraph)

The CEH conclusion was based on the fact that the Mayan people, who were targeted in each village, included everyone in the village, not only those who posed a military threat. Frequently, military patrols would gather the whole community together or surround the village before unleashing a hail of bullets on the helpless victims. The military patrols would raze abandoned villages and fire on groups of refugees attempting to escape the very fate just inflicted on them. As well, the Mayans were victims of cruel treatment such as torture and other degrading acts for the purpose of terrorizing the entire Mayan population. The razing of villages, worked fields, and harvests were acts that constitute the "deliberate infliction on the group of conditions of life" whose purpose was to bring about "its physical destruction in whole or in part."

With respect to the issue of intention, the CEH concludes that the acts of destruction inflicted on the Mayan population:

> [They] were not isolated acts or excesses committed by soldiers who were out of control, nor were they the result of possible improvisation by mid-level Army command. With great consternation the CEH concludes that many massacres and other human rights violations committed against these groups obeyed a higher, strategically planned policy, manifested in actions which had a logical and coherent sequence.

(*Historical Clarification Commission*, Christian Tomuschat, Otilia Lux de Cotí, Alfredo, Balsells Tojo)

Moreover, the COHA condemned the treatment of the Mayans by the government and military as genocide. In an open letter to the *Financial Times*, COHA reports that "...Guatemala was Latin America's most notorious human rights violator, launching a *genocide* [emphasis mine] which killed tens of thousands of indigenous peoples from 1969 until the mid-1990s."

Some of the victims have requested that the Center for Human Rights Legal Action represent them in pressing charges against high-ranking military officers for "war crimes and crimes against humanity, including genocide, committed in the early 1980s" (*Guatemala: Political Violence Unchecked*, Human Rights Watch News).

It is undeniable that the government of Guatemala was guilty of committing genocide against the native population, but furthermore, it can be demonstrated that the Government of the United States was also complicit in the genocide.

The United States unequivocally participated in an act of genocide. American involvement included military advisors, military aid, economic aid, and training both at the School of the Americas and in Guatemala.

David Model

American participation in military and economic aid is outlined in the following table:

U.S. economic and military assistance (millions of dollars, 1970 rate)

	Average per year
1946–1949	2.3
1950–1954	1.1
1955–1959	23.1
1960–1964	20.6
1965–1969	30.4
1970–1974	21.0
1975–1979	13.7
1980–1984	6.9*
1985–1989	46.7
1990–1994	24.9

*embargo

(*Accord Guatemala Project*, Historical Background)

To prove that the participation was intentional, refer back to the State Department and CIA documents reporting on the progress of the counter-insurgency campaign. According to the CEH:

> The United States demonstrated that it was willing to provide support for strong military regimes in its strategic backyard. In the case of Guatemala, military assistance was directed towards reinforcing the national intelligence apparatus, and for training the officer corps in counterinsurgency techniques, key factors which had significant bearing on human rights violations during the armed confrontation.

(*Historical Clarification Commission*, Guatemala Memory of Silence)

Similarly, Human Rights Watch reports that:

Successive U.S. administrations supported this regime [Castillo Armas] as it engaged in widespread human rights violations. Although direct U.S. military assistance to Guatemala ended in the late 1970s, the U.S. government continued to provide significant financial support, including publicly defending Guatemala's human rights record.

Whether or not successive U.S. administrations harbored genocidal intent is irrelevant, because it is only necessary to prove that the U.S. administrations had knowledge of the genocidal intent of the Guatemalan government and military. It is clear from State Department and CIA reports that the administration was well aware of the efforts of the Guatemalan forces to search for villages with the intent of murdering everyone in the village, irrespective of whether or not they were guerillas. That particular strategy, if followed to its logical conclusion, would have eliminated most of the Mayan population. For example, a CIA report states that:

> Since the operation began, several villages have been burned to the ground, and a large number of guerrillas and collaborators have been killed. Comment: When an army patrol meets resistance and takes fire from a town or village it is assumed that the entire town is hostile and it is subsequently destroyed.

(CIA secret cable, February 1982)

Another declassified CIA document reveals that:

> The Guatemalan military's plans to begin sweeps through the Ixil Triangle area which has the largest concentration of guerrillas and sympathizers in the country, could lead not only to major clashes, but serious abuses by the armed forces...it will probably be necessary to destroy a number of villages.

(CIA Top Secret Report, February 5, 1982)

Combined with previous declassified documents cited in this chapter, these documents definitively establish that the State Department, CIA, and embassy staff in Guatemala were fully aware of events in Guatemala. They knew that the counter-insurgency forces were destroying entire villages in order to eradicate the Mayan population. Incredibly, the total number of villages destroyed was 626 (CEH).

According to the criteria in the Genocide Convention, the United States has committed a punishable act in the convention, namely complicity. U.S. administrations were aware of the intentions of the counter-insurgency forces in Guatemala to eliminate as many Mayan villages as possible but nevertheless supported successive governments both militarily and economically. They knew that the very arms they were sending to Guatemala would be used to destroy Mayan villages. Therefore, the United States is complicit in the genocide against the Mayan people in Guatemala.

In fact, throughout the 1950s to the end of the 1970s when Carter introduced the embargo, U.S. governments preferred that dictators ruled Guatemala. The whole point of overthrowing the democratically-elected Arbenz, who was setting a dangerous example in Latin America, was to support leaders who would be subservient to the United States and who would adopt social and economic policies more amenable to American policymakers. Corrupt dictators serve that purpose extremely well.

Therefore, in order to ensure a compliant government in Guatemala, the United States set in motion a sequence of events that ultimately led to the death of 200,000 people. Apparently, human rights and democracy are shibboleths that American leaders grandstand about at home but are totally indifferent to in other countries.

3

VIETNAM: DESTROYING A NATION TO SAVE IT.

Nguyen Ai Quoc, a young kitchen assistant at the Ritz in France in 1919, would become involved in three genocides forty years later. The three genocides were committed by the United States in Vietnam, Cambodia, and Laos, resulting in the death of over four million people.

South Vietnam was to be the bulwark against communism. American fears about the domino effect in Southeast Asia, where the loss of South Vietnam to communism would result in the fall of all of Southeast Asia, induced American leaders to launch an all-out effort to save South Vietnam. The result of this effort was three to four million Vietnamese deaths and approximately 55,000 American deaths. Shortly after the last few Americans remaining in Vietnam climbed into a helicopter on the American Embassy roof, Nguyen Quoc, or Ho Chi Minh, the popular leader of North Vietnam, became ruler of a united Vietnam.

When the Vietnamese, led by Ho Chi Minh, defeated the French colonizers at Dien Bien Phu in 1954, the Americans moved in to assume control of South Vietnam and maintain a succession of dictators in power until the end of the Vietnam War. These dictators did not serve the public weal of Vietnam but only their own well-being and the interests of the United States. As a result, the people of South Vietnam were provoked into attempting to overthrow these dictators and to forming the core of a resistance movement against both the dictators and American intervention. Vietnamese peasants formed the base of support for the Viet Cong. They were themselves disgruntled peasants of the South who became the primary opposition to American dominance in their country. The North Vietnamese joined the struggle and together successfully forced the Americans to retreat in humiliation.

During the war, American forces discovered that they needed to destroy the base of their enemy's support. Hence, they launched a search and destroy program in which they massacred all inhabitants of a village (to save it), destroyed their food, and razed their shelters. Furthermore, in order to fight the war on their terms, U.S. bombing missions attempted to defoliate the country with napalm and Agent Orange to undermine the strategy of the Viet Cong, who were fighting guerrilla warfare. Another American strategy was to mercilessly bomb North Vietnam into submission.

The outcome of American intervention in Vietnam was genocide. Although their motivation was not to kill all the South Vietnamese, the known consequences of their actions were bound to result in massive civilian casualties.

Ho Chi Minh returned to Vietnam on February 28, 1941, to fight the Japanese and the French and to create a broad front of patriots, peasants, workers, merchants, and soldiers who became known as the Viet Minh. He selected North Vietnam as his base because of its proximity to China, where he could easily obtain weapons.

At first he lived on the run to escape French patrols, but in 1945 Ho and the Viet Minh were able to seize power in Hanoi where he established the Democratic Republic of Vietnam (DRV). In 1946, a full-scale war broke out between the French and the Viet Minh.

In 1946, the United States was ambivalent about events in Vietnam, but when the nationalist government in China was taken over by the communist government of Mao Zedong, the United States claimed that the Viet Minh were part of the worldwide communist conspiracy.

The change of governments in China influenced the American attitude about the war in Vietnam, and when the French began losing battles to the Viet Minh, the United States sent American bombers, military advisors, and $1.4 billion in assistance. At the same time, China was aiding the Viet Minh.

As the war raged on and the Viet Minh forces were threatening to defeat the French, the United States decided that neither a French loss nor a negotiated settlement was a viable option. Both options risked a communist government in Vietnam. A National Security Council paper stated that "it was U.S. policy to accept nothing short of a military victory in Indo-China…[The] U.S. actively opposes any negotiated settlement in Indo-China at Geneva [location for upcoming peace talks]."

The French fought the climatic battle of the war against the Viet Minh between March 17 and May 7, 1954, at Dien Bien Phu, a remote valley in North Vietnam. After a long, hard-fought battle, the Viet Minh defeated the French.

On February 18, 1954, the United States, Great Britain, and France announced a meeting in Geneva for late April where a settlement would be negotiated to end the wars in Southeast Asia. Most of the nine countries represented at the conference in Geneva were not willing to engage in direct contact. The Vietminh officials boycotted the French, the Russians were disdainful of the Chinese, the Americans shunned the Chinese, the French resented the Americans, and the Americans were angry with the French.

After fierce bickering, the representatives reached an agreement on a few issues while most remained unresolved. The only documents signed by all parties were ceasefire accords ending hostilities in Vietnam. An agreement was reached between France and the Viet Minh (DRV) that provided for a temporary division of Vietnam to be drawn at the seventeenth parallel. Ho Chi Minh and his government would rule North Vietnam and Ngo Dinh Diem would rule a noncommunist state in the South. Diem had just been appointed prime minister of South Vietnam. Both North and South Vietnam were required to hold a nationwide election in 1956, at which time the people would vote for the government of their choice in a reunited Vietnam. Neither the Americans nor Diem signed the commitment to hold elections as they feared that the outcome would be a united communist Vietnam.

When Diem refused to sign the Accords, he was supported by the United States. Diem had been Washington's choice of a surrogate leader, but not without serious reservations. John Foster Dulles, Secretary of State, lamented that the Americans would underwrite Diem "because we knew of no one better."

The truth of the matter was that although Eisenhower insisted that aid would depend on Diem's "standards of performance," he was already receiving assistance. Both Donald Heath, U.S. Ambassador to South Vietnam, and John Foster Dulles, Secretary of State, agreed that Diem was a poor choice but approved of a $300 million aid package as a time-buying measure. With American backing, Diem was able to fend off his enemies and consolidate his power. As well, his position was secured when the United States and Diem ignored the call for elections in 1956 for fear the popular Ho Chi Minh would win by a large margin.

His greatest enemy was in his own backyard: the Viet Minh militants, who had gained a stronghold in villages in the Mekong Delta. During French rule, the Viet Minh had set up religious, peasant, and youth associations. They distributed pamphlets emphasizing the importance of maintaining unity in the struggle against the French. Many of the Viet Minh had become village leaders and implemented progressive agrarian policies. At the same time, many members of the Viet Minh were either communists or converts to communism.

After the French defeat, the Viet Minh turned their attention to the repressive regime of Diem. Diem feared the Viet Minh and felt that they had to be eliminated. Diem's soldiers scoured the countryside for either members of the Viet Minh or anyone else who had fought the French. They were tortured and frequently murdered, and those members of the Viet Minh who survived fled. By 1956, Diem had eliminated most of the Viet Minh in the Mekong Delta.

The Viet Minh veterans who had survived Diem's purge became the nucleus of the National Liberation Front (NLF), whose purpose was to lead guerrilla warfare against Diem. Diem referred to them as the Viet-cong or Vietnamese Communists, but many noncommunists joined the NLF because of their hatred of the Diem Regime. As early as 1957, Hanoi instructed the communists in South Vietnam to organize thirty-seven armed companies, most of them in the marshes and forests of the Mekong Delta. Even though the NLF was receiving some of its orders from Hanoi, their primary purpose was to overthrow the repressive, corrupt government in Saigon. Notwithstanding that Hanoi's goal may have been to create a united Vietnam under Ho Chi Minh, a goal that would have been achieved through the Geneva Accords, the Viet Cong were more interested in overthrowing a repressive regime in the South.

Diem's government became a small oligarchy composed of his brother, wife, and other relatives who refused to delegate power, thus limiting their base of support. Diem did seek support of the wealthy landowners, and most of his policies favored them while alienating the peasants. He did not implement any reforms to redistribute land and antagonized the peasants by requiring them to pay for it, in contrast to the Viet Minh who had given them the land at no cost during the war with the French.

Another major miscalculation involved the transfer of peasants to farm communities known as agrovilles in an attempt to separate the rural population from the communists. Uprooting peasants from their native villages and ancestral graves disrupted their traditional social patterns. Often more peasants were forced to abandon their villages to build an agroville than could be accommodated, causing many peasants to become homeless. In many villages, the Vietcong were welcomed as liberators. Philippe Devillers, in *The Pentagon Papers*, observed that:

> It was thus by its home policy that the government of the South finally destroyed the confidence of the population, which it had won during the early years, and practically drove them into revolt and desperation. The Communists (and even the anti-Communists) opposition had long been aware of the turn events were taking. But at the beginning of 1960 very many elements, both military and civilian, in the Nationalist camp came to a clear realization that things were moving from bad to worse, and if nothing were done to put an end to the absolute power of Diem, then Communism

would end up gaining power with the aid, or at least with the consent, of the population.

(*The Pentagon Papers*, Volume 3, Chapter 4)

Furthermore, Diem alienated the middle class professionals including doctors, lawyers, and teachers because he rejected even the façade of democracy in the 1959 elections. In those elections, the peasants were coerced into voting for Diem and those in the cities were denied the vote if they were suspected of opposing Diem.

It was during this period of maelstrom that JFK assumed the presidency and was confronted with the question about the degree of support that should be offered to Diem. He immediately rejected neutrality for South Vietnam despite the fact that Hanoi had offered such a proposition. He believed that he could counteract the threat of communism without a great cost to the United States.

JFK decided to launch a counter-insurgency program in the South by creating a task force to search for ways to prevent communist domination. Finally, Kennedy implemented a strategy to improve conditions in South Vietnam by increasing assistance to Vietnam through a counter-insurgency plan that offered Diem support for a 20,000-man increase to his army. He increased the number of American advisors to 3,000, and the figure climbed to 16,000 over the next two years.

The military assistance, in itself, could not win the war because the real problem was the loyalty of the vast majority of peasants in the countryside. Notwithstanding the fact that the agroville plan had been a complete failure, Diem was determined to create a similar program, not just to separate the communists and the peasants, but also to pacify the peasants and win them over.

To gain control of the population, the Government of South Vietnam (GVN) gathered people from areas threatened by guerrillas and relocated them to fortified hamlets. Once physical security was established, the peasants would then be subjected to a pacification program that was designed to encourage the peasants to identify with the Diem government. The strategy of controlling the rural population was called the Strategic Hamlet Program. In August 1962, Diem had created 2,500 hamlets and 2,500 more were under construction.

The Strategic Hamlet Program failed because the peasants resented displacement from their land and coercion into settling into hamlets. They were also frustrated over the inadequate materials they were provided with for building shelters and fortifications. Diem's emphasis on security meant that there was little money for schools, hospitals, and other social programs. As well, rice, cash grants, and fertilizers were often stolen by government officials. The hamlet program converted many of the peasants into Vietcong sympathizers as they frequently demonstrated a contrived loyalty to Diem's troops during the day but supported the Viet Cong at night.

The Strategic Hamlet Program was one of many problems plaguing Diem, and Kennedy's response was to send General Maxwell Taylor on October 18, 1961, to compile a report and make recommendations on possible solutions. General Taylor submitted his report on November 3, 1961, in which he proposed that the United States show its commitment to Diem while on the other hand persuade him that he must endeavour to win the support of the people through progressive reforms. In terms of the commitment to Diem, the report recommended an increase in the number of military advisors, a shipment of three squadrons of helicopters, and 8,000 U.S. combat troops.

Even with American military assistance, Diem's army proved to be ineffective in fighting the Vietcong. Vietcong contingents defeated larger South Vietnamese divisions who became more reluctant to confront the Vietcong and preferred instead to depend on American air support and artillery fire.

While Diem was losing on the battlefield, ultimately he was buried by a religious issue. In April 1963, Diem banned the traditional Buddhist flag just prior to a major festival to celebrate Buddha's birthday. There were between 300,000 and 400,000 practicing Buddhists in South Vietnam, and 80 percent of the population were nominal Buddhists. Buddhists in Hue, the center of Buddhist learning, defiantly flew their flags despite the order. The local administration's failure to take action encouraged the Buddhists to continue to fly their flags. Diem viewed the flags as a challenge to his authority and ordered local authorities to disperse the crowds. When local officials needed assistance, government troops arrived and killed nine demonstrators and wounded fourteen. Buddhists reacted by launching a nationwide protest. Rioting quickly spread from Hue to Saigon, becoming a full-blown political crisis when 350 Buddhist monks demonstrated in front of the National Assembly and announced a forty-eight-hour hunger strike. Approximately two weeks later, a Buddhist monk poured gasoline on himself and set himself on fire.

The United States pressured Diem to resolve the Buddhist crisis but feared that Diem was incapable of conciliating dissident groups and had to be removed from power. When Diem and his family persisted in alienating the Buddhists, Kennedy and his staff began to consider replacing Diem.

Although some of Diem's generals were turning against him, his collapse would not have been possible without American complicity. Kennedy had finally come to the realization that the war could not be won with Diem and asked Henry Cabot Lodge, the U.S. Ambassador to Saigon, to support overthrowing Diem's government. Henry Cabot Lodge was in complete agreement with Kennedy and said that:

> We are launched on a course from which there is no respectable turning back; the overthrow of the Diem government…there is no possibility, in my view, that the war can be won under a Diem Administration.

Lodge encouraged Diem's senior officers to stage a coup. The U.S. government was involved in orchestrating the coup, and on October 25, 1963, a State Department document recommended the:

> Cessation of all U.S. aid to Diem Government and announcement thereof. U.S. facilities in Viet-Nam (military advisors, transport, communication, etc.) in support of coup group…Once the coup group has seized power, the

U.S. rallied promptly to its support with statements and assistance.

(*Check-List of Possible U.S. Actions in Case of a Coup*, Department of State Guidelines)

Lieutenant Colonel Lucien Conein, an experienced CIA agent, maintained close contact with the generals as they were plotting the coup and met with General Minh, the most senior and respected general in South Vietnam, to advise him that unless the coup was executed soon, the war would be lost. On November 1, 1963, General Minh carried out the coup, and Diem and his brother were murdered.

L. B. Johnson became president following Kennedy's assassination and inherited a number of problems in Vietnam. Following Diem's downfall, a number of disturbing developments would force President Johnson and his advisors to carefully rethink their policies in Vietnam. Reports from Vietnam had been overly optimistic about the progress of the war, about the military and political leadership, and about the success of the pacification program. The Vietcong were gaining strength, and the Government of South Vietnam was losing popular support to the Vietcong.

Political instability in South Vietnam, caused by frequent change in leadership, was further undermining the peasants' confidence in their government. General Khanh followed Minh in January 1964, and Nguyen Cao Ky became Prime Minister in February 1965 while Colonel Nguyen Van Thieu became head of state.

All these problems in the war precipitated some soul searching by war planners in Washington in the quest for a new strategy. They came to the inevitable conclusion that at some unspecified point in the near future, the United States would have to implement a series of gradually mounting air strikes against the North and would have to begin increasing American troop levels in the South.

One of the most critical developments in the war occurred in August 1964, just prior to the presidential elections in November. This development was the commitment to a massive increase in the number of American troops in the South.

Events leading up to the expansion of American troop levels began in 1954 when the CIA trained squads of anticommunist South Vietnamese to assassinate and abduct officials in North Vietnam, destroy military installations, establish bases, and organize local cadres. This covert intelligence campaign was code-named Operation Plan 34A, or 34 Alpha.

The CIA and South Vietnamese forces launched a covert marine and airborne operation, inserting agents in the North to collect intelligence, recruit support, and carry out psychological operations along enemy lines.

In June 1962, after losing the naval vessel *Nautelas II* and four commandos, the United States initiated a succession of hit-and-run attacks along the coast of North Vietnam. In addition to the covert operations, the United States launched DeSoto Patrols, which were naval intelligence collection operations used to gather signals from North Vietnam.

Moreover, to intimidate the North Vietnamese, Washington ordered Commander-in-chief Pacific, Admiral Ulysses Grant Sharp, Jr., to station a task force in the Gulf of Tonkin to conduct aerial reconnaissance. The carrier *Ticonderoga* and the destroyer *Maddox* were stationed in the Gulf. Authority to expand 34 Alpha operations was granted, and American naval ships began shelling radar sites, defense posts, and other coastal targets.

The North retaliated by launching an unsuccessful attack on the *Maddox*, and two North Vietnamese boats were severely damaged in the exchange. On August 4, 1964, the National Security Agency (NSA) warned the *Maddox* of another possible attack, and an hour after NSA's warning, the *Maddox* claimed she had radar contact with three or four unidentified vessels in the Gulf of Tonkin.

The pivotal incident, which vastly transformed American involvement in South Vietnam, occurred when several unidentified vessels allegedly attacked the *Maddox*. The *Ticonderoga* sent aircraft to assist the *Maddox* and *C. Turner Joy*, also a destroyer, but stormy seas, low clouds, and thunderstorms thwarted any attempts to locate the unidentified vessels. Captain John Herrick, captain of the *Maddox*, recommended a thorough investigation of reports from the radar crew of radar contact with the hostile vessels and weapons fire. According to Captain Herrick, the sightings and weapons fire could have been attributed to the stormy seas, darkness, or inexperienced or nervous crewman. Furthermore, there was no damage to either destroyer. Assuming that there had been North Vietnamese vessels in the Gulf, they would have had every right to fire on hostile vessels in their territorial waters committing hostile acts.

Despite the request for an investigation by Captain Herrick, who was not convinced that there had been an attack, President Johnson exploited the incident to convince the public and Congress that there was a need to step up America's war effort in Vietnam. He sent Robert McNamara to Congress to report that there was "unequivocal proof" that there had been a second unprovoked attack on American vessels in international waters. He denied any involvement in South Vietnamese operations, including 34 Alpha and the DeSoto operations.

At the request of President Johnson, Congress passed the "Gulf of Tonkin" Resolution, which stated that "Congress approves and supports the determination of the President...to take all necessary measures to repel any armed attack against the forces of the US and to prevent further aggression" (The American War Library).

Based on the Resolution, President Johnson began shipping more troops overseas, beginning with sending two marine battalions on March 8, 1965, to Da Nang to protect the airbase. In response to a request from Ambassador Taylor for more soldiers to protect the base, another forty-four battalions were shipped to Da Nang. By 1966, there were 184,000 troops in Vietnam, which climbed to a staggering 542,000 by 1969.

To alleviate President Johnson's apprehensiveness about the safety of American troops, the military developed the enclave strategy, which based troops in coastal enclaves where they established safe perimeters of fifty miles. The underlying rationale was to restrict the fighting to relative low-risk areas.

It was becoming increasingly obvious that the enclave strategy would not produce a victory but only a holding pattern. General Westmoreland developed a more aggressive strategy called "search and destroy." According to *the Pentagon Papers*:

> The basic idea behind the strategy was the desire to take the war to the enemy, denying him freedom of movement anywhere in the country and taking advantage of the superior firepower and maneuverability of U.S. and Third Country forces to deal him the heaviest blows.

(*The Pentagon Papers*, Volume 3, Chapter 4)

The basic function of "search and destroy" was to destroy the Vietcong base of support, without which they would be unable to operate successfully. The Vietcong base of support was the peasants who lived in villages that dotted the landscape and who provided the Vietcong with supplies, intelligence, soldiers, and shelter. General Westmoreland defined the objective of "search and destroy" as a strategy to "search out and destroy communist forces and infrastructure in South Vietnam by offensive military operations." Westmoreland describes the enemy as communists, concealing the fact that the real targets were the peasants who refused to live under a corrupt, brutal dictatorship supported by the Americans. In actual fact, the real enemy was not communists but the corrupt regime in Saigon.

Westmoreland's objective was to target the peasant population in a war of attrition in which all Vietnamese people were perceived as fair game. Underlying the "search and destroy" strategy was a widespread racist attitude toward the Vietnamese, who were referred to as "gooks," "slants," and "dinks." The racism poured down from the top, including General Westmoreland, who said that the "Oriental doesn't value life the same way as a Westerner" (*Hearts and Minds*, Peter Davis).

His plan was to flush out the NLF from the villages and destroy them with American airpower. Frequently, a group of U.S. soldiers would enter a village to massacre all the inhabitants who were either Vietcong or their supporters. The most notorious example was the case of My Lai in March 1968 when Charlie Company led by Captain Earnest Medina and Lieutenant William Calley entered a village and slaughtered over 350 unarmed women and children. After My Lai became public knowledge when Lieutenant Calley and Captain Medina were brought to trial, the public was given the impression that these were rogue officers and My Lai was an aberration. Smaller, unreported My Lais occurred throughout the war. James Duffy, a machine gunner on a Chinook helicopter for Company A of the 228th Aviation Battalion, 1st Airborne Division, testified at the "Winter Soldier" investigation in 1971 that:

> I swung my machine gun into this group of peasants and opened fire…But my mind was so psyched out into killing gooks that I never even paid attention to look around and see where I was. I just saw gooks and I wanted to kill them.

(*Testimony of the 1st Air Cavalry Division, Part II*, Winter Soldier Investigation)

Other similar incidents included E Company, 4th Battalion, 31st Infantry Brigade and 23rd Infantry Division, who swept through the Que Son Valley on September 29, 1969, burning homes, slaughtering animals, raping women and a girl, and executing members of the village. As well, B Company, 4th Battalion, 3rd Infantry Division killed an undetermined number of women and children in My Khe on March 16, 1968. Soldiers tossed grenades into shelters, shooting women and children as they ran for cover. These were but a few of the villages subjected to the savage treatment of U.S. forces on "search and destroy" missions.

According to the U.S. Subcommittee on Refugees, artillery fire, bombing, and massacres on the ground were responsible for at least 400,000 dead, 900,000 wounded, and 6.4 million refugees by 1971, all in an attempt to destroy the Vietcong's base of support and wear down the peasantry.

In addition to the "search and destroy" strategy, U.S. objectives included a bombing campaign in both North and South Vietnam. The purpose of the bombing campaign in the North was to force Ho Chi Minh into submission and to terminate the shipment of supplies to the South on the Ho Chi Minh Trail, which ran along the border of Vietnam, Cambodia, and Laos. The objective of the bombing campaign in the South was to defoliate the jungles and forests to deprive guerrilla fighters of cover and food.

Rolling Thunder, the bombing campaign in the North, included such targets as transportation routes, supply routes, munitions dumps, oil-storage facilities, power plants, factories, and airfields. A CIA study discloses that by 1968 there had been approximately 36,000 casualties, 29,000 of whom were civilians. As well, according to William Wilson in *Rolling Thunder*, by 1968, the number of bombing missions over the North was 148,000 per year, which dropped 128,000 tons of bombs.

The bombers also dropped two internationally banned chemicals, Agent Orange and napalm, both used to defoliate jungles and forests. The objective in bombing the South was to create a level playing field so that American troops were not disadvantaged by the guerrilla warfare tactics of the Vietcong. American troops were not trained for guerrilla warfare, and the Vietcong were no match for American technological superiority. To fight the war on their terms, the Americans decided to defoliate the South.

Napalm, a mixture of gasoline and a chemical thickening agent, is a highly flammable substance used as an incendiary bomb. Agent Orange is an herbicide containing one of the deadliest substances known, dioxin, which was used as a defoliant. Both these substances are not only deadly to human beings but are extremely destructive to the environment.

President Kennedy authorized the use of herbicides in 1961 as part of the counter-insurgency campaign. Between 1962 and 1970, U.S. bombers and helicopters dropped a total of 100 million pounds of Agent Orange and other types of herbicides over four million acres of land covering 10 percent of the landmass of South Vietnam. The quantity of chemicals dropped in the South is equivalent to 300 pounds of high explosives for every man, women, or child in South Vietnam. By the end of the war, an astounding twenty-five million acres of farmland and twelve million acres of forest had been destroyed.

Shockingly, the result of the spraying was a massive number of deaths and injuries, the loss of valuable farmland, irreparable damage to the environment, and lingering contamination, which still causes death and disease to the Vietnamese people today. The heavy human toll exacted since 1961 from spraying includes the deaths of 400,000 people, 500,000 birth defects, multiple miscarriages, and cancer. Today, Vietnam has the highest concentration of dioxin on the planet. The pain and suffering directly attributable to these chemicals has been horrific and unconscionable, violating every tenet of international law.

American bombers also dropped cluster bombs on both South and North Vietnam, a weapon that has since been banned internationally due to the fact that it kills indiscriminately, destroying anyone within its range. Cluster bombs are dropped from bombers or launched from the ground, and before hitting their target, eject multiple small submunitions or bomblets, which range over a wide area, killing anyone in their path. Another impact is that a high percentage of the bomblets fail to explode. The result is that landmines or unexploded ordnance become time bombs, waiting to be triggered by some unsuspecting innocent person.

Overall, the U.S. Air Force dropped 82.6 million cluster bombs on both South and North Vietnam, with approximately 800,000 still in the soil that have not yet exploded. Consequently, 35 percent of the land in Central Vietnam cannot be farmed. An estimated 38,000 people have been killed by cluster bombs, while 65,000 have been injured by unexploded submunitions since the war ended.

Among the primary targets, the Vietcong were all members of the NLF, the political wing of the movement whose objective was to overthrow the totalitarian government in South Vietnam. One method of rooting out members of the NLF civilian infrastructure and NLF sympathizers was a paramilitary operation in which CIA agents identified possible NLF suspects, who were then tortured and executed. Named Operation Phoenix, it was authorized by President Johnson in May 1967. CIA operatives set up offices throughout South Vietnam to conduct intelligence operations as well as advise South Vietnamese soldiers who were part of the operation. According to former CIA director William Colby, who was testifying before the 1973 Church Committee of Congress:

> The function of the Phoenix offices was to collate intelligence about the Vietcong infrastructure, interrogate civilians picked up at random by military units carrying out sweeps through villages, and "neutralize" targeted members of the NLF.

Once the civilians were rounded up, they were held without due process and then tortured and murdered. William Colby claimed that 20,587 persons were murdered as a result of the Phoenix program.

CIA operatives in the Phoenix Program were allocated quotas of 1,800 civilians a month, a target that was exceedingly difficult to fill, thus encouraging agents to be overly zealous in identifying suspects. As well, members of the NLF civilian infrastructure were impossible to distinguish from the general population, resulting in the death of many people who were not members of the NLF.

Not all the battles were fought in villages and the jungle. On January 21, 1968, approximately 70,000 Vietcong and North Vietnamese soldiers launched a surprise offensive of extraordinary intensity aimed at South Vietnamese urban areas. They invaded thirty-six of the forty-four provincial capitals along with numerous other towns. The purpose of the offensive was to draw American forces to urban centers, where they would be bogged down trying to prevent a calamitous defeat. Although the Vietcong and North Vietnamese forces were spread too thin to capture any of these urban centers, they accomplished their goal of winning the countryside and destroying the pacification program. Their losses in the cities were more than compensated for by recruiting new troops in the countryside.

The Tet offensive and the progress of the war in general

persuaded President Johnson to renew an offer he proposed in the fall of 1967, to stop bombing North Vietnam in exchange for productive discussions. North Vietnam responded to the offer by insisting that the bombing stop before any discussions could begin. In his Address to the Nation on March 31, 1968, President Johnson reported that:

> Their [Vietcong and troops from the North] attack—during the Tet holidays—failed to achieve its principal objectives. It did not collapse the elected government of South Vietnam… The Communists were unable to maintain control of any of the more than 30 cities that they attacked. And they took very heavy casualties.

President Johnson maintained the myth that the government of South Vietnam had been democratically elected and referred to the enemy as communists, ignoring the fact that the people the Americans were fighting were the people of South Vietnam. He also suggested that the "Communists" were unable to achieve any of their objectives when, in fact, their objective was not to capture any of the cities but to win in the countryside.

In renewing his offer to talk, he proposed that:

> Tonight, I renew the offer I made last August—to stop the bombardment of North Vietnam. We ask that talks begin promptly, that they be serious talks on the substance of peace. We assume that during those talks Hanoi will not take advantage of our restraint. We are prepared to move immediately toward peace through negotiations.

Talks began in Paris in 1969 after R. M. Nixon won the presidential election and included representatives from Saigon and the Vietcong. Preparing the way for eventual withdrawal, Melvin Laird, the new Defense Secretary under Nixon, invented the term Vietnamization, which was a face-saving measure. It was defined as a process of turning over the responsibility of defending South Vietnam to South Vietnamese troops with full knowledge that the North would easily overrun the South after an American withdrawal.

David Model

Henry Kissinger, the new National Security Advisor under Nixon, conducted secret negotiations with Le Duc Tho, the North Vietnamese negotiator. Both the official and secret sets of talks underwent a series of vicissitudes until Kissinger and Le Duc Tho finally signed an initial agreement on January 8, 1973. Cease-fire agreements were then formally signed in Paris on January 27, 1973. American troop strength had been dwindling since 1969, and the remaining American troops were shipped home March 29, 1973.

Vietcong and North Vietnamese troops captured Saigon on March 25, 1975, achieving the united Vietnam that the Geneva Accords could not achieve seventeen years earlier due to U.S. opposition. During that harrowing seventeen years, the United States committed genocide in South Vietnam.

The victims of genocide were the rural population, members of the NLF and Vietcong. The United States had installed and supported a succession of dictatorships in the South who were subservient to U.S. imperatives. These dictatorships were corrupt and did not serve the interests of the population. They did not implement an effective land reform or agrarian policy or any other political, social, or economic reforms that would have ameliorated the life of the peasants of South Vietnam. After the insurgency began, the government forcibly removed peasants from their land and transferred them to central locations for the pacification program. The conditions in these central hamlets were poor, and the peasants deeply resented their evacuation from their homes.

All the peasants' grievances with their government incited many of them to either join the Vietcong or support them. The Vietcong themselves were the military wing of the NLF, whose purpose was to overthrow the brutal and corrupt dictatorship propped up by the Americans.

The peasants were the obstacle to American dominance of South Vietnam. They threatened American objectives, which were to establish a base of operations in Asia, and to prevent Vietnam from becoming an example of a socially just alternative to American free market ideology.

Therefore, it became necessary to attack the people who posed the threat to their objectives, namely the rural population, the Vietcong and NLF who were South Vietnamese, and the soldiers from the North who were supporting the insurgency. If the only enemy was North Vietnam, then the Americans were throwing the baby out with the bath water, or in other words, destroying the very people they were trying to save. In either case, the victims were the people of South Vietnam.

The issue of "in whole or in part" can be resolved by examining the strategy of the United States. They started by supporting the army of South Vietnam with advisors, military and economic aid, and intelligence (CIA). They initiated a bombing campaign against the South (and North) using conventional weapons, cluster bombs, and then chemical weapons, all of which were aimed at the Vietcong and peasants who were supporting them. Finally, they shipped a massive number of troops to the South, many of whom were engaged in "search and destroy" missions designed to kill Vietcong and the rural peasantry who supported them.

American efforts to achieve their goal of obliterating the insurgency continually escalated as it became clear that more force was needed to accomplish their goals. Force applied by the United States resulted in an exorbitant mounting death toll. Had the war continued, the death toll would have risen proportionately. The aim was to destroy the insurgency, whose numbers increased with every atrocity committed by American forces or the Saigon government. As the objective was to kill as many peasants as necessary to destroy Vietcong operations, the "in part" represents the death of over four million people. Therefore, the "in whole or in part" requirement of the Genocide Convention is clearly met.

When examining the issue of "intention," it is important to remember that motivation is sufficient if "actions or omissions of such criminal negligence or recklessness that the defendant must reasonably be assumed to have been aware of the consequences of his conduct." Based on the evidence presented in this chapter, there is no question that American war planners were well aware of the approximate number of people in the South who were casualties of American war efforts.

President Kennedy authorized the use of chemical weapons, which were to be dropped indiscriminately on heavily populated areas. The consequences of these weapons could have easily been predicted. The indiscriminate use of cluster bombs had well-known consequences and was mainly used to kill people. Operation Phoenix was authorized by President Johnson, and its function was to capture "suspected" members of the NLF, "interrogate" them, and "neutralize them." According to former CIA Director William Colby, CIA operatives were to "interrogate civilians picked up at random…and neutralize targeted members of the NLF." "Search and destroy" missions were the conception of General Westmoreland but were authorized by President Johnson. Sending a massive number of troops into villages searching for Vietcong who were indistinguishable from the peasants had well-known consequences. General Westmoreland defined the purpose of these missions as a means, "to search out and destroy communist forces and infrastructure by offensive military operations." American soldiers on these missions would have had no method for distinguishing a so-called communist from a peasant, and therefore everyone was "fair game."

In the South, villages were burned and were subject to massive bombardments. As well, cattle were killed, vegetation was destroyed by defoliants, and any food stores of the villagers were destroyed. The consequences of these actions would have been predictable given the war strategies adopted by the Americans. The intent may not have been to commit genocide, but the motivation to destroy the Vietcong and their base of support inevitably resulted in a massive number of casualties.

The argument that the United States was defending South Vietnam from North Vietnam is specious for a number of reasons. General Eisenhower refused to sign the 1954 Geneva Accords and pressured South Vietnam to refrain from participating in the election process called for by the accords. If the will of the people of South Vietnam was to be united with the North, then the United States had no right to intervene because they were threatened by the probable outcome. Peasants in the South and the NLF, not the North Vietnamese, started the insurgency due to the corrupt and undemocratic puppet government in Saigon. Originally, the North did not attack the South.

In fact, part of the problem was American interference in the political process in South Vietnam to ensure that U.S. interests were served. First, the United States rejected the 1954 Geneva Conventions and thereafter insured that "their man" ruled in the South, perpetuating governments that were not serving the interests of the people.

The final toll of death and suffering was astronomical, and the carnage is one of the worst humanitarian disasters since World War II. Possibly, only the Congo can match the horror show in Vietnam. One of the tragic ironies of the war is that American governments were claiming to be securing the freedom for the people in South Vietnam when, in fact, they imprisoned them in a cesspool of horrors and barbarity.

4

CAMBODIA: DOUBLE JEOPARDY.

On May 29, 1928, Saloth Sar, the youngest of seven children, was born near the town of Kompong Thom, Cambodia. Although Saloth Sar's father owned nine hectares of rice land, he never worked a single day in a rice field nor knew peasant life. As part of the privileged middle class, he was fortunate enough to attend high school and then learn carpentry in the capital, Phnom Penh, until he received a scholarship to study radioelectricity in Paris. After failing three years in a row in Paris, he returned home. Those who knew him said that he would never kill a chicken and described him as charming and self-effacing, yet between 1975 and 1979 Saloth Sar was directly responsible for the murder of 1.5 million people. He became known as Pol Pot.

Surprisingly, his rise to power in Cambodia could be attributed to a large extent to American intervention, which consisted of invasions by American and South Vietnam troops, scorched earth bombing, and interference in the political process of the country.

Cambodia was a victim of both the Vietnam War and cold war politics. The Ho Chi Minh Trail, which ran along the Cambodian border, was a supply route for North Vietnamese troops, and Washington reproved of Cambodia's efforts to remain neutral in the miasma of Cold War politics in Indochina.

Despite Cambodia's neutrality, the United States engaged in a scorched earth bombing campaign to destroy North Vietnamese sanctuaries in Cambodia. American bombing was directly responsible for the deaths of 600,000 peasants and destruction of massive tracts of farmland on which the peasants depended for survival. As a result of the bombing, many of the displaced peasants joined an extremist revolutionary group called the Khmer Rouge, and the remainder fled to the city with no means of survival. Many of the peasants strongly resented the American-supported government in Phnom Penh, who turned a blind eye to the bombing. Consequently, peasants were either impelled to join the Khmer Rouge or to become their base of support. When the Khmer Rouge finally did succeed in attaining power, they perpetrated one of the bloodiest carnages since World War II. They emptied the cities, tore apart families, forced men, women, and children to work long hours in rice fields without adequate food, and savagely butchered 1.5 million people.

American actions in Cambodia attest to the guilt of American leaders in genocide because of their direct intervention in Cambodia and also attest to their complicity in the genocide committed by the Khmer Rouge. As a result of their actions, the United States is either directly or indirectly responsible for the deaths of over 1.5 million people.

American involvement in Cambodia began while the country was still a French colonial protectorate, as it had been since 1863. The French decided to abandon any attempt to hold onto Cambodia as a colony in 1953 in the face of a growing insurgency and the all-consuming war with the Viet Minh in Vietnam.

The insurgency movement seeking independence changed direction when Prince Sihanouk, who had been appointed king by the French, decided to pursue the route of negotiation rather than armed conflict. As the opposition became more impatient, Sihanouk dissolved the Assembly and declared martial law in 1952. When the French conceded in 1953, Sihanouk became king of an independent Cambodia.

One of the groups struggling for independence was a communist organization called the Khmer People's Revolutionary Party (KPRP). Pol Pot eventually captured the leadership, and in 1966 the name of the Party was changed to the Communist Party of Kampuchea (CPK). CPK formed an armed resistance movement against Prince Sihanouk and called themselves the Khmer Rouge.

The movement's growing strength partly contributed to Prince Sihanouk's ambition to establish a neutral and unaligned state, which was reinforced when the Geneva Accords of 1954 confirmed Cambodia's neutrality. Sihanouk's aspirations for a nonaligned state were hampered by his decision to rig the 1955 elections, thereby denying seats to parties in the center and left, and by closing opposition newspapers.

Further antagonizing the United States, he criticized the newly formed Southeast Asia Treaty Organization (SEATO) created by the United States and its allies, who were seeking a bulwark against Communist China. At the same time, he visited Peking, where he agreed to peaceful coexistence with China and accepted economic aid from them.

In retaliation for his accommodations with China, the United States cut off aid to Cambodia while Thailand and South Vietnam imposed a blockade severing vital transportation routes throughout these two countries.

Moreover, American apprehensiveness about Cambodia's political leanings induced Americans to ensure that Cambodia did not interfere with American aims in the region. South Vietnam army units invaded Cambodian border areas to prevent Vietcong or North Vietnamese soldiers from operating in relatively safe territory. To compound the problem, Thai and South Vietnamese forces supported, armed, and trained by the CIA were encroaching on Cambodian territory. As well, since the early sixties, U.S. Special Forces had been engaging in secret reconnaissance and mine-laying missions in Cambodian territory. By 1967, these missions, code-named Salem House, numbered about 800. The name was changed to Operation Daniel Boone and the number of missions doubled by 1969. By March 1970 there had been 1,000 additional missions.

All of these encroachments on the territorial integrity of Cambodia violated international law, as did any acts of war carried out inside Cambodia. These incursions were strongly proscribed by international law because they were perpetrated against a neutral country not at war.

The continuing efforts to pressure Sihanouk to forsake his neutrality backfired as he dug in his heels by implementing a program of economic reforms and rejecting American military and economic aid. In 1964, he even threatened to sever diplomatic relations with the United States if they supported any further violations of Cambodian territory.

American frustration with Vietcong and North Vietnamese incursions into Cambodian territory persuaded the United States to launch a bombing campaign initially just inside the Cambodian border. Following through with his threat, Sihanouk broke off relations with the U.S in 1965 as bombing of Cambodian villages continued.

As in Vietnam, Washington stepped into the exigency of war to transform Cambodia into an ally of the U.S. American policymakers would not even tolerate a neutral Cambodia and were determined to ensure that Cambodian territory was not available to Vietcong or North Vietnam forces.

The ongoing forays conducted by the Americans, now in conjunction with the South Vietnamese, steamrolled further and further into Cambodian territory in search of enemy supply lines and sanctuaries. Shockingly, the United States was also dropping napalm on Cambodian villages.

Throughout the 1960s, the violations of Cambodian sovereignty in search of the enemy amounted to 1,864 border violations, 165 sea violations, 5,149 air violations, 293 Cambodian deaths, and 690 Cambodians wounded (*Far East Economic Review*, T. D. Allman).

In addition to the violations of Cambodian territory, Cambodia was suffering from declining stocks of rice to feed its peasants and from decreasing revenues from taxes on the export of rice. This problem corresponded to the continually increasing number of American and North Vietnamese troops in Vietnam, all of whom required food.

Cambodia experienced record rice harvests in 1963 and 1964, which made the balance of trade in rice positive. In 1965, American troop levels increased from 20,000 to 300,000; thus the recruitment drives of the NLF quadrupled. A large quantity of Cambodian rice was smuggled across the border to feed the soldiers on both sides, resulting in less rice for Cambodian peasants and reduced tax revenues from rice exports (*The Pol Pot Regime*, Ben Kiernan).

Sihanouk now had severe problems for several reasons: first because of the rice shortage and second because the U.S. clearly would not tolerate his neutrality any further. The opportunity for change materialized when Lon Nol, Premier of Cambodia and former Minister of Defense with close ties to the American military, began plotting a coup to overthrow Sihanouk.

The United States was connected to these plans, and there is incontrovertible evidence that in 1969, Lon Nol was approached by agents of American military intelligence who asked him to overthrow Sihanouk (*The Price of Power*, Seymour M. Hersh). According to Samuel R. Thornton, an intelligence officer operating inside Cambodia, Lon Nol was seeking a guarantee from Washington that after the coup he would receive military, political, and economic support. Thornton also claimed that approval for the planned coup came from Washington, where interest in the coup lay "at the highest levels of government." Furthermore, Frank Snepp, a strategic analyst for the CIA, claimed that if Sihanouk was replaced by Lon Nol, "he would welcome the United States with open arms and we would accomplish everything" (*Sideshow*, William Shawcross, p. 115).

On March 18, 1970, Sihanouk was deposed from power in a military coup led by Lon Nol. Within hours of the coup, American and South Vietnamese forces stationed inside Cambodia contacted Cambodian commanders to extend the hand of cooperation.

With Lon Nol as the new head of state, war planners believed that they now had a freer hand in fighting the war on communism. In January 1969, the military had more to celebrate when a new American government took office. The crisis of troop incursions, bombing, and rice smuggling all pale in comparison to the policies implemented by the newly elected President, Richard Nixon, and his National Security Advisor, Henry Kissinger, in 1969.

During Kissinger's first week in office, the Pentagon reported to the White House that a defector had pinpointed the exact location of the Central Office for South Vietnam (COSVN), Vietcong headquarters, located inside the Cambodian border. The legitimacy of the information was supposedly verified by other intelligence sources. General Earle G. Weaver, Chairman of the Joint Chiefs of Staff, advocated a "short-duration, concentrated B-52 attack" on COSVN in order to counter an imminent North Vietnamese offensive.

Although Kissinger received conflicting advice about the plan to bomb COSVN, he decided to proceed on the condition that the operation would be conducted in the utmost secrecy, thereby concealing the mission from Congress and the American people. The obsession with secrecy became an imperative, because the United States was planning to bomb a neutral country with which it was not at war.

To preserve the secrecy of the operation, Kissinger was prepared to bypass the Strategic Air Command's normal command and control system. His preoccupation with secrecy was so strong that he did not want even the crews bombing Cambodia to be aware of their targets.

Nixon and Kissinger asked Air Force Colonel Ray B. Sitton, an aide to the Joint Chiefs of Staff (JCS), to devise a reporting scheme for American bombers dropping bombs on Cambodia that would ensure absolute confidentiality.

The clandestine operation began with a cable from President Nixon to Ambassador Ellsworth Bunker (American Ambassador to South Vietnam), explaining that all discussions about the bombing of Cambodia were to be absolutely secretive.

Not everyone approved of the project, as was the case with the Secretary of Defense, Melvin Laird, who was more skeptical. Despite his reservations, Laird agreed that if COSVN was actually destroyed, it would justify the bombings.

COSVN was located in an area designated as Area 353. To maintain the secrecy of the operation, sixty B-52 aircraft were sent on a regular bombing mission to legitimate targets in South Vietnam. Forty-eight of the planes would then be diverted to targets inside Cambodia in "Operation Breakfast."

Critical to the operation was the dual reporting system created by Sitton. Before takeoff, the B-52 crews were given their normal briefing for targets in South Vietnam, most of which were cover targets. After their usual briefing, the pilots and navigators of the planes heading for Cambodia were pulled aside by their commanding officer and were told to expect special instructions from a ground radar station inside Vietnam. Computers at the radar station would take control of the navigation system in the planes and guide them to their real targets in Cambodia and compute the precise moment at which the bombs were to be released.

After the bombing had been completed, the bomber's radio operator would call his base to report that the mission had been accomplished, and the intelligence division at the base would enter the South Vietnamese coordinates rather than the Cambodian coordinates in the official report. Major Hal Knight, commander of the radar crews, would collect any paperwork related to the real targets and burn it.

At the completion of the missions, the pilots would return to their home base for a debriefing on the cover targets in South Vietnam. The evaluation of the bombing mission would then be reported in the Pentagon's secret command and control system as if the mission had taken place over South Vietnam. The men who worked on the ground radar sites in South Vietnam would be provided with top-secret target instructions a few hours before each mission by a special courier flight from Saigon. The radar operators in South Vietnam knew the real targets but maintained secrecy until the Watergate hearings in 1973.

Area 353 bombing mission operated on the same plan, and when it was completed, Kissinger received a cable reporting that the bombing mission had been an unqualified success. During their debriefings, the crew members had reported seventy-three secondary explosions, signaling a direct hit on Viet Cong headquarters and their stores of munitions.

To verify destruction of COSVN, the United States sent a "Daniel Boone" team into Area 353 to assess the damage. The mission was carried out by two or three Americans, wearing nondescript uniforms to protect their identity, and up to ten local mercenaries. After the helicopters had dropped the intelligence team and departed, communists hiding behind trees began firing at the team, who immediately dispersed and called for help. A helicopter landed through weapons fire to rescue the four survivors.

Many American and Cambodian lives would have been spared had the planners of the secret operation to destroy COSVN in Cambodia been aware of the fact that there were no stationary headquarters. COSVN never remained in one location for more than ten days. It moved constantly, leaving a false trail for American intelligence.

Initially, General Creighton Abrams had hoped that a single attack would destroy COSVN, limiting the number of violations of Cambodia's territorial integrity. When it became clear that Vietcong headquarters had eluded American bombers, more bombing missions inside Cambodia became necessary.

The next target selected, Base Area 609, code-named "Lunch," was also suspected of harboring COSVN, not to mention the 198 Cambodians who lived there. After the mission was completed, American intelligence discovered that they had missed COSVN again. In total, there were fifteen targets in this project where they suspected COSVN was located, code-named "menu," but discovered afterwards that they had failed to bomb Vietcong headquarters.

As Vietcong and North Vietnamese headquarters penetrated further into the interior, American bombing missions had to expand their scope of operations. Nixon and Kissinger approved 3,530 flights, which dropped 100,000 tons of bombs over Cambodia between February 1969 and April 1970.

Many of the residents of the towns that were bombed took refuge in the forest, seething with rage at the people who were destroying their villages and property. Many of the peasants were radicalized by the American bombing, and some, in resentment and anger, joined the CPK. Many who didn't join became a base of support.

By the end of 1970, Cambodia was reeling from a shortage of rice, destruction of towns and villages, a growing number of refugees, and the extension of the Vietnam War into Cambodian territory. American leaders were well aware of the devastation that they were inflicting on Cambodia as indicated by a declassified CIA document which warned that:

> Cambodia is showing the strains of the growing military, political and economic pressures of the war. The surge of national spirit and euphoria that followed the coup against Sihanouk in March 1970 has been dampened by the grim realities of casualty lists, refugee movements, and economic strains.

(*Taking Stock in Cambodia*, Central Intelligence Agency, February 18, 1972)

Furthermore, in the transcript of a tape, recording a conversation between President Nixon and Henry Kissinger, the President demanded, "…a plan where every goddamn thing that can fly goes into Cambodia and hits every target that is open."

American leaders were also aware of the growing strength of the Khmer Rouge and the threat they posed to Lon Nol. According to a declassified CIA document:

> There has also been considerable expansion of the indigenous communist apparatus and guerrilla force—the Khmer Rouge (KR). Estimates of KR strength vary widely, but a functioning KR apparatus now exists in most and possibly all the Cambodian provinces…The KR organization includes a combat force of some 15–50,000, concentrated primarily near the major communist bases in the northeast…they present a persistent challenge to government control in the lightly defended countryside…"

(*Taking Stock in Cambodia*, Central Intelligence Agency, February 18, 1972)

Frustration over the failure of the heavy bombing to destroy COSVN convinced Kissinger and his staff that a broad ground attack was absolutely necessary to achieve their objective. Nixon believed that if South Vietnamese troop forces were attempting to destroy the enemy's sanctuaries, it seemed strategically sound to use American forces as well. Two of the targets were Area 352 and Area 353, where Abrams believed COSVN was still operating despite the fact that 29,000 bombs had already been dropped there. On April 29, 1970, American ground forces invaded Cambodia.

The United States dispatched 5,000 U.S. troops into northeastern Cambodia, 1,500 into the Fishhook area, and opened a new front with 6,000 troops. In total, there were 25,000 American troops in Cambodia by May 1970. The end result was destruction of a number of towns and most of their citizens simply because they were suspected communists. American and South Vietnamese forces committed acts of rape, looting, and burning villages, forcing about 50,000 Cambodians to seek safety in overcrowded refugee camps in South Vietnam. In total, the invasion created 130,000 refugees (*The Pol Pot Regime*, Ben Kiernan).

Although U.S. ground forces withdrew from Cambodia in 1973, the scorched earth policy continued on a massive scale. By the end of 1973, U.S. B-52s had bombed Cambodia for 160 consecutive days, dropping in excess of 240,000 tons. At one point, the bombing reached a level of 3,600 tons a day.

As the bombing escalated, the number of people from destroyed villages who took refuge in Phnom Penh increased, and the recruitment efforts of the Khmer Rouge became more successful.

The CIA's Director of Operations commenting on the impact of the bombing on the strength of the Khmer Rouge reported that:

> They are using damage caused by B-52 strikes as the main theme of their propaganda campaign. The cadre tell the people that the Government of Lon Nol has requested the airstrikes and is responsible for the damage and the "suffering of innocent villagers"…The only way to stop "the massive

destruction of the country is to...defeat Lon Nol and stop the bombing."

This approach has resulted in the successful recruitment of a number young men ...Residents say that the propaganda campaign has been effective with the refugees and in areas... which have been subjected to B-52 strikes.

(*The Pol Pot Regime*, Ben Kiernan, p. 22)

The U.S. House of Representatives blocked any further funding for the bombing of Cambodia on May 10, 1973, but in fact, it did not actually end until August 15 of the same year. During the American bombing, the United States dropped 2,756,941 tons of explosives and flew 230,516 sorties over Cambodia on 113,716 targets.

Following the end of American intervention in Cambodia, Lon Nol fought a losing battle with the Khmer Rouge until they successfully marched into Phnom Penh on April 17, 1975. American occupants of the U.S. Embassy had already evacuated the building on April 12. Cambodia now belonged to the Khmer Rouge.

By 1975, Cambodia was a country in ruins where leveled villages littered the countryside, one million refugees had fled to Phnom Penh, and much of the farmland had been destroyed in the wake of carpet bombing. With crops unsowed and a shortage of food, hundreds of thousands of people died from starvation and disease.

The scale of the death and destruction from the bombing was shockingly massive. The Finnish Inquiry Commission estimates that 600,000 Cambodians died out of a population of seven million and two million refugees sought safety in either the cities of Cambodia, South Vietnam, or Thailand. The Commission referred to the atrocities in Cambodia as genocidal.

To simplify the analysis, the atrocities in Cambodia are divided into three genocides. The devastation caused by the invasion and bombing perpetrated by the United States meet the criteria of the Genocide Convention and thus qualifies as genocide. As well, the United States contributed to strengthening the Khmer Rough by bombing farmland and driving peasants into their waiting arms. Furthermore, the Khmer Rouge exploited the bombing in a propaganda campaign to win new recruits. American atrocities had incited such an impassioned fury over the loss of life and land that the peasants became a base of support for the Khmer Rouge. Once in power, the Khmer Rouge committed genocide. The United States is complicit in the genocide committed by the Khmer Rouge. The third genocide occurred after the American bombing, which resulted in destroyed farmland, food shortages, and peasant refugees in Phnom Penh and other cities. To exacerbate the problem, American aid was terminated at the same time. The impact of the bombing precipitated conditions that would inevitably cause starvation and disease well after the Americans left. These conditions and the destruction they wrought qualify as genocide.

The bombing and invasion targeted the rural population of Cambodia because that is where the Vietcong and North Vietnamese were located. The "whole or in part" criteria is based on the clause, "The accused aimed to destroy a large part of the group in a particular community." In this case "community" is those Cambodians who live in rural areas.

Six hundred thousand people who were killed in the rural community constitute a sufficient number to qualify as genocide based on precedents already established. As well as killing members of the group, the bombing inflicted, "…on the group conditions of life calculated to bring about its physical destruction in whole or in part." A CIA document clearly shows that the U.S. government was well aware of the hardships inflicted on the rural community when it states that, "Cambodia is showing the strains of the growing military, political, and economic pressures of the war" (see *Taking Stock in Cambodia* above).

Intent is clearly established by the elaborate planning of the bombing missions and by the words of President Nixon when he demanded that the bombers "hit every target that is open." Furthermore, in a telephone conversation between Nixon and Kissinger, Nixon blusters that:

> The point of the matter is—oh Goddammit Abrams can do more and that damned Air Force can do more about hitting Cambodia with their bombing attacks....I want them to hit everything. I want them to use big planes, the small planes, everything that will help out here and let's start giving them a little shock.

(*Henry A. Kissinger Telephone Transcripts*, Nixon Presidential Materials Project, December 9, 1970)

As well, the outcomes of the bombing were well known according to the declassified CIA documents cited above.

Moreover, the American bombing "deliberately inflicted on the group conditions of life calculated to bring about its physical destruction in whole or in part." The consequences of bombing rice farms were well known because part of the U.S. strategy was to deny food to the Vietcong and North Vietnamese troops in addition to destroying Vietcong sanctuaries. At the same time, bombing would have reduced rice supplies for the people of Cambodia due to the loss of farmland. Furthermore, peasants who flocked to the cities deprived the countryside of farmers. Therefore, American atrocities in the bombing of Cambodia qualify as genocide.

The fact that the United States did not intend to commit genocide when it destroyed the countryside is irrelevant, since the predictable consequences of their actions would have been massive destruction and death.

The genocide caused by the bombing was followed by the genocide perpetrated on the people of Cambodia when Pol Pot and the Khmer Rouge took power. The Khmer Rouge's first course of action was to evacuate Phnom Penh and all other cities and towns so that people could work the land. Cambodians were expected to work long hours from 5 am until dark with inadequate food and medicine. Family units were separated, family names abolished, and the onus was placed on individual will power to overcome hardships in order to survive.

The Khmer Rouge were obsessively driven by an ideology that

included the creation of a classless, agrarian society where everyone would speak the same language and lose their individual identity. Strict adherence to the ideology was demanded of every citizen, and anyone who was even slightly suspected of expressing any resistance or dissent was immediately executed.

The Party leadership exercised very tight control over the population, as pointed out by Ben Kiernan when he observed that:

> Despite its underdeveloped economy, the regime probably exerted more control over its citizens than any state in world history. It controlled and directed their public and private lives more closely than government had ever done.

(*The Pol Pot Regime*, Ben Kiernan, p. 464)

Estimates of the number of deaths vary significantly from study to study, but I am relying mainly on the estimates of Ben Kiernan, one of the leading experts on the subject of Cambodia. According to his research, 1.5 million people died during the Pol Pot reign of terror.

To prove that American actions contributed to the genocide of the Khmer Rouge, it is first necessary to prove that the Khmer Rouge did, in fact, commit genocide. To substantiate this, it is only necessary to refer to a panel created by the United Nations called the Group of Experts who were commissioned to examine all available evidence in order to determine whether or not the Khmer Rouge leaders should be charged with the crime of genocide. The Group of Experts concluded that the Khmer Rouge had "subjected the people of Cambodia to almost all the acts enumerated in the Convention" (*The Pol Pot Regime*, Ben Kiernan). They also concluded that:

> [The] evidence suggests the need for prosecution to investigate the commission of genocide against the Cham, Vietnamese and other minority groups, and the Buddhist monkhood. The Khmer Rouge subjected these groups to an especially harsh and extensive measure of the acts enumerated in the Convention. The requisite intent has support in direct and indirect evidence, including Khmer Rouge statements,

eyewitness accounts and the nature and number of victims in each group...

(*The Pol Pot Regime*, Ben Kiernan)

The requirement that the victims of the genocide conform to one of the groups in the Convention is met because the Chams, Vietnamese, and other minority groups living in Cambodia were targeted. On the surface, it might appear that the Khmer Rouge were targeting those who manifested any disapproval of their ideology, or in other words, a political group. It has been proven by the Group of Experts that the targeted groups were in fact ethnic or national groups, which meet the criteria of the Convention. As well, Ben Kiernan in an exhaustive study concluded that "there is no question that Democratic Kampuchea waged a campaign of genocide against ethnic Vietnamese...Now there is no doubt that Democratic Kampuchea regime intended to destroy the Cham Muslim religious group 'as such'" (*The Pol Pot Regime*, Ben Kiernan, p. 460–462).

To demonstrate American complicity, it is also essential to prove that they participated in some way and had knowledge of the genocide perpetrated by the Khmer Rouge. The American contribution to the Khmer Rouge genocide is related to their direct responsibility for the expansion of Khmer Rouge strength and for creating a base of support that they enjoyed before imposing their ideology on the people of Cambodia. Jon Swain of the *Sunday Times* (London) reported that:

> The United States has much to answer for here, not only in terms of human lives and massive material destruction; the rigidity and nastiness of the un-Cambodian like fellows in black who run this country now, or what is left of it, are as much a product of this wholesale American bombing which has hardened and honed their minds as they are a product of Marx and Mao...The entire countryside has been churned up by American B-52 bomb craters, whole towns and villages razed.

(*Sunday Times*, Jon Swain, "Diary of a Doomed City")

David Chandler in *Public Affairs* observed that:

Aside from killing and maiming tens of thousands of Cambodians who never fired a shot at an American, the bombing had several political effects, all beneficial to the C.P.K. [Khmer Rouge]. One was to demonstrate the party's contention that Cambodia's principal enemy was the United States. Another was to turn thousands of young Cambodians into participants in an anti-American crusade.

(*Public Affairs*, David Chandler, "When was the Birthday of the Party?")

Further, Ben Kiernan claims that:

Although it was indigenous, Pol Pot's revolution would not have won power without U.S. economic and military destabilization of Cambodia, which began in 1966 after the American escalation in next-door Vietnam and peaked in 1969–73 with the carpet bombing of Cambodia's countryside by American B-52s. This was probably the most the most important single factor in Pol Pot's rise.

(*The Pol Pot Regime*, Ben Kiernan, p. 16)

Taylor Owen and Ben Kiernan substantiate the claims above by pointing out that:

Civilian casualties in Cambodia drove an enraged populace into the arms of an insurgency that had enjoyed relatively little support until the bombing began, setting in motion the expansion of the Vietnam War deeper into Cambodia, a coup d'état in 1970, the rapid rise of the Khmer Rouge, and ultimately the Cambodian genocide.

(*ZNET*, Bombs over Cambodia)

As well, Noam Chomsky observed that:

[W]e must bear in mind that part of the death toll under phase II [the genocide committed by the Khmer Rouge] must be attributed to the conditions left by the U.S. war. As the war ended, deaths from starvation in Phnom Penh alone were running at about 100,000 a year, and the U.S. airlift that kept the population alive would result in one million deaths in Cambodia if U.S. aid were to cease....The U.S. embassy estimated that available rice in Phnom Penh would suffice for at most a few weeks. The final U.S. AID report observed that the country faced famine in 1975...The report predicted "widespread starvation"...assessing these various elements, it seems fair to describe the responsibility of the United States and Pol Pot atrocities during "the decade of genocide" as being roughly the same range.

(*Manufacturing Consent*, Noam Chomsky, p. 263)

Therefore, it is undeniable, based on the above evidence, that the U.S. bombing in Cambodia was a major factor in the rise of the Khmer Rouge.

Moreover, Washington was also very aware of the rapid growth of the Khmer Rouge as revealed in a declassified CIA document, which reported that "there has also been considerable expansion of the indigenous communist apparatus and guerrilla force (KR)" (see above, *Taking Stock in Cambodia*).

Finally, the last step in proving American complicity in genocide is to demonstrate that the American leadership had knowledge of the murderous nature of the Khmer Rouge. It must be shown that the Americans could have predicted that the Khmer Rouge would inflict atrocities on the Cambodian people to such an extent that their actions would constitute genocide. In a Senate report dated March 21, 1975, the Committee on Foreign Relations reported that:

Throughout the Committee's discussion of this decision [on U.S. involvement in Cambodia] the primary concerns of its members was how the present and prospective bloodshed in Cambodia could be minimized. In this respect the possibility that an insurgent victory would be followed by a bloodbath weighed heavily on the minds of the members. Reference was made to testimony on this point before the Committee by

Members of Congress who recently visited Southeast Asia. On March 6, 1975, for example, Representative Millicent Fenwick testified as follows:

There is no doubt that the horror, the terror, of the Khmer Rouge is something that I have never witnessed....Nobody knows exactly why this terror has reached the atrocities and the pitch in a place that was supposed to be composed of peaceful people.

Other testimony which committee members found impressive was that of Representative Paul N. McCloskey who stated that Cambodian refugees told him:

When the Khmer Rouge came into the village, they had summarily called out people to be executed, school teachers, two people in one village, and ten in another, all government civil servants anyone who the communists side could expect to ultimately be an opponent of the communist government.

(*Committee on Foreign Relations*, Supplemental Assistance for Cambodia, March 21, 1975)

A cable from the American embassy in Laos to the Department of State on March 12, 1975, reported that:

Khmer Rouge have also occupied West Bank of Mekong, encroaching on areas in which many Lao families live. He added that they have been "murdering" the people using 82 mm mortars to attack the villages...

(*American Embassy Cable Vientiane*, Lao Deputy Alleges Khmer Encroachments, March 12, 1975)

U.S. actions strengthened the Khmer Rouge to the point where they were empowered sufficiently to win control of the country.

It is now conclusive that Pol Pot committed genocide after the Americans were primarily responsible for the rise of the Khmer Rouge, and at the same time, the Americans were aware of the murderous intent of the Khmer Rouge. Therefore, America must share complicity in the genocide perpetrated by Pol Pot.

The third commission of genocide resulted from the conditions that Americans created before Pol Pot assumed control of the country. They were responsible for peasants leaving their farms to escape the bombing and for destroying the land on which the peasants worked. The peasants then swarmed the cities with refugees who had no shelter or food. It has been estimated that massive food shortages and disease were responsible for 100,000 deaths before the Khmer Rouge committed their own genocide.

John Rogers, in a *Washington Post* article, stated that:

Diplomats and officials of international relief organizations... point to the food crisis in Phnom Penh in the months preceding the Khmer Rouge victory as a further indicator of what must be happening now...[O]ne relief official [said,] "When you look at the facts, it is difficult to believe there is not mass starvation."

(*Washington Post*, John Rogers, "Cambodians are Starving, Refugees Say")

In a report to Congress, the Office of the Inspector-General of Foreign Assistance warned that:

In Phnom Penh, there are between one and two million refugees [from the U.S. bombing war] in a city that had a pre-war total of about 375,000. The added hundreds of thousands of destitute victims have proven a burden with which relief programs cannot cope.

William Shawcross reported that:

Throughout 1975 the population (particularly the "new people" from the towns) suffered terribly from lack of food; hundreds of thousands may well have died of starvation and disease.

(*Sideshow*, William Shawcross, p. 375)

To prove genocide, it is essential to demonstrate that American leaders were aware of the consequences that would befall the people of Cambodia after they withdrew. All the reports cited above clearly describe conditions in Cambodia before Pol Pot took power. Washington knew exactly what they had done, as illustrated by John Rogers's remarks when he noted that "Kissinger has been actively leaking White House intelligence on the tragic sufferings of the Cambodian people, including predictions that one million Cambodians will die in the next twelve months" (*Far Eastern Economic Review*, "Cambodia on the Rack," July 25, 1975).

The group who suffered from the American bombing were the peasants living in the countryside who were forced to move to cities, many of whom died after the Americans withdrew from Cambodia. American attacks "aimed to destroy a large part of the group in a particular community." They were also "inflicting on the group conditions of life calculated to bring about its physical destruction in whole or in part."

It is also clear from the above citations that the U.S. leaders fully intended to cause the destruction inflicted on the Cambodian people. Nixon ordered that "they have to go in there and I mean really go in…I want anything that can fly to go in there and crack the hell out of them." American actions produced conditions that caused severe suffering after American withdrawal. These actions constitute genocide.

In Cambodia, the United States was directly guilty of two genocides and complicit in a third, all three of which in total claimed over two million victims. All these people died needlessly because the United States did not want the "evil communists" to rule Southeast Asia, and in particular, Cambodia. It is true that the Khmer Rouge, who ultimately assumed power in Cambodia, murdered approximately 1.5 million people, but these were not the communists whom the Americans feared for a number of reasons. They started out as a marginal group who did not have the strength to take over the country. Moreover, they were not really communists as much as an extreme ideological group who believed in a utopian agrarian society. They were not even remotely interested in an international communist conspiracy, if one ever existed.

The turning point in this period of Cambodia's history occurred when the Americans overthrew Sihanouk. At that point, Cambodia was not in any grave danger of suffering the huge losses that they suffered after American intervention. From the "official" perspective, Cambodia needed to be destroyed in order to be saved: echoes of Vietnam.

5

LAOS: INNOCENT BYSTANDER.

A pattern can be identified in the two genocides in Vietnam and Cambodia that repeats itself in Laos. Washington's ultimate objectives in all three countries were to prevent a communist takeover while maintaining power over an American-friendly government.

To accomplish these objectives, the United States had to forestall a political settlement that would have allowed a left-wing party to gain control of a government that was not American-friendly. In the case of Laos, the Americans had to violate the 1954 Geneva Accords, which defined Laos as a neutral, independent state. Neutrality in Laos imports a coalition government consisting of both right- and left-wing parties that were impervious to American influence peddling. Part of the pattern in these countries involved overthrowing recalcitrant governments and installing a subservient dictator who would suspend the interests of his own people in order to satisfy American imperial interests.

To protect the government from insurgents or revolutionary forces, the United States provided military support, usually beginning with advisors to avoid the optics of intervention. In Laos, advisors were sent in 1955 to train the Lao army.

Advisors were usually followed by one of the most powerful levers available to the United States for influencing governments, military and economic aid. The U.S. signed an economic assistance agreement with the Laos government, which was to form the basis of American aid for many years. In 1955, the American government opened the U.S. Operation Mission in Laos to channel aid to the government that could be withdrawn or increased to influence decision making in Laos as in Vietnam and Cambodia.

Ultimately, insurgencies grew sufficiently strong to pose a threat to the United States, as was the case in Vietnam with the Vietcong and

Cambodia with the Khmer Rouge. In Laos, the insurgency was called the Pathet Lao who ultimately won control of the country. As in the case of Vietnam and Cambodia, the Lao insurgents were characterized as communists who posed a threat not only to the country but to all of Southeast Asia. To eliminate the communist "threat" in all three cases, the United States embarked on a bombing campaign to eliminate the growing cancer threatening peace, stability, and development. In reality, in all cases, the insurgents were not interested in a worldwide communist conspiracy as much as establishing a democratic government representing all elements in society, which would serve the interests of the Laotian people, not the United States. Bombing the insurgents in Laos was responsible for the deaths of 350,000 people and constituted genocide.

The targeted group in Laos, the Pathet Lao, began as a resistance movement seeking independence from French colonial rule. The seeds of the Pathet Lao first sprouted during French rule, when a group of French officers persuaded the King of Laos to dismiss the Viceroy, Phetsarat. Phetsarat subsequently formed a resistance movement called the Lao Issara or the Free Lao Movement along with his two half brothers, Prince Souvanna Phouma and Prince Souphanouvong. After joining with a group of Lao nationalists, the Lao Issara denounced all treaties with France, deposed the king for his continued subservience to the French, and set up Phetsarat as head of a provisional government. In 1946, the French defeated the Lao Issara, forcing Phetsarat and his followers to flee to Bangkok.

While the Lao Issara were in exile, a constitution was proclaimed in Laos in 1947 and a parliamentary system of government was created. Shortly thereafter, the French declared Laos an independent state within the French Union. The Lao Issara decided to compromise with the French and returned to Laos to join the Royal Lao Government (RLG). However, not all members of the Lao Issara were satisfied with the accommodation that put Laos in the French Union rather than granting complete independence. Prince Souphanouvong and other dissatisfied members of the Lao Issara refused to participate in the RLG and settled in Northern Laos, where they eventually became known as the Pathet Lao.

In an effort to end hostilities in Southeast Asia, Laos, Vietnam, and Cambodia participated in the 1954 Geneva Conference for the purpose of signing an armistice agreement. An International Control Commission was charged with monitoring the ceasefire.

After Prince Souvanna Phouma became prime minister in 1956, he invited the Pathet Lao and other leftist groups to participate in negotiations, the result of which was the first coalition government in 1957 including two Pathet Lao cabinet ministers. The popularity of the Pathet Lao and their platform of corruption and government indifference were reflected in the election results in May 1958 when they won thirteen out of twenty-one contested seats and Souphanouvong became Minister of Economic Affairs.

American political leaders, who were already referring to the Pathet Lao as communists, were alarmed at their presence in such large numbers in the Lao government. Eisenhower embarked on a campaign to sabotage the coalition government by forming a political pressure group, the Committee for the Defense of National Interests (CDNI), reputed to have the backing of the CIA. As well, Eisenhower stopped all payments to the RLG and disseminated propaganda.

In July 1958, Souvanna Phouma lost a vote of confidence in the National Assembly and was forced to resign. He was replaced by Phoui Sananikone in a right-wing government in which the Pathet Lao were excluded, facilitating U.S. support for the new government. After assuming office, Phoui shifted policy to the right, dissolved the National Assembly, and repudiated the 1954 Geneva truce.

In the same year, the North Vietnamese army occupied a number of villages in Laos near the border, claiming they belonged to North Vietnam. The RLG responded by sending troops in order to drive the North Vietnamese troops back to North Vietnam; however, they were unsuccessful. In a pattern that was to repeat itself in Northern Laos, once the North Vietnam troops had secured the Lao towns, the Pathet Lao moved in to occupy them. When the Royal Lao Army (RLA) attempted to recover the occupied towns, the United States provided military assistance through the private sector by hiring Civil

Air Transport (CAT). CAT planes were flown by American civilian pilots to fly U.S. advisors and intelligence officers into war zones in support of the Royal Lao Army. To further support the right-wing government, the United States shipped a number of short takeoff and landing aircraft to transport supplies and personnel wherever the RLA needed them.

U.S. intervention in Laos was clearly intended to maintain a right-wing pro-American government in power through economic aid and military assistance. Part of the plan was to exclude the Pathet Lao from winning seats in the National Assembly, where they might advocate policies that were in the interest of the people of Laos but not in the interests of the United States. The Pathet Lao, having been excluded from government, decided to embark on an insurgency campaign to overthrow the American-supported government.

North Vietnam was determined to protect the Ho Chi Minh Trail and was sympathetic to the cause of the Pathet Lao because of their own struggle in Vietnam against American imperialism. Although the North Vietnamese had no right to intervene in Laos, their presence did not imply that the Pathet Lao were communists with subversive intentions. The Pathet Lao began as an independence movement against France, but when they were excluded from the pro-American government, they reacted by forming an insurgency movement fighting for a neutral, independent Laos.

As the April 1960 elections approached, the right-wing government led by Phoui implemented a number of measures to rig the election in favor of right-wing candidates. Phoui engaged in gerrymandering to strengthen the chances of right-wing candidates, flew village chiefs to the capital to meet with government officials, imprisoned a number of Pathet Lao leaders to prevent them from running in the election, and rigged the balloting. As a result, all fifty-nine seats were won by right-wing candidates, ensuring a pro-American, anticommunist government.

Disapproving of the pro-American government, Captain Kong Le led the Second Paratroop Battalion in a coup d'état followed by the installation of Souvanna Phouma as prime minister. Subsequently, a number of opposing forces fought for control of the government, including rightist, centrist, and leftist elements.

At the same time, the Pathet Lao were on the march to gain control of as much of Laos as possible, winning control in the north and the east. The Soviet Union, who was supporting struggles of liberation, airlifted heavy military equipment to the Pathet Lao in the Plain of Jars, where the Ho Chi Minh Trail cuts through Laos.

North Vietnam was also supporting the Pathet Lao because they sympathized with their struggle of liberation but more importantly to protect a vital stretch of the Ho Chi Minh Trail in the Plain of Jars along which they shipped supplies and troops to South Vietnam.

To defeat the insurgents and the North Vietnamese, the United States had depended heavily on the RLA up to this point. In addition, acting as a surrogate force for the Americans, the Hmong were a 4,000-year-old culture that originated in the mountainous regions of China where they lived until they migrated to Southeast Asia in the seventeenth century.

The Hmong, under General Vang Pao, held North Vietnamese forces at bay in Northern Laos for ten years with support from the United States. Observing and destroying that section of the Ho Chi Minh Trail that ran through Laos was a vital contribution to America's war in South Vietnam. They also defended an ultra-secret CIA-U.S. Air Force location at the summit of a Hmong Mountain called Lima Site 85 where U.S. forces directed around-the-clock precision bombing strikes against the Pathet Lao and North Vietnamese in Northern Laos.

Additionally, as mountainous people, Hmong troops were placed at strategic points in the Plain of Jars to fight the North Vietnamese and the Pathet Lao in 1960. Led by Vang Pao, they asked the United States for military aid, food, and refugee assistance. According to Jane Hamilton-Merrit:

> "Vang Pao's force—consisting of less than 7000 volunteer soldiers—would be the bulwark of freedom. The Americans reasoned that these "little guys" with U.S. assistance and training would hold off the North Vietnamese Army of "national liberation" to buy time to try for a political solution.

(*Tragic Mountains*, Jane Hamilton-Merrit, p. 95)

By the spring of 1961, the U.S. government concluded that the Pathet Lao were in a position to take over the whole country due to its strength in the countryside in addition to its support from the Soviets and North Vietnamese. At this point, the American's contribution to defeating "communist" forces consisted of a number of pilots from the CIA's Air America, 2,000 Americans serving primarily as advisors, and 2,000 more in other countries who were providing logistics.

American apprehension over a possible Pathet Lao victory in Laos resulted in an agreement to participate in a conference scheduled in Geneva in 1961. As a backup, Washington put Task Force 116 in Okinawa on alert for deployment in Laos, ordered the Seventh Fleet to move into the Gulf of Siam, planned an airborne invasion to occupy the Plain of Jars, and sent a squadron of helicopters to an air base in Thailand on standby.

After prolonged negotiations, the three Lao factions in Geneva agreed to form a coalition government with Souvanna Phouma as prime minister. Despite the agreement, the forces of the three opposing groups continued to fight each other, forcing another conference in Geneva in 1962. Although a neutrality declaration was agreed to, each side maintained its own soldiers in territory under its control and continued to fight one another. Civil war resumed with increasing intervention from the United States and North Vietnam.

As a result of the new coalition, the Americans now believed they could work with Souvanna Phouma. U.S. interference in the political affairs in Laos was a necessity so that Washington could exclude leftist groups from participating. A report of the minutes of a White House meeting on June 13, 1962, which included the President, Secretary of

State Rusk, and Secretary of Defense McNamara, disclosed that:

> The President raised the question of working out some
> arrangements with Souvanna and the West...Governor
> [Harriman-New York] noted that much of the responsibility
> in this respect might rest with CIA and the Agency had
> some plans to implement this...The President requested a
> memorandum from the Department on political actions that
> the US was planning with respect to the new government of
> Laos.

(*Memorandum for the Record*, Report of Meeting at the White House,
June 13, 1962)

In the spring of 1964, North Vietnamese and Pathet Lao
forces had secured the vital Plain of Jars. Fearing communist control
of the Plain of Jars, Souvanna Phouma authorized unarmed U.S.
reconnaissance flights over the Plain to provide intelligence for the
RLA.

The conflict in Laos had reached a critical point for American
leaders, who were absolutely determined to ensure an American-
friendly government in Vientiane.

An example of that determination can be found in a
memorandum of conference on January 19, 1961, between President
Eisenhower and President-Elect Kennedy when Eisenhower stated
that:

> The United States was determined to preserve the
> independence of Laos. It was his opinion that if Laos should
> fall to the Communists then it would just be a question of
> time until South Vietnam, Cambodia, Thailand and Burma
> would collapse. He felt that the communists had designs
> on all of Southeast Asia, and that it would be a tragedy to
> permit Laos to fall.

(*The Pentagon Papers*, Memorandum of Conference on January 19,
1961)

Eisenhower's perspective, while not atypical, was shaped by cold war mythology and in particular a belief that there was a worldwide communist movement seeking to take over the world. He also believed the domino theory that if one country fell to communism, they all would fall. He failed to recognize that in each country in Southeast Asia, the United States had meddled in a political system with the ultimate goal of establishing a government that would serve American interests at the expense of the people in each country. The result of these policies was an insurgency that fought to defeat the American-supported leaders in order to replace them with a democratic system of government. Inevitably, these insurgencies received support from one or more communist countries that feared the growing American empire. Once the communist support was evident, it was easy for American leaders to point their finger at the communist enemies who were part of a conspiracy to spread communism.

Another myth created by American leaders was that the United States was fighting for an independent Laos. An independent Laos was completely anathema to U.S. objectives, demonstrated by American attempts to destroy broadly based coalitions in favor of right-wing governments friendly to the United States.

At this point in the struggle to defeat communism (the insurgency) in Laos, it was clear that the United States would have to escalate their military efforts. Up until this point, American support for the RLG consisted of development grants (totaling U.S. $8 million), government budget support (U.S. $320 million), and military assistance (U.S. $152 million). American personnel were limited to advisors, CIA agents, and civilian pilots.

U.S. military planners were preparing to intervene. A report from the Pentagon discloses that:

> Through the last half of April, the conditions in Laos continued to worsen...As developments in Laos appeared headed towards a climax at the end of April, PACOM [Pacific Command] elements moved into forward positions, anticipating possible intervention orders.

(*Pentagon Report*, Summary of Observations on the U.S. Command Experience in Laos, October 17, 1963)

In 1965, American ground troops arrived in South Vietnam, and air force fighting squadrons were stationed in Northern Thailand. From their bases in Thailand, American bombers began their campaign of brutality.

Throughout the 1960s, American contribution to the war in Laos was clandestine and was referred to as the "the Secret War." The secret reporting procedures used in the bombing of Cambodia were adopted in the bombing of Laos.

American objectives in bombing Laos were to destroy the Ho Chi Minh Trail linking North and South Vietnam through Laos, to destroy the physical and social infrastructure of the Pathet Lao, to obliterate Pathet Lao supply routes and troop concentrations, and to allow the RLA to move into the area. To kill enemy troops, the U.S. bombers used defoliants to expose hidden supply routes, including the Ho Chi Minh Trail. According to a telegram sent by General Westmoreland: "During all phases, there will be an intensification of psychological warfare and herbicide operations...through the Laotian Panhandle...We must use all assets at our disposal to block, deny, spoil and disrupt this infiltration" (*FRUS-State Department*, Telegram from General Westmoreland to the Commander in Chief, Pacific).

In planning the bombing, the State Department sent a telegram to the embassy in Laos which stated that:

> Our preliminary views as to possible air attacks are as follows:
>
> a. The military objective would be to interdict and destroy facilities supporting infiltration into SVN [South Vietnam]...
>
> b. Armament would be napalm unless politically unacceptable, in which case armament would be less effective conventional bombs...

(*The Pentagon Papers*, Telegram from the State Department to the Embassy in Laos Proposed Bombing in Laos, July 26, 1964)

Furthermore, a cable from the U.S. Embassy in Laos to the State Department in 1964 reported that:

> As earlier noted I believe we could gradually establish [a] pattern [of] U.S. suppressive strikes in panhandle without adverse Souvanna reaction and this perhaps [would] even truer of T-28 [aircraft used by CIA] strikes. Even though strictly speaking suppressive strikes would not be in response to RLG request nevertheless [I] believe Souvanna would back U.S. up if we represented them as being authorized by RLG.

(*The Pentagon Papers*, Cable from U.S. Embassy to the State Department on Proposal to Initiate Bombing in Laos, August 17, 1964)

Notice that the United States was planning bombing attacks in Laos supposedly on behalf of the RLG, but there was never any intention to consult with the government first.

To recapture territory lost to the PL or North Vietnamese, U.S. bombing cleared the territory of enemy forces followed by the occupation of the area by the RLA under American close tactical air support. As a result of this strategy, large areas in Northeastern Laos were depopulated and scarred by bomb craters.

Operating from bases in Thailand and from aircraft carriers, American bombers inflicted massive suffering on the people in Northern Laos and in particular in the Plain of Jars, where bombs rained down on average every eight minutes on people who were either killed, driven out as refugees, or forced to lived in caves to survive. Approximately 793,000 refugees had to flee from Northeastern Laos. A U.S. Senate Subcommittee on refugees and casualties in Laos reported that:

> In Laos we are witnessing the familiar pattern of Vietnam, in the destruction of the countryside, the generation of refugees, and the occurrence of civilian war casualties... Based on field reports available to the subcommittee, as

well as the press commentary and official reports from our government, there is reason to believe that human suffering has vastly increased as a result of this escalation and the nature of American involvement. More than our national leadership cares to admit, the intensive bombing of Laos since 1968 has dramatically increased the flow of refugees, and inevitably, the toll of civilian casualties. There are even suggestions that we deliberately set about to remove population from Pathet Lao areas.

(*Senate Hearings*, Refugee and Civil War Casualties in Laos and Cambodia, 1970)

In another Senate subcommittee hearing, it is reported that:

I am concerned that a very real possibility exists that a State Department–controlled aerial bombardment of villages in Northern Laos has been the compelling reason for the 100,000-plus refugees generated during 1968 and 1969... An estimated 1 million people may have once lived in these villages; in the last 10 years perhaps 700,000 of these people have become refugees (page 31, hearing record) moving into the Western portions of Laos controlled by the Royal Laotian Government...It is clear that the air force is only following orders and that all targets are cleared and approved by the State Department...With reference to the facts set forth above, the significant and incontestable conclusion is that at least 76 percent of 96 small villages in Northern Laos were destroyed by bombing in 1969. Cluster bombs and white phosphorous were used against the civilian population...

(*Hearings Before the Subcommittee to Investigate Problems Connected with Refugees and Escapees*, War-related Civilian Problems in Indochina: Part II Laos and Cambodia)

In addition to defoliating large tracts of land in Laos and destroying villages, the bombing targeted enemy crops, depriving the civilians of food. By September 1969, 20,485 acres of land had been destroyed. Between 1965 and 1966, about 200,000 gallons of herbicide including Agent Orange were dropped on eastern Laos by

U.S. bombers, and by 1970, 537,495 gallons were sprayed. As a direct result of defoliants, people still suffer today from birth defects and cancer.

The bombing intensified rapidly in Laos, reaching between 17,000 and 27,000 sorties a month following President Johnson's bombing halt in Vietnam in 1968. Napalm, phosphorous, and cluster bombs unleashed atrocities on the helpless people of Laos.

The inevitable response of the PL was to escalate their counter-attacks on the ground, resulting in numerous RLA strongholds being lost to the insurgents. With the PL in control of much of the country, they proposed terms for a political solution to the civil war, which included the cessation of American bombing, withdrawal of pro-American troops, a prisoner exchange, and the formation of a provisional government. A representative of the PL political wing was dispatched to hold discussions with Prime Minister Souvanna Phouma, and both sides agreed to peace negotiations, which took place in the summer of 1972. Despite many breakdowns, ultimately both sides were able to agree to a ceasefire, which was to become effective on February 21, 1973, after which all American military operations in Laos were to come to a complete halt. When military clashes extended past the deadline, Washington became impatient and threatened to withdraw aid to the RLG unless they settled quickly with the PL. Thus, the RLG agreed to grant equal power to the PL in a new coalition.

Finally, in June of 1974, the remaining American military personnel exited from Laos, although approximately 40,000 North Vietnamese troops remained. The Lao Peoples Revolutionary Army (PL) took power in December 1975 and Laos became a communist state.

A communist government in Laos in 1975 is a tragic irony given the U.S. extreme efforts to destroy a coalition government representing all political ideologies. U.S. forces then engaged in relentless, unconscionable bombing to destroy the left, exacting an enormous toll. The tragic irony was that they were forced to withdraw with a communist government in power. The same catastrophic twist was also true in Vietnam and Cambodia. The very scenario that the Americans feared the most came to pass because of their intervention to prevent it.

Between 1965 and 1973, American bombers unloaded more than two million tons of bombs in over 600,000 sorties, considerably more than the United States had dropped on Germany and Japan in World War II. Villages were leveled and countless people were buried alive, burned by napalm and white phosphorous, or riddled with pellets from cluster bombs.

A total of ninety million cluster bombs rained down on Laos of which 20 to 30 percent did not explode, creating a minefield for future generations. Out of 236,000 square kilometers of land, 12,000 square kilometers were heavily impacted and 74,786 were moderately impacted. Nine out of fifteen provinces were severely hit.

The damage caused by American intervention was massive in scale and included a huge death toll, displacement of people in bombed-out areas, destruction of rural areas, and a legacy of disease, birth defects, and cancer. Thousands of people die each year from these unexploded ordnances, and one out of every 384 people in Laos is an amputee. By the end of 1998, 38,248 people had been killed and 64,064 injured (*Landmine Monitor*, 2003). The bombing resulted in 350,000 dead, and according to the Finnish Kampuchea Inquiry Commission, two million people became refugees.

The group that was destroyed in "whole or in part" was the Pathet Lao, whose origins can be found in the war against the French but shifted to the RLG from which they had been excluded. As well, American forces, including their surrogates, the Hmong, who were supporting the RLG, became the enemy. Although the Pathet Lao were frequently defined as a political, nationalist, and communist group, they were, in fact, either those who opposed the RLG and Americans or anyone living in areas occupied by the Pathet Lao. In this sense, they can be considered a community of Lao people representing "part of the total population." They can also be considered an ethnic group consisting of the Lao Loum people who lived in the lowlands, representing 68 percent of the population. The other two ethnic groups include the Lao Theung, who lived in the uplands, representing 22 percent of the population, and the Lao Soung, who lived in the highlands, representing 10 percent of the population. The Lao Soung included the Hmong and Meo people.

The number of people killed easily meets the criteria of the Genocide Convention given previous examples. Intent can be clearly established by examining the orders given by senior military officers, the President and the State Department. For example, consider General Westmoreland's comment above about the use of herbicides and a memo from the American Embassy in Laos to the State Department calling for "suppressive strikes." There is no doubt that American leaders were aware of the carnage they were responsible for as disclosed in the Senate Subcommittee hearings.

American actions definitely meet the criteria of the Genocide Convention. The multiplicity of deaths and refugees in Laos was part of the overall cost paid by the people of Southeast Asia for American's misplaced ambition to save these countries from communism. Nevertheless, Vietnam, Cambodia, and Laos, having wound up with communist governments, raise questions about military intervention, the use of force, and the ignorance of leaders who feared a chimerical threat that existed more in the minds of American leaders than in reality. Furthermore, it can be argued that the Americans invented the threat and exploited it to advance American interests.

6

INDONESIA: OUR SON OF A BITCH.

Killer chameleon is the most accurate description of Haji Mohammad Suharto. He was born on June 8, 1921, in Central Java, Indonesia, the son of simple peasants, although there are suspicions that he was the illegitimate son of somebody well placed. In 1940, he enlisted in the Dutch colonial army and attended military school. A week after the completion of his training, the Japanese invaded Indonesia and Suharto joined the occupation police force, rising to the level of a battalion commander in 1943. After Japan surrendered in 1945, Suharto joined the Indonesian army in order to fight in the war for independence. Ultimately, he became leader of Indonesia and was simply referred to as General Suharto. Once in power, he became a genocidal killer who murdered between 300,000 and 600,000 of his own people and 200,000 people in East Timor.

During his reign, Suharto was courted and tolerated by Western governments. Indonesia was a bountiful prize coveted by a number of countries, including the United States, who had their foot in the door as early as 1912 when Rockefeller was able to build a subsidiary of Standard Oil in Central Java.

Not only is Indonesia rich in resources, but it is strategically located for military and economic objectives. It would serve as a base of operations for projecting force in Southeast Asia.

As such a rich bounty, it seemed inevitable that the United States would endeavour to gain control over the government and its resources while ensuring it remained noncommunist. In fact, Indonesia represented a major threat in the region due to the fact that it had the strongest communist party in the noncommunist world. With the threat of Southeast Asia succumbing to communism, Indonesia represented an important potential bulwark against the voracious red monster.

To colonize Indonesia in the modern sense, the United States began supporting a right-wing group in the armed forces led by General Suharto with the objective of instigating a coup. When General Suharto finally became the president of Indonesia, he established close ties with the United States, offering enormous investment opportunities and natural resources in exchange for military and economic aid.

With the support of the United States, Suharto was able to launch a campaign to eradicate the huge communist and left-wing community in Indonesia. In the process of destroying the communist element, the armed forces and militias acted on their Chinese racism by treating them as the enemy as well, resulting in 500,000 to one million deaths overall. In addition to killing the Chinese, Suharto passed a set of laws that were crafted to destroy all facets of their culture. Both Suharto and the United States are guilty of genocide for the deaths of members of the Chinese community and for eradicating their culture.

As well, Suharto and the United States are guilty of genocide in East Timor. Before 1975, East Timor was an ancient culture that did not pose a threat to other countries in any sense. Their great misfortunate was to have rich offshore oil reserves. Australia and the United States preferred to negotiate an oil deal with Indonesia rather than East Timor due to the fact that East Timor had a left-wing government that might not cooperate with the United States. To solve this problem, the United States armed Indonesia and encouraged them to invade East Timor. The result was the destruction of the East Timorese culture and the death of 200,000 people. This genocide will be discussed in detail in the next chapter.

During many centuries of colonial rule, Indonesia was exploited primarily by the Dutch for its natural resources. In the early twentieth century, a number of large American corporations began operating in Indonesia, such as Standard Oil and Goodyear Tire Rubber Company.

After World War II, U.S. policymakers were supportive of Indonesia becoming an independent nation under the strict condition that the Dutch maintain influence in order to protect the country from communist influences. In fact, the Dutch were unwilling to relinquish their colony and fought intermittent warfare with the pro-independence movement led by Sukarno.

Washington refrained from supporting either side and refused to provide assistance requested by Sukarno. Nevertheless, the United States ultimately offered to mediate a compromise when it appeared that the Dutch might actually win. U.S. strategy was to ensure that an American-friendly government was installed in an independent Indonesia. Washington believed that Indonesia was a key asset in American global policy as revealed by President Eisenhower when he remarked that:

> So when the U.S. votes $400 million to help that war [in Indochina], we are not voting a giveaway program. We are voting for the cheapest way that we can prevent the occurrence of something that would be of a most terrible significance for the United States of America, our security, our power and ability to get certain things we need from the riches of the Indonesian territory and from Southeast Asia.

(*Remarks at the Governors' Conference, Seattle, Washington*; Dwight D. Eisenhower Presidential Library, August 4, 1953)

After negotiations with the Dutch in 1948, the Indonesia pro-independence movement signed the Renville agreement while the Communist Party in Indonesia (PKI) opposed it and demanded land reform. Failing to win any concessions, the PKI rebelled in Madiun, an agricultural city in Java, refusing an order from Sukarno to disband, resulting in violence. A number of PKI guerrillas were killed and 36,000 were imprisoned, virtually destroying the PKI leadership. Although Sukarno was a nationalist and neutral, he became acceptable to the United States after the Madiun uprising because he employed strong measures to suppress the PKI.

Finally, in 1949 when Indonesia agreed to hold the status of Irian Barat (New Guinea) in abeyance as a concession to the Dutch, Indonesia was granted sovereignty. As discussions over Irian Barat reached a stalemate, the United States sent a mediator to The Hague, where negotiations were taking place. The objective of the mediator was to influence the outcome in order to protect American interests.

Protecting American interests depended heavily on the leadership of the government, and when Sukarno first took office in 1949 he was acceptable, though his attempts to grant concessions to both the PKI and the army were disconcerting. As well, Sukarno nationalized private holdings of the Dutch, visited the Soviet Union, and bought arms from Eastern Europe, calling into question his loyalty to the West.

In the early 1950s, Washington decided to guard against the PKI gaining control over the government to ensure that Indonesia did not fall into the communist camp. The U.S. National Security Council (NSC) and the CIA embarked on a campaign to strengthen other sources of power as insurance against Indonesia leaning too far to the left. Under the Eisenhower administration in 1953, the NSC proposed "appropriate action in collaboration with other countries, to prevent communist control of Indonesia." According to declassified documents, the National Security Council in NSC 171/1 had "decided that the US would use 'all feasible covert means' as well as overt, including 'the use of armed force if necessary,' to prevent the richest parts of Indonesia from falling into Communist hands" (*Confronting the Third World*, Gabriel Kolko, p. 174). Also, NSC 171/1 recommended military training of right-wing officers in the Indonesian armed forces as a counterbalance to the PKI.

Another strategy implemented by the United States to entrench American ideology in Indonesian elites was to influence their postsecondary education. Dean Rusk, Secretary of State, understood the value of capturing the minds of the new generation of Indonesian leaders and spelled it out by observing that, "Communist aggression" in Asia required not only that Americans be trained to combat it there, but "we must open our training facilities for increasing numbers of our friends from across the Pacific" (*Department of State Bulletin*, Foreign Policy Decisions in the Pacific, November 1951). A number of American foundations and think tanks such as the Rand Corporation and the Ford Foundation donated money to the cause of educating future Indonesian leaders.

CIA operations in Indonesia also contributed to the effort to buttress anticommunist forces against the danger of the PKI capturing control of the country. The Church Report of 1975 mentioned that:

> In addition to the plots discussed in the body of the report, the Committee received some evidence of CIA involvement in plans to assassinate President Sukarno of Indonesia... Former Deputy Director...Richard Bassett testified that the assassination of Sukarno had been "contemplated" by the CIA but planning had proceeded no further than identifying an "asset" whom it was believed might be recruited to kill Sukarno. Arms were supplied to dissident groups in Indonesia...

> (*An Interim Report of the Select Committee to Study Governmental Operations*, Alleged Assassination Plots Involving Foreign Leaders)

In the 1955 election campaign, the CIA donated a million dollars to the Masjumi Party, a coalition of Muslim organizations for the purpose of denying Sukarno's Nationalist Party and the PKI a victory. The PKI emerged as the most powerful party, further creating divisions among the various forces vying for power despite the efforts of various agencies of the American government. According to a NSC document:

> The Chairmen reviewed current election prospects and prognosticated that the elections would probably be held in the middle of August. Courses of action in the paper were discussed and it was agreed that they were in accordance with NSC 171/1;...it was further agreed that they should be listed in the minutes of the meeting for the mutual information of the various agencies engaged in carrying out the courses of action. They were:

> 1. The embassy should provide continuing estimates and recommendations on courses of action as to Indonesian elections as they draw near;

2. Encouragement should be given to all possible indigenous elements to attack the Communist Party on the grounds that it represented foreign control and it was a false national front.

(*Memorandum of a Meeting of the OCB Working Group on NSC 171/1*, National Security Council, March 8, 1955)

The most significant conflict developed between the center of power, Java, and the outer islands such as Sumatra and Sulawesi, where most of the natural resources were located. The outer islands resented the government in Java for squandering their wealth. As a result of this rift, regional commanders in these outer islands, whose popularity was based on their leading role in the independence movement, began to oppose the centralizing policies of Army Chief of Staff Abdul Haris Nasution. Acting out of resentment of Java for squandering their wealth, these colonels in the outer islands chose to engage in smuggling to earn profits from the sale of resources rather than the central government.

Sukarno's response to the increasing efforts of the outer islands' bid to achieve independence was to institute a system of "Guided Democracy" in which the PKI would be included in a cabinet of national unity. When the regional commanders strongly opposed Sukarno's plan, Nasution urged Sukarno to declare martial law on March 14, 1957, ending parliamentary democracy in Indonesia. Growing opposition to Sukarno's heavy-handed policies led to an assassination attempt on his life.

Americans were becoming very apprehensive about the strength of the PKI at the center and the instability caused by the conflict between the regions and Java. To protect their interests, the United States decided to support the independence movement of the commanders of the regions where all the resources were located and where anticommunist sentiment ran high. One of the actions undertaken by the CIA was to arm and train Indonesians as mercenaries in order to bring down Sukarno. Joseph Burkholder Smith, a CIA officer involved in the Indonesian operations, stated that:

...before any action against Sukarno's position could be taken, we would have to have the approval of the Special Group—the small group of top National Security officials who approved covert action plans. Premature mention of such an idea might get shot down...In many instances, we made the action programs up ourselves after we had collected enough intelligence to make them appear required by the circumstances. Our activity in Indonesia in 1957–1958 was one such instance.

(*Portrait of a Cold Warrior*, Joseph Burkholder Smith)

Another action undertaken by the CIA was to send approximately a dozen B-26s to the rebel forces, who were trained to fly the planes in the Philippines. When Allen Pope, a CIA contractor, was shot during an attack in the Southern Moluccas, the CIA's cover was blown. This was made worse when secret CIA documents were discovered.

The CIA and State Department believed that it was essential to support the rebel forces on the outer islands to safeguard against a communist government gaining control over their resources. Thomas Ross and David Wise point out the rationale for supporting the rebel colonels:

> And many in the CIA and the State Department saw merit in supporting these dissident elements. Even if Sukarno were not overthrown, they argued, it might be possible for Sumatra, Indonesia's big oil producer, to secede, thereby protecting private American and Dutch holdings. At the very least, the pressures of rebellion might loosen Sukarno's ties with the Communists and force him to move to the right. At best, the Army, headed by General Abdul Haris Nasution, an anti-communist, might come over to the rebels and force wholesale changes to the liking of the United States.

(*The Invisible Government*, Thomas Ross and David Wise, p. 139)

On January 9, 1958, the colonels who were leading the dissident forces met on Sumatra where they served an ultimatum to Jakarta calling for a new central government. If Jakarta refused, they would proclaim full independence. At the same time, the first secret shipment of small arms and equipment was sent from Subic Bay, a U.S. base in the Philippines. The colonels were also reassured that they would receive U.S. recognition as soon as they became independent.

Nasution mobilized his troops and air force to battle the insurgency on the outer islands, resulting in defeat for the insurgent forces. Overcoming the rebellion had a number of negative impacts from the U.S. perspective. These included increasing the prestige of Sukarno, who was credited with a major role in defeating the rebels and strengthening the unity and power of Nasution's armed forces, which consolidated their control over the economy. Another impact was to augment support for the PKI, who lambasted the United States for their imperial intervention, and to weaken the forces that were hostile to the PKI.

When President Kennedy took office, he was confronted with problems bequeathed to him from the Eisenhower administration. The underlying problem was the standoff between the army and PKI as Sukarno struggled to maintain equilibrium. Moreover, the U.S. government continued to assess Sukarno's political posture to determine whether or not they could depend on him to stop communism. Two other problems left over from the Eisenhower Government that needed resolution were the conflict between Indonesia and the Dutch over Irian, the western half of New Guinea, and the level of American military and economic aid.

Both Indonesia and the Dutch were building up their forces for a war over Irian, resulting in the first armed clashes in January 1962. Sukarno recognized that the acquisition of Irian would be a symbolic victory in his struggle for the complete independence of Indonesia while the Dutch were determined to hold onto the remaining vestige of its empire. Kennedy finally resolved the conflict by persuading the Dutch to cede Irian to Indonesia.

Kennedy now decided that economic aid was the most effective avenue for enhancing U.S. influence on social, economic, and political matters. Achieving this objective was based on the hope that America's support in the Irian affair and in strengthening aid programs would turn Indonesia to the West. The strategy was called "the Action Plan for Indonesia."

Another foundation of the plan was to maintain a "toehold" in Indonesia, or in other words, to maintain contact with anticommunist forces, mainly political and military figures. In addition to maintaining contact, the United States offered to extend military aid to these same elements. Between 1962 and 1965, the United States gave Indonesia $39.5 million in military assistance (*The United States and the Overthrow of Sukarno*, Peter Dale Scott).

Anticipating an inevitable confrontation between communist and anticommunist forces, the United States used the extended military aid as a signal to anticommunist elements and the right-wing generals as to whom they would support.

Despite all the American efforts to "save" Indonesia from communism, Sukarno increased his ties with the People's Republic of China and admitted to increasing the number of communists into his government.

Nevertheless, U.S.-Indonesian relations improved for a while until late 1963 when Sukarno and the PKI united in opposition to the British-sponsored creation of the Federation of Malaysia, consisting of Malaya, Singapore, and the British colonies of North Borneo. Indonesia opposed the British plan because it had hoped to integrate the same colonies into an Indonesian federation. During the brief campaign General Suharto, who was leading the Indonesian forces, secretly established contacts with American intelligence to end the war. Suharto knew that it was a losing cause and wanted to redeploy his troops on Java and Sumatra to keep the PKI in check.

Washington was opposed to Indonesia's ambitions in the South Pacific, and as a result relations between the two began to deteriorate. With the PKI gaining in dominance, the United States needed to align itself more closely with anticommunist forces. James C. Thomson,

Jr., of the National Security Council staff sent a memorandum to the President's Special Assistant for National Security Affairs stating that:

> At the working level in Defense, however, it is suggested that it might be wise…to have our military people in Djakarta (Colonels Harvey and Benson) go to Nasution and Jani for a candid "where-the-hell-do-we-go-from-here" session in which we might obtain a better reading on the military's real hopes and needs. After all, it is argued, our military training program has been the most vital part of our Indonesian assistance in terms of future pay-off.

(*National Security Council*, Johnson Library National Security File, August 25, 1964)

A memorandum from the Joint Chiefs of Staff to Secretary of Defense Robert McNamara states that:

> Contacts maintained between the US and Indonesian military personnel have been beneficial from an intelligence gathering aspect, as well as for maintaining US influence among the Indonesian military leaders. Desirably, this link should be continued insofar as possible.

(*Joint Chiefs of Staff*, Washington National Records Center, August 26, 1964)

When President Johnson took office, relations between Indonesia and the United States were on the brink of collapse. This was due to the PKI's surge toward dominance, Sukarno's shift to the left, the dispute over Malaysia, and the degenerating Indonesian economy. To prevent the PKI from attaining power, Johnson adopted two initiatives, which included withdrawing economic aid to further destabilize the country and create conditions for a possible army coup and strengthening support for anticommunist forces in the army.

These actions were laying the groundwork for an eventual military takeover by anticommunist elements in the military. A memorandum from the Director of the United States Information

Agency to Secretary of State Dean Rusk in 1965 recommends the following course of action:

> Anti-American activities in Indonesia, particularly those directed against USIS [United States Information Service] during the last six months, have created a situation that I can describe only as intolerable. I believe that American interests and our national dignity, not only in Indonesia but elsewhere, require that action now be taken to indicate that we will not allow such actions to continue unpenalized. I realize that our long-suffering patience has been due in large part to our desire to keep Indonesia out of the communist orbit at virtually any cost, but it seems that the Indonesian government is abusing our patience to its advantage—and thus our present predicament...Whatever remains in the way of a U.S. economic assistance program in Indonesia, including training, supplying of spare parts, civic action, malaria eradication, etc., should be terminated immediately, with attendant wide publicity.

(*Johnson Library National Security File*, Memorandum from Director of the United States Information Agency to Secretary of State Rusk, February 16, 1965)

In a memorandum prepared for the 303 Committee (counter-insurgency group reporting to the Secretary of State) by the State Department, the new strategy is clearly elucidated:

> [The problem is] to counter the growing strength and influence of the Communist Party over Indonesian foreign and domestic affairs...One of the main factors bearing on the problem is the close affinity between the current objectives of Sukarno and Red China and the support provided to Sukarno by the PKI in contrast to the lack of coordination and common ground for action among the various anti-communist elements in Indonesia...[Operation directives include to] provide covert assistance to individuals and organizations capable of and prepared to take obstructive action against the PKI...Identify and cultivate potential leaders within Indonesia for the purpose of ensuring an

orderly non-communist succession upon Sukarno's death or removal from office.

(*National Security Council*, Memorandum prepared for the 303 Committee, February 23, 1965)

Frustration and impatience in the ranks of anticommunist army officers, notably General Suharto and General Nasution, was due to the strength of the PKI. Sukarno, who supported the PKI, was fomenting so much discontent that anticommunist officers with the support and encouragement of the CIA began to develop a plan for taking over the country. These officers joined together in a "General's Council" to plan for the eventuality that Sukarno would be removed from office or die. The "General's Council" met in Jakarta on September 30, 1965, leading to speculation that these army officers were plotting a coup for Armed Forces Day, October 5, 1965, when many of their troops would be brought into the city on the pretext that they were there to parade.

One of the problems confronting Suharto and others in the "General's Council" was a group of high-ranking officers such as the Army Chief of Staff General Yani who were unwilling to take any action against Sukarno. On September 30, 1965, a group of officers loyal to Suharto abducted and killed six generals, including Yani, and seized key points in the capital. This alleged coup attempt was referred to as the Gestapu. It was successful for not only eliminating neutral generals but for creating an opportunity to blame the entire operation on the PKI and then, as a solution to the threat posed to Sukarno by the communists, the Gestapu officers planned to kill the so-called "coup plotters" (PKI). The U.S. government was aware of Suharto's plans to deal harshly with the communists as stated in a Department of State memorandum:

> The Indonesian army, having countered what appears to have been a leftist coup on 1 October, is for the first time being firmly in control of Indonesia. It would likely use the opportunity to take strong steps against the Indonesian Communist Party (PKI) and elements allied with it.

(*Department of State*, Intelligence Memorandum, October 6, 1965)

The CIA had its fingerprints all over this operation in order to assess the level and type of support that could be offered to the real coup plotters. According to the propaganda, the group of junior officers responsible for the "coup attempt" were really acting on behalf of the PKI in an attempt to take control of the government. The role of the CIA was described by a former CIA officer Ralph McGehee:

> The Agency seized upon this opportunity [Suharto's response to Gestapu] and set out to destroy the PKI... Media fabrications played a key role in stirring up popular resentment against the PKI. Photographs of the bodies of the dead generals—badly decomposed—were featured in all the newspapers and on television. Stories accompanying the pictures falsely claimed that the generals had been castrated and their eyes gouged out by Communist women. The cynically designed campaign was designed to foment public anger against the Communists and set the stage for the massacre.

(*The C.I.A. and the White Paper on El Salvador*, Ralph McGehee, p. 423)

As well, a memorandum prepared by the CIA advises that:

> ...the Army leaders appear determined to seize the opportunity of the current confused circumstances to break the organizational back of the PKI, to eliminate it as an effective political force, and to prevent emergence of any crypto-Communist successor party...In short, we must be mindful that in the past years we have often wondered when and if the Indonesian Army would ever move to halt the erosion of non-Communist political strength in Indonesia. Now that it has seized on the fortuitous opportunity afforded by the PKI's error on the September 30 affair and is asking for covert help as well as understanding to accomplish the very task, we should avoid being too cynical about its motives and its self-interest, or too hesitant about the propriety of extending such assistance provided we can do so covertly, in a manner which will not embarrass our government.

(*Department of State Historical Files*, Memorandum Prepared in the Central Intelligence Agency, November 9, 1965)

Murdering six generals was a strategy to pave the way for anti-Sukarno forces to grab power. The alleged purpose of the Gestapu coup was to kill generals loyal to Sukarno and to create the impression that the PKI were responsible because they had ambitions to take over the government. In fact, the coup was carried out by anti-PKI forces whose purpose was to blame the PKI for the coup as an excuse to destroy them.

Suharto and the other coup plotters brought army units loyal to Suharto to Jakarta for the October 5 Armed Forces Day Parade in order to supply the necessary army support for the coup.

On October 1, 1965, General Suharto announced on the radio that six generals had been killed by the PKI and officers in the air force. He further stated that he was in control of the army, which would suppress the coup attempt to protect Sukarno. As well, he declared that Gestapu was transferring power to a fictitious "Revolutionary Council," which did not include Sukarno, but that Sukarno would still be allowed to remain as titular head of the government (*The United States and the Overthrow of Sukarno*, Peter Dale Scott).

On October 5, 1965, the army made the decision to implement plans to destroy the PKI and its supporters. Three days later the first attacks began. Indonesia plunged into a systematic killing crusade against the PKI, supporters of the PKI, and the Chinese, organized by Suharto and the army. Although the massacre was organized by Suharto and the army, it was carried out by Muslim youth, civilians recruited and trained by the army, and groups supported by the CIA.

The American government was well aware of the killings in Indonesia as revealed by a telegram from the Department of State to the Embassy in Indonesia, which pointed out that, "[The] PKI [are rushing] headlong in [the] face of mass attacks encouraged by [the] Army" (*National Archives and Records Administration*, Telegram from the State Department to the Embassy in Indonesia, October 29, 1965). Another telegram states that, "[It] appears from here that Indonesian military leaders' campaign is moving swiftly and smoothly." As well, a telegram from the consulate in Medan, Indonesia, notes that:

Two officers of Pemuda Pantjasila (Muslim Youth Group) separately told Consulate officers that their organization intends to kill every PKI member they can catch. November 14 Secretary Medan City Pemuda Pantjasila said [their] policy is to ignore public calls for calm and order by Sukarno and other leaders. He stated Pemuda Pantjasila will not hand over captured PKI to authorities until they are dead or near death. He estimated it will take five years to eradicate all PKI. Similar statements were made [a] few days earlier by [the] leader [of] North Sumatra cultural arm of Pemuda Pantjasila.

(*National Records and Archives Administration*, Telegram from the Consulate in Medan to the Department of State, December 16, 1965)

Pemuda Pantjasila was one of the Muslim groups recruited, trained, and armed by Suharto along with the Army to kill the PKI. They refused to obey orders given by Sukarno, who at this point was only a figure head.

Many of the people carrying out the slaughter were poorly armed, sometimes only with knives, and lacked communication equipment. This resulted in a request by the Indonesian generals for more American equipment. According to Gabriel Kolko:

> Since "elimination of these elements" was a precondition of better relations, the United States quickly promised covert aid—dubbed "medicines" to prevent embarrassing revelations. At stake in the army's effort was the "destruction," as the CIA called the undertaking, of the PKI, and "carefully placed assistance which will help the army cope with PKI."

(*Confronting the Third World*, Gabriel Kolko, p. 181)

Washington's support for the massacre of the PKI extended beyond providing arms to the army. The United States actually provided them with the names of Communist Party leaders. Kathy Kadane released a study in May 1990 in which she discovered that:

> The U.S. government played a significant role by supplying the names of thousands of Communist Party leaders to the Indonesian army, which hunted down the leftists and killed them, former U.S. diplomats say…As many as 5000 names were furnished to the Indonesian army, and the Americans later checked off the names of those who had been killed or captured, according to U.S. officials.

(*Year 501: The Conquest Continues*, Noam Chomsky, p. 131)

Between 1965 and 1966, the army and Muslim youth traveled from village to village over 13,000 islands spread along 3,000 miles on the equator and systematically slaughtered innocent people who were suspected communists or supporters of the PKI. Also targeted were the Chinese residents of Indonesia, who had always been victims of discrimination.

Estimating the total number of people killed is impossible, but the range is between 300,000 and 600,000, although some scholars place the number at one million. CIA estimates of the number of people imprisoned during the massacre were between 150,000 and 200,000.

There is irrefutable evidence that the Americans were most definitely aware of the carnage in Indonesia. A paper prepared for the Department of State in 1966, claims that:

> Between October 1 and the middle of March of this year [1966] the Communist Party was virtually eliminated as an effective political organization, perhaps as many as 300,000 Indonesians were killed—the great bulk of whom we believe were in fact associated with the Communist apparatus.

(*Memorandum from the President's Special Assistant (Rostow) to President Johnson*, Johnson Library, National Security File, June 8, 1966)

In August of 1967, Suharto placed all armed forces under his control and won the presidential election on March 21, 1968. Sukarno later died in 1971.

Once again, the United States has blood on its hands. General Suharto committed genocide against the Chinese population in Indonesia, and the United States is complicit in this genocide.

In proving that there was a targeted group who meet the criteria of the Genocide Convention, it is necessary to establish that a group was intentionally targeted and that it is one of the four groups described in the convention. The evidence clearly confirms that a massacre took place, but it might seem, on the surface, that it was a political group and not one of the groups described in the convention. In fact, there was more than one group targeted, and one of the groups was the Chinese national group living in Indonesia.

Declassified documents make clear reference to the massacre that had taken place, including the paper prepared for the State Department where there is a reference that "as many as 300,000 Indonesians were killed." Many of the other documents cited in this chapter support the conclusion that a massacre took place.

Next, it is imperative to authenticate that one of the groups targeted for elimination was the Chinese Nationals in Indonesia. Not only were they targeted to be killed, but Suharto passed a series of laws to assimilate the Chinese Nationals into Indonesian life. This is also a form of genocide carried out by destroying their culture.

Targeting of Indonesians of Chinese origin was described in a letter to Glele Ahanhanso, UN Special Rapporteur on Racial Discrimination:

> We the undersigned—organizations of the international community, write this letter to you in regard to the continued acts of racial discrimination against Indonesian citizens of ethnic Chinese origin...[T]he Indonesian Chinese community has been intentionally and violently targeted in numerous riots that swept across the archipelago.

> The discrimination against ethnic Chinese is deeply entrenched. Anti-Chinese discrimination dates back to the Dutch colonial period, but the process of a systematic

campaign against ethnic Chinese Indonesian citizens became particularly blatant since Suharto's rise to power in 1967 on the pretext of suppressing a suspected communist coup….The massacre included Chinese Indonesians who were wrongfully blamed as communists.

(*United Nations High Commissioner for Human Rights*, Open letter from Mr. Maurice Glele Ahanhanso)

Human Rights Watch also reported that:

In periods of social upheaval or in specific incidents of unrest in Indonesia, the ethnic Chinese have often become a target, in part because of their domination of the economy. They were targeted by the armed forces during the anti-communist pogroms of 1965–1966.

(*Human Rights Watch*, Human Rights Watch Report—Indonesia, May 16, 1994)

The discriminatory practices implemented by Suharto to destroy the Chinese culture included a ban of their language; a ban of their religion and culture; prohibiting them from painting their places of worship red; replacing Chinese names with Indonesian names; limiting the number of students who were admitted to state schools or universities; a ban of Chinese language publications; prohibiting Chinese schools; prohibiting the celebration of the Chinese New Year; and a ban on the building of Chinese temples.

The intention of Suharto and the army to destroy the Chinese community is evident in the letter to the UN High Commissioner for Human Rights (above) and in the report of Human Rights Watch (above). Kathy Kadane's study cited above refers to the "Indonesian Army which hunted down the leftists and killed them." Suharto and the Army unmistakably intended to destroy the PKI and Chinese as well.

After examining all the evidence above, it is undeniable that Suharto's intention was to destroy the PKI and to eradicate Chinese culture, and thus the "in whole or in part" criteria is met.

To show American complicity in the genocide, it must first be verified that there was intentional participation in the killing. It is not necessary to show that the Americans themselves intended to commit genocide, but only that they were aware of the genocidal intentions of Suharto and the army.

One way in which the United States participated in the genocide was the handing over of a list of 5,000 names of PKI members to the Indonesian army. Kathy Kadane stated that "as many as 5000 names were furnished to the Indonesian army" (see above). Moreover, the United States had been supplying Suharto and the army with arms for many years, as discussed earlier in this chapter. For example, Gabriel Kolko reported that "the United States quickly promised covert aid." They believed that "carefully placed assistance...will help the army cope with PKI" (see above).

It is also evident from the facts in this chapter that the United States was well aware of the intentions of General Suharto and the army. For example, a memorandum from the American Consulate to the Department of State explained that "their organization (Muslim youths) intends to kill every PKI member they can catch" (see above). As well, a State Department paper prepared for President Johnson reports that "as many as 300,000 Indonesians were killed."

All the criteria for complicity in Suharto's genocide have been met, and therefore the United States is guilty of complicity.

This case is an example of the United States thwarting any possible attempt of communists attaining power in Indonesia and threatening American interests. Saving Indonesia from the "scourge" of communism cost hundreds of thousands of lives, not to mention political and economic freedom trumpeted at home as one of the underlying principles of American democracy. Americans faced a fictitious enemy in the form of a fictitious international communist conspiracy with the fictitious objective of overthrowing fictitious democracies but costing real lives.

7

EAST TIMOR: WHERE HAVE ALL THE VILLAGES GONE?

East Timor is a small island 400 kilometers north of Australia inhabited by people who in 1975 were still practicing many of their ancient customs with no ambitions beyond maintaining their communal village life. Many villagers walked four miles on mountain paths to fetch water and trekked many miles every Sunday to the market in order to purchase needed items while socializing with people from other villages. Most East Timorese people lived in huts and set aside one hut where mothers could nurse their babies. Serious crimes such as rape and murder were virtually nonexistent.

It was an idyllic life until it was invaded and occupied by Indonesia in December 1975, armed and supported by the United States. The crimes of East Timor were that it was endowed with offshore oil, was located strategically for military objectives, including a deep seaway passage for American submarines, and was situated near the Indonesian archipelago.

Just prior to the invasion, East Timor had been a Portuguese colony struggling for independence against the opposition of Portugal and Indonesia. Preparing for independence led to the formation of three political parties. However, Indonesia intervened in the political affairs of East Timor to undermine its attempts at becoming a sovereign state. Indonesia was planning to integrate East Timor into the Indonesian Republic, and Timorese sovereignty would undermine that endeavor.

A short civil war ensued in September 1975 between two of the political parties. It was won by Fretilin, a left-of-center party, who immediately set up a de facto government in the absence of the Portuguese, who withdrew during the civil war. As well, to advance the decolonization process, Fretilin called a peace conference with Portugal and Indonesia, but due to Portugal's procrastination, unfortunately it never took place.

When Indonesia commenced attacks on towns near the West Timor border and threatened an invasion, Fretilin hastily declared the independence of the Democratic Republic of East Timor.

A few days later, on December 7, 1975, Indonesia invaded East Timor with bombers, paratroopers, and marines who fired indiscriminately into crowds of men, women, and children. Fretilin appealed to the outside world through radio broadcasts to intervene and end the invasion, but the silence was deafening. The United States knew months in advance about the invasion and had been supplying Indonesia with arms. An Indonesian victory would confer upon the United States and Australia the rights to the offshore oil.

President Ford and Henry Kissinger, Secretary of State, were in Indonesia on the day before the invasion and had given the green light to Suharto. In addition, the United States supplied almost 90 percent of the weapons used by Indonesia in the invasion and military occupation.

For the next twenty-four years, Suharto attempted to integrate East Timor into Indonesia as the twenty-seventh province but was unable to defeat the resistance movement. On August 30, 1999, the people voted for independence but had already suffered the unbelievable loss of 200,000 people. During their departure, the Indonesian soldiers embarked on a killing spree, murdering as many people as possible before they left.

Indonesia is guilty of committing genocide against the people of East Timor not only for killing 200,000 people but for sterilizing women and destroying their culture. The United States is guilty of complicity in this genocide for supporting Suharto and for providing most of the arms for the invasion and occupation.

Both Dutch and Portuguese empires exploited Timor as early as 1515 for sandalwood and slaves until 1913 when Timor was divided into West Timor under control of the Dutch and East Timor under control of the Portuguese.

East Timor contributed very little to the Portuguese economy and was one of the least developed colonies in Southeast Asia. During World War II, the Japanese were able to gain control only after a violent struggle. Caught between Japan and the Allies in World War II, East Timor suffered as a result of Japanese brutality and Allied bombing. At the end of the war, Portugal regained control of its colony, East Timor, and West Timor became part of the Indonesian Republic.

The majority of the population of East Timor was unaffected by European civilization and had maintained the same lifestyle, customs, and myths for centuries, exemplified by the fact that many Timorese lived in villages of twenty-five people where mutual support, sharing, and cooperation formed the basis of their culture. Ancient dances, carrying water for many miles to the village in mountainous terrain, and ancient myths attracted archeologists from around the world to study this pristine culture.

In addition to the villagers, an educated class had emerged who were determined to break away from Portugal in order to become an independent nation. As the Timorese people inched closer to independence, three political parties had formed, including UTD (The Timorese Democratic Union), Fretilin (The Front for an Independent East Timor), and Apodeti (Timorese Popular Democratic Association). UTD was conservative and pro-Portuguese, Fretilin advocated socialism and democracy, and APODETI supported autonomous integration with Indonesia. Fretilin, the most popular party, agreed to join with UTD in a coalition that was planning to work with Portugal on achieving independence for East Timor. Facilitating the process was the overthrow of the fascist government in Portugal by a group of left-leaning officers who called themselves the MFA (Armed Forces Movement).

Indonesia feared an independent nation on its border and had hopes of integrating East Timor into the Indonesian Republic. To obstruct the independence movement, Indonesia launched "Operation Komodo" consisting of border incursions into East Timor from West Timor. As well, Indonesia persuaded conservative members of UTD that a coalition with Fretilin would imperil the struggle for independence.

As a result, UTD carried out a coup in Dili, the capital of East Timor, but failed due to the superior strength of Fretilin. By September 1975, Fretilin has gained control over most of East Timor.

Fretilin invited Portugal and Indonesia to a peace conference where decolonization meetings would begin, but repeated postponements by Portugal forced Fretilin to become a de facto government. At the same time, Indonesia was stepping up its raids on border towns as a precursor to a full-scale invasion. Fearing an Indonesian invasion, Fretilin declared the independence of the Democratic Republic of East Timor on November 28, 1975.

A few days later, on December 7, 1975, at 2 am, Indonesia invaded East Timor when Indonesian ships began to bombard the capital, Dili. At 5 am, paratroopers who were dropped near the waterfront marched toward Dili firing indiscriminately at men, women, and children. After massacring people in Dili for a few days, the 10,000 Indonesian troops attacked other major towns and pushed further inland.

Many of the villagers, Fretilin supporters in particular, sought refuge in the mountains to escape the killing, rape, and murder, although conditions were very inhospitable there due to a deficiency of food. Many of those in the mountains died of starvation or disease. In 1978 and 1979, Indonesian troops launched a constant heavy bombing campaign to destroy Fretilin and their supporters or drive them out of the mountains.

Frustrated with their efforts to defeat Fretilin, Indonesian forces began a campaign of terror against the villages, murdering the men, raping the women and children, and applying horrifying torture techniques. Along the path towards the villages, cropland was defoliated and livestock killed.

From 1978 until 1979, Indonesia decided to destroy Fretilin supporters in the mountains in an "Encirclement and Annihilation" campaign that consisted of saturation bombing and defoliation. Saturation bombing, hunger, and disease forced many of the East

Timorese to come down from the mountains in order to surrender to the Indonesian troops. They were greeted with a hail of bullets.

When the bombing campaign had reached its peak, Indonesian troops forced those living in villages to move to resettlement camps. They were not allowed to leave the camps, and the only food available to them was what they were able to cultivate. Many of the people in the camps were tortured, murdered, or raped. By 1979, estimates ran as high as 300,000 people living in the camps (USAID). Concentrating the population in fifteen resettlement camps to facilitate the ability to maintain tight control over the population opened up the opportunity to socialize the Timorese into Indonesian culture. In addition to assimilation, birth control was forced on the Timorese to reduce their numbers. Another method to limit the number of Timorese was to sterilize the women and girls with pills or injections without their knowledge.

In the late 1970s and early 1980s, Fretilin fought a number of battles throughout the country, putting Indonesian leaders on the defensive. By the end of 1984, Indonesian soldiers were unable to achieve any gains despite the fact that they had been reinforced with 20,000 troops.

One technique adopted by the Indonesians to locate guerrillas was to flush out the Fretilin from their hiding places by forcing Timorese in the resettlement camps to march ahead of the Indonesian troops. Once caught, Fretilin soldiers were either tortured or shot.

Furthermore, Indonesian military leaders implemented a number of measures to control the population in the cities. These controls included setting a 7:00 pm curfew, breaking up small groups in the streets, prohibiting foreign broadcasts, censoring mail, and forbidding the use of Portuguese. Children were terrified by groups of security forces who patrolled the streets at night, frequently shooting on sight. These children behaved as Indonesians to escape the danger of instant execution.

Resettlement was ongoing in the 1980s to supply forced labor for growing cash crops for export. By 1990, almost all the East Timorese were living in these resettlement camps. Another purpose of forcing farmers to abandon their farms for resettlement camps was to free up available fertile land for transmigrants from Indonesia. These transmigrants, who were from all the islands of Indonesia, were encouraged to move to East Timor to assume ownership of the land abandoned by the East Timorese farmers. This migration was part of the process of assimilating East Timor into Indonesian culture. By 1992, approximately 100,000 Indonesians were living in East Timor.

Despite all the efforts of Indonesia to annihilate Fretilin and to transform the culture of East Timor, the armed opposition continued to fight for independence and was able to focus world attention on their cause.

On November 12, 1991, an incident occurred that drew the world's attention to the human rights violations and illegal occupation of East Timor. A group of mourners gathered at a local parish church to attend a memorial mass for Sebastiao Gomes, a pro-independence activist who had been killed in the same church. Accompanying the mourners were journalists from the United States, Great Britain, and Australia to cover the memorial ceremony. After the mass, the mourners marched toward Santa Cruz Cemetery waving banners and shouting pro-independence slogans despite the fact that Indonesian troops lined the streets.

At the cemetery, a number of people went to the graveside while others waited outside the walls. Without warning and without provocation, Indonesian soldiers opened fire at the crowd, shooting at everyone present. This resulted in young boys and girls fleeing the scene while being chased by Indonesian soldiers who began shooting people in the back. This resulted in 250 dead and hundreds more wounded.

When the massacre was reported in the Western media, it provoked moral outrage. European Parliaments and Congress passed resolutions condemning Indonesia for its flagrant violation of human rights, and the Western media began to call for East Timorese independence

Moreover, the attitude of Indonesia toward East Timor critically shifted after the removal of President Suharto from power in May 1998. Combined with Indonesia becoming more open as well as the promise of elections, the new leader, B. J. Habibie, found himself in the middle of a pervasive economic crisis. He desperately needed outside assistance such as loans from the World Bank and aid from major Western powers. Habibie recognized the urgency in convincing the international community that corruption, mismanagement, and ineffective social and economic policies had ended with his ascendancy to the presidency.

With an increasing number of images of brutality appearing on television screens around the world, support for a referendum in East Timor became stronger. World pressure forced Indonesia to promise a referendum to determine whether the people of East Timor were in favor of independence. The response of the Indonesian military in East Timor was to threaten "liquidation" for all pro-independence supporters. In May 1999, Indonesia ordered that massacres should be carried out from village to village if East Timor voted for independence. After the result was announced on August 30, 1999, that 78 percent had voted for independence, the Indonesians began a new wave of mass killings. Only after the United Nations become involved did the mass killing finally come to an end.

The number of East Timorese who were killed and the number injured or raped can be found in the *Commission for Reception, Truth and Reconciliation in East Timor* set up in 2000 by the United Nations. The report, released on October 31, 2005, accused Indonesia of a number of human rights violations such as:

> Indonesian security forces systematically: Failed to discriminate between civilian and military targets in conducting repeated large-scale bombings…Destroyed food sources by burning or poisoning crops and food stores. Slaughtering herds of livestock…Refused to allow access to international aid organizations.

The Commission finds that the only logical conclusion that can be drawn from these actions is that the Indonesian security forces consciously decided to use starvation of East Timorese civilians as a weapon of war.

The Commission finds that during the invasion and occupation members of the Indonesian security forces summarily executed thousands of East Timorese non-combatants.

The Commission finds that imposition of conditions of life which could not sustain tens of thousands of East Timorese civilians amounted to extermination as a crime against humanity committed against the East Timorese population.

Throughout the period of the conflict members of the Indonesian security forces systematically raped and imposed conditions of sexual slavery on thousands of East Timorese women.

(*Commission for the Reception, Truth and Reconciliation in East Timor*, October 31, 2005)

As well, the Commission reports the number of deaths, injuries, rapes, and torture:

The Commission finds that the Government of Indonesia and the Indonesian security forces are primarily responsible and accountable for the death from hunger and illness of between 100,000 and 180,000 Timorese who died as a direct result of the Indonesian military invasion and occupation.

(Ibid.)

The Commission further documented the use of illegal weapons:

The Commission has found that at times ABR/TNI [Indonesian forces] used weapons which are prohibited by international laws governing armed conflict. These include

chemical weapons which are used to poison water supplies
and kill crops and vegetation, and resulted in the deaths by
poisoning of hundreds of civilian victims.

(Ibid.)

These findings confirm that Indonesia committed genocide
in East Timor. They planned the invasion well in advance with the
intention of destroying the population of East Timor. East Timorese
were either killed by Indonesian security forces, subject to socialization
into Indonesian culture, or forced to practice birth control, or take
pills or injections for sterilization. In other words, Indonesia intended
to "destroy in whole or in part" the people of East Timor or to
impose "measures intended to prevent births in whole or in part." The
Indonesian security forces also "inflicted conditions of life calculated to
bring about its physical destruction in whole or part."

The U.S. complicity in the genocide in East Timor is based
on their full awareness of the intentions of General Suharto as well as
supplying Suharto with 90 percent of the military equipment that he
then used to perpetrate the genocide. The *Commission for Reception,
Truth and Reconciliation in East Timor* condemns the United States for
the critical part it played in the atrocities committed against the people
of East Timor:

> The Commission finds that the United States of America
> failed to support the right of the East Timorese to self-
> determination, and that its political and military support were
> fundamental to the Indonesian invasion and occupation....
> President Gerald Ford met President Suharto twice in 1975.
> The second meeting was in Jakarta on 6 December, the day
> before the Indonesian invasion of Dili, when the impending
> invasion was discussed. The Commission finds on the basis
> of the available documentary evidence that the United States
> was aware of Indonesian plans to invade Timor-Leste. It
> also finds that the United States was aware that the military
> equipment supplied by it to Indonesia would be used for
> this purpose...the United States decided to turn a blind eye
> to the invasion, even though US-supplied arms and military
> equipment were sure to be used.

(Ibid.)

In addition to the Commission's report, there is a mountain of declassified documents that definitively prove that the United States was fully aware of Indonesia's intentions and that the United States supplied military equipment to Indonesia with full knowledge that it would be used to kill East Timorese.

In one recorded conversation between President Ford and General Suharto, Suharto was seeking reassurance that if he invaded East Timor, President Ford would not object:

> Suharto—It is now important to determine what we can do to establish peace and order for the present and the future in the interest of security of the area of Indonesia. These are some of the considerations we are now contemplating. We want your understanding if we deem it necessary to take rapid or drastic action.
>
> Ford—We will understand and will not press you on the issue. We understand the problem you have [with East Timor] and the intentions you have.

(*Telegram from Embassy in Jakarta to Secretary of State*, Gerald R. Ford Library, December, 1975)

A telegram from the Secretary of State to the embassy in Jakarta advised against the invasion beginning while the president was still in Jakarta:

> By now you will have seen [deleted] regarding a "decision" by Suharto to initiate a major military intervention in Timor between December 6–8, and to foreshadow such action in an announcement December 5 "to dissociate Indonesian military intervention from President Ford's visit." ...It continues to be our judgment that the Indonesians are unlikely to launch a major military intervention in Timor prior to the President's departure from Jakarta. However, they could make the proposed announcement which it seems to us would be a serious embarrassment for the President's

visit...Send an urgent message to the Indonesians... requesting the Indonesians to make no announcement and to take no military action until well after the President's departure from Jakarta.

(*Telegram from the State Department to the Embassy in Jakarta*, National Security Archives, December 6, 1975)

American officials not only encouraged the invasion but supported the military occupation, which served their purpose of maintaining access to East Timorese oil. At the same time, U.S. leaders were well aware of the atrocities perpetrated by the Indonesians as confirmed by declassified documents such as a telegram from the U.S. Embassy in Jakarta to the Secretary of State:

> The information provided was based largely on a special briefing [deleted] outlined the strategy and results of the recent operation to eliminate Fretilin remnants. Moving in an East to West sweep which covered the Eastern half of the province, GOI [Indonesian army] forces killed 450 of an estimated 900 Fretilin guerrillas and captured 4,500 civilian sympathizers...Nevertheless from this description there seems to be little doubt that normal life and agricultural activity in the Eastern half of the province would have been seriously disrupted by an operation of that scale and nature

(*Briefing on the Military Situation in East Timor*, Telegram from Jakarta Embassy to State Department, November 1981)

In another telegram from the Jakarta Embassy to the State Department, it was reported that:

> Indonesian soldiers died [15]. Sources in East Timor reported that in retaliation for the killings, and especially for villagers' direct role in killing an Indonesian soldier who nearly escaped, Indonesian forces carried out reprisals two days later against the villagers. The information reaching [deleted] claimed that up to two hundred villagers died.

(*Views on East Timor Developments*, Telegram from Jakarta Embassy to State Department, September 1983)

Note that the embassy is treating this as a war between Indonesia and East Timor rather than an invasion and a military occupation.

The United States provided 90 percent of the weapons used by Indonesia in perpetrating genocide in East Timor. In a memorandum from Clinton E. Granger, member of the National Security Council, to Brent Scowcroft, Ford's National Security Advisor, the issue of MAP (Military Assistance Program) equipment used in East Timor by the Indonesians was discussed:

> The ex-USS Claud Jones class destroyer…has been involved in coastal shelling since November 22 [1975]…Two other ex-U.S. ships…have participated in coastal patrols… Transportation throughout the operations has been provided by ex-US 511 class LSTs…Five C-47 transport aircraft that were MAP supported have been identified in support operations…Seven U.S. MAP and one FMS provided Hercules participated in paradrops on Dili and Baucau… Defense believes that both brigades are using their U.S.-supplied equipment and have not substituted domestically produced Indonesian weapons. The arms inventory of these two brigades follows:
>
> M-16A1 rifle…………..3332
>
> M-60 machine gun………..180
>
> M-79 grenade launcher…108
>
> 81-mm mortars…………..18
>
> 90-mm recoilless………..10
>
> 3.5-inch rocket launcher…86
>
> U.S. parachutes………..3332

(*Memorandum from Clinton E. Granger to Brent Scowcroft*, Gerald R. Ford Library, December 12, 1975)

The annual arms transfer from the United States to Indonesia is very indicative of the level of American support for the invasion and occupation:

Arms transfers to Indonesia 1975–1995

(in millions of current dollars)

YEAR	TOTAL
1975	$ 65.0
1976	37.3
1977	27.0
1978	127.0
1979	56.8
1980	26.2
1981	52.6
1982	54.8
1983	40.0
1984	26.2
1985	49.0
1990	52.0

(*Pentagon Foreign Military Sales*, Commercial Arms Sales Program, U.S. Department of Defense)

The evidence clearly proves that the invasion and occupation by Indonesian forces resulted in genocide. As well, the evidence irrefutably establishes that the United States was aware of the genocidal intentions of the Indonesians.

Washington's primary interest in East Timor was in offshore oil and not in committing genocide. Although the United States did not have genocidal intentions, it had full knowledge of the atrocities perpetrated by Indonesia and supplied the arms. America's role in the genocide incriminates them in complicity in genocide.

It seems that oil, leftist governments, and strategic locations are the bane of countries that lack the resources to defend themselves against exploitative powers. An innocent, ancient civilization had to be sacrificed on the alter of corporate interests while the governments who act on behalf of these corporate interests are the high priests who plunge the economic and humanitarian dagger into the victim so that corporate interests can earn higher profits. Profits are the golden calf to which most of the Western World pays homage with the glitter of gold blinding them to their own in humanity.

8

IRAQ – 1990: RICHES TO RAGS.

Former President George H. Bush discovered a method for traveling back in time in Iraq. Before bombing Iraq in 1991, the country was very prosperous compared with other countries in the Middle East, with a growing economy built on a sound infrastructure and modern industries. People had access to a good healthcare and a decent educational system, and women enjoyed the most progressive policies toward women in the Middle East. The one major drawback in Iraq was the lack of political, legal, and civil rights due to the brutal dictatorship of Saddam Hussein.

In 1980, the United States encouraged Iraq to declare war against Iran, which had become an enemy state after overthrowing the Shah and holding members of the American Embassy hostage. Despite the fact that the United States was ostensibly supporting Iraq and supplying Saddam with military equipment for the war against Iran, the United States hypocritically sold arms to Iran.

After a bloody, vicious eight-year war in which one million people died, Saddam had at best achieved a stalemate but had weakened the Iraqi economy by borrowing money to buy arms. Between the end of the Iran-Iraqi war in 1988 and 1990, the American attitude towards Saddam completely shifted. Iraq was not sufficiently subservient to U.S. imperial designs, and furthermore, Washington had been seeking control of Iraqi oil for many years. Additionally, Iraq had become too strong militarily because of the weapons supplied to Saddam during the war with Iran.

American policymakers decided that the solution to the Iraqi "problem" was to launch a massive bombing campaign against the Iraqis to accomplish the above goals. Needing a pretext for attacking Iraq, Bush and his advisors devised a clever scheme to lure Iraq into invading Kuwait, giving the United States the opportunity to march into Kuwait as knights in shining armor to rescue the Kuwaitis.

Bush convinced Kuwait to increase its supply of oil to lower the price, thus depriving Iraq of desperately needed oil revenues in order to make payments on Iraq's debt. To encourage Saddam even further, the American ambassador to Iraq conveyed the impression that the United States would not intervene if Iraq invaded Kuwait.

Saddam took the bait, and all his efforts to avoid America's planned invasion were futile. The United States bombed Iraq for forty-two days, during which over 100,000 people were killed and the entire infrastructure of Iraq was destroyed. Iraq had been bombed back into the pre-industrial age, thereby causing a severe shortage of electricity, clean water, sewage-treatment plants, and modern industries. Bush's time-machine consisted of millions of tons of bombs that transformed a modern industrial economy into virtually a pre-industrial economy. The result was a monstrous act of genocide.

During World War II, Britain invaded Iraq and established a pro-British government after Prime Minister Rashid Ali Al-Gaylani supported Nazi Germany. In 1958, the monarchy in Iraq was overthrown and King Faisal was executed. The new Prime Minister, Abdul Karim Qassem, resisted the monopolies of Western oil companies and contributed to the foundation of the Organization of Petroleum Exporting Companies (OPEC) in 1961.

Control over Arab oil reserves was a major foreign policy objective of France, Britain, and the United States. When Qassem thwarted attempts to gain control of Iraqi oil, a CIA-supported coup assassinated Qassem and his supporters in 1963.

The assassination was followed by a series of military coups until 1968 when Ahmed Hasan al-Bakr of the Baath party assumed power. The Baath party was socialist with strong nationalist convictions. In an attempt to gain control over its oil reserves, the Iraqi government nationalized the U.S.-British-owned Iraqi Petroleum Company. Due to the nationalist inclination of the Baathist Party and nationalization of oil, the United States embarked on a campaign in 1972 to destabilize Iraq by encouraging the leaders in Northern Iraq to rebel against the Iraqi government. Events in Iran led to a major U.S. policy shift in the

Middle East. Iranian support for American ambitions in the Middle East, and in particular for the campaign to overthrow the government in Iraq, suddenly ended with the overthrow of the Shah of Iran by the Ayatollah Khomeini. With the loss of a major ally, the United States decided to turn to Iraq for support in 1979, the same year that Saddam Hussein came to power.

Iran's transformation into an Islamic republic was alarming both to the United States and to Iraq. American attitudes towards Iran underwent a complete reversal as the Khomeini regime was now considered a major threat to American objectives in the Middle East. In 1980, with encouragement from the United States, Iraq declared war on Iran. American support for Iraq consisted of six Lockheed L-100 civilian transport aircraft, six small jets, forty-five large Bell helicopters, and most significantly, massive amounts of financial aid. Further, American allies in the Middle East, Saudi Arabia, and Kuwait contributed billions of dollars to Iraq's war effort.

Paradoxically, the Reagan administration was forced to sell weapons to Iran in order to acquire funds to buy weapons for the Contras who were stationed in Honduras and Costa Rica to fight a war of attrition against the Sandinistas in Nicaragua. Surreptitious methods for arming the Contras were needed after Congress had cut off all their funding when the Boland Amendment was approved by Congress.

When the war finally ended in 1988, none of the issues between Iran and Iraq had been resolved. Shockingly, Iraq had suffered approximately 375,000 casualties and Iran 300,000, while 500,000 people were injured.

By the end of the war, Iraq had become a relatively strong military power in the Middle East. The United States and regional allies had supplied Iraq during the war with military equipment and weapons and also with the precursor chemicals for chemical weapons. An imbalance in the military power equilibrium in the Middle East was not consistent with American plans for the region. American policymakers were apprehensive about a strong Iraq, which could potentially pose a threat to America's complete control of the Middle East.

U.S. policymakers were also disconcerted and angry over Saddam's refusal to cooperate with the American economic blueprint for Iraq. The United States was campaigning to establish the same relationship with Iraq as it had with Saudi Arabia. Washington would offer Iraq U.S. government securities in exchange for petrodollars. The interest on the securities would then be paid out to American companies to improve Iraq's infrastructure and build new cities. In addition, the United States would sell Saddam tanks and fighter planes and build chemical and nuclear power plants. The purpose of this plan was to entrap Saddam in an American economic web from which there was no escape (*Confessions of an Economic Hit Man*, John Perkins, pp. 214–216).

As well, Iraq was situated in a very strategic location bordering a number of oil-producing nations and highly suitable for American military bases. A closer relationship with Saddam would create the opportunity to build these bases.

Furthermore, as Iraq was the second-largest oil-producing nation, the United States was maneuvering to gain control over the oil reserves in the Middle East in order to achieve a competitive advantage over upcoming economic powers such as China.

For all the above reasons, the United States embarked on a campaign to weaken Iraq. One method was to economically weaken Iraq by convincing Kuwait to produce an oversupply of oil to drive down the price. A lower price for oil would impair Iraq's ability to pay back the huge debt accumulated during the Iran-Iraqi war. Iraq had amassed this debt during the Iran-Iraqi war totaling over $80 billion, of which $30 billion was owed to Kuwait. Iraq offered to repay the debt after rebuilding its economy, but Kuwait demanded repayment immediately.

To further exacerbate Iraq's debt problem, Kuwait increased oil output excessively on August 8, 1988, one day after Iraq and Iran agreed to a ceasefire. Crude oil prices fell from $21 to $11 a barrel, and Iraq's oil revenues declined $14 billion a year (*The Fire This Time: U.S. War Crimes in the Gulf*, Ramsey Clark, p. 14).

David Model

Ultimately, the United States intended to declare war on Iraq but first devised a subterfuge to provoke Iraq into invading Kuwait in order to furnish a rationale for a declaration of war. The United States would then search for allies to form a coalition that would seek authorization from the Security Council. Moreover, Washington would launch a major propaganda campaign to sell the war to the American people.

Iraq already had one grievance against Kuwait due to Kuwait's decision to ratchet up the supply of oil. Additionally, Kuwait had stolen $2.4 billion worth of oil from the Rumaila oil fields, which ran beneath the vaguely defined border between Iraq and Kuwait. Kuwait had moved the border and claimed an additional 900 square miles of the Rumaila field. Kuwait was also stealing oil that clearly belonged to Iraq by using American-supplied slant-drilling technology. As well, two Gulf islands blocked Iraq's access to the Persian Gulf, and Iraq insisted that these islands belonged to them.

The economic warfare against Iraq also consisted of a set of sanctions imposed by the United States and other Western countries, although they were not approved by the United Nations until 1990. The total impact of economic warfare was devastating to the Iraq economy, which had already suffered severely from the war with Iran.

Recognizing the hardships in Iraq imposed by sanctions and a large debt, other nations in the Middle East undertook a number of efforts to resolve the dispute over oil prices between Kuwait and Iraq. Other Arab nations also suffered economically from the Kuwaiti spike in oil prices, which were in violation of OPEC's production quotas. In frustration, Iraq dispatched envoys to several Arab nations appealing for new quotas that would allow a modest increase in the price of oil. However, Kuwait refused to comply.

Further, it became clear that Kuwait was determined to increase oil supplies without regard for the other oil-producing nations in the Middle East. It was also clear that Kuwait was unconcerned about the consequences of refusing to comply with OPEC quotas or an invasion from Iraq because the Emir of Kuwait had received assurances from the United States that they would defend Kuwait. Washington had patently orchestrated the Kuwaiti oil policy as a means to prod Iraq into an invasion of Kuwait. When Sheikh Sabah of Kuwait was urged by Jordan to treat the Iraqi threats to launch an invasion more seriously, he reported that "we are not going to respond to [Iraq]…If they don't like it, let them occupy our territory…We are going to bring in the Americans" (*The Village Voice*, April 5, 1991, in an interview with King Hussein of Jordan).

Ultimately, Saddam Hussein was not prepared to invade Kuwait without either the approval or the indifference of the United States. Saddam met with the American Ambassador to Iraq, April Glaspie, on July 25, 1990, to seek out the U.S. position on an Iraqi invasion of Kuwait. The following is part of the transcript of the conversation:

> U.S. Ambassador Glaspie—I have direct instruction from President Bush to improve our relations with Iraq. We have considerable sympathy for your quest for higher oil prices, the immediate cause of your confrontation with Kuwait. As you know, I have lived here for years and admire your extraordinary efforts to rebuild your economy. We can see that you have employed massive numbers of troops in the south. Normally that would be none of our business but when this happens in the context of your threats against Kuwait, then it would be reasonable for us to be concerned. For this reason, I have received instructions to ask you, in the spirit of friendship—not confrontation—regarding your intentions. Why are your troops massed so very close to Kuwait's border?

> Saddam Hussein—As you know, for years I have made every effort to reach a settlement in our dispute with Kuwait. There is to be a meeting in two days. I am prepared to give negotiations this one more brief chance. But if we are unable to find a solution, then it would be natural that Iraq will not accept death.

> U.S. Ambassador Glaspie—What solutions would be acceptable?

Saddam Hussein—(A list of conditions). What is the United States opinion on this?

U.S. Ambassador Glaspie—We have no opinion on your Arab-Arab conflicts, such as your dispute with Kuwait. Secretary of State James Baker has directed me to emphasize the instruction first given to Iraq in the 1960s, that the Kuwait issue is not associated with America.

(*The New York Times International*, September 23, 1990, p. 19)

April Glaspie's statements in her conversation with Saddam Hussein are a singular example of American deviousness and hypocrisy when she reported to him the position of Washington with regard to the invasion of Iraq. She wove the final skein in the web of deceit to entrap Hussein into invading Kuwait.

With Iraqi troops stationed on the Kuwait border and Saddam now convinced that the United States would not interfere if Iraq invaded Kuwait, the invasion of Kuwait was imminent. Other Arab nations fervently hoped that a war between Iraq and Kuwait could be avoided, but with Kuwait's intransigence over the price of oil, war seemed inevitable. In one final effort to avoid war, King Hussein of Jordan and King Fahd of Saudi Arabia beseeched the Emir to attend a mini-summit on July 31 in Jidda, Saudi Arabia. Although the invitation was addressed to the Emir, he sent the Prime Minister in his place. The Emir had instructed the prime minister to be "unwavering in your discussions." Kuwait, under instructions from the United States, refused to negotiate, and the mini-summit was a failure.

Without any hope of resolving the issues through negotiations and with the apparent indifference of the United States toward "Arab-Arab conflicts," Iraq invaded Kuwait on August 2, 1990. On the same day, the United Nations Security Council passed Resolution 660, which stated that:

...The Security Council, alarmed by the invasion of Kuwait on August 2, 1990, by the military forces of Iraq:

1. Condemns the Iraq invasion;

2. Demands that Iraq withdraw immediately and unconditionally...

3. Calls upon Iraq and Kuwait to begin immediately intensive negotiation...

Notwithstanding that Saddam had bitten the bait, Washington would not declare war on Iraq until a propaganda campaign had succeeded in "manufacturing consent" for the expenditure of funds and the risk to American lives in a confrontation with Iraq. On August 2, 1990, U.S. Deputy Press Secretary Popadiuk released a statement:

> The United States is deeply concerned about the blatant act of aggression and demands the immediate and unconditional withdrawal of all Iraqi forces...we are urging the entire international community to condemn this outrageous act of aggression.

Demanding "unconditional withdrawal" was a clever ploy to guard against the danger that Saddam might offer to withdraw but under reasonable conditions. American intentions were etched in concrete, and the United States was determined to bomb Iraq regardless of Saddam's response. The United States had to guarantee that all attempts by Iraq to settle its disputes with Kuwait were doomed to failure.

As part of the propaganda campaign, condemnations of Saddam spewed out of Washington to demonize the leader of Iraq. He was repeatedly criticized, and to exploit this characterization to the fullest, he was even compared to Hitler.

Saddam's illegal invasion of Kuwait would form the foundation of the propaganda campaign. The problem was that Kuwait presented a public relations challenge to the Bush administration because it was a small Arab sheikdom ruled by a family oligarchy. Since 1961, the emirate had been ruled by the Sabah family, who had dissolved the National Assembly. The Assembly had not been a paragon of democracy, since only 65,000 males and zero women out of a population of two million were allowed to participate in the political process. Moreover, political dissent was not tolerated. On January 22, 1990, the government brutally attacked a pro-democracy demonstration with tear gas and batons and several politicians were beaten. As well, Kuwait depended on foreign workers to provide the labor in Kuwait's oil fields, and they were treated as slaves who were systematically abused by burning, blinding, and fatal beatings.

To win the support of the American people, Washington hired a number of public relations firms to "educate" the public about the necessity of declaring war against Iraq. Kuwait funded an estimated twenty public relations firms, lobby groups, and law firms including the Redon Group (public relations) for a retainer of $100,000, Neill & Co. (lobbyists) for $50,000 per month, and Hill & Knowlton (the world's largest public relations firm at the time), who served as the mastermind of the Kuwaiti campaign. Some of their activities included arranging media interviews with visiting Kuwaitis, setting up days of observance such as National Free Kuwaiti Day, organizing public rallies, distributing news releases and information kits, contacting politicians at all levels, and producing dozens of video news releases that were distributed to the media.

The coup de grace in the propaganda campaign was a story invented by Hill & Knowlton that evoked a strong emotional response from the public. On October 10, 1990, the Congressional Human Rights Caucus on Capitol Hill held a hearing on Iraqi human rights violations. Although the hearing bore a resemblance to a Congressional proceeding, this ad hoc Human Rights Caucus was, in fact, nothing more than a meeting of politicians, not a committee of Congress with legal accoutrements. The caucus was chaired by Democrat Tom Lantos and Republican John Porter, who were also co-chairs of the Congressional Human Rights Foundation. The Human Rights Foundation was occupying offices rent-free in Hill & Knowlton's Washington office.

Hill & Knowlton's public relations stunt involved an emotionally charged horror story that came from a fifteen-year-old Kuwaiti girl named Nayirah who supposedly could not reveal her last name for fear of putting friends and family who were still in Kuwait at risk. She tearfully recounted that she had witnessed Iraqi soldiers taking babies from incubators and leaving them on the cold floor to die. To publicize the story, she provided written testimony packaged into media kits prepared by Citizens for a Free Kuwait. The story was repeated frequently by President Bush, who claimed that 312 babies had suffered the same fate. It was also repeatedly retold on television, radio, and at the Security Council.

Hill and Knowlton had omitted one minor detail about the identity of the fifteen-year-old girl, namely that she was, in fact, the daughter of Saud Nasir al-Sabah, the Kuwaiti ambassador to the United States. They also failed to mention that she had been coached by Hill & Knowlton before her appearance in front of the Caucus.

After the war, human rights investigators and reporters completely discredited the story. John Martin, an ABC news reporter, traveled to Kuwait on March 15, 1991, and interviewed Dr. Mohammed Matar, director of Kuwait's healthcare system, and his wife Dr. Fayeza Youseff, chief of obstetrics at the maternity hospital. They both denied any knowledge of babies being snatched from incubators. Martin also visited al-Addan hospital, where Nayirah had claimed she had witnessed the removal of fifteen babies from incubators. Dr. Fahima Khafaji, a pediatrician at the hospital, also completely refuted the stories.

In actual fact, the real horror story was not about the babies and incubators but about how the U.S. government manufactured a lie to sell a war in which over 100,000 people died, as was the case in 2003 when George W. fabricated the grand deception about weapons of mass destruction in Iraq.

While the propaganda campaign was underway, the Pentagon was preparing for war. The buildup of American forces in the Persian Gulf began on the same day that Iraq invaded Kuwait. On August 2, a group of seven warships led by the USS *Independence* headed toward the Persian Gulf followed by another aircraft carrier and an assault ship on August 5.

The United States needed a base of operations in the Persian Gulf, and Saudi Arabia was the preeminent location. To overcome the Saudis' reluctance to serve as a base for U.S. military operations against Iraq, a fellow Arab state, the United States lied to Saudi Arabia by warning the Saudis that Iraqi troops were lined up on the Saudi border. On August 3, Defense Secretary Dick Cheney and the Chairman of the Joint Chiefs of Staff met with Prince Bandar bin Sultan, the Saudi Ambassador to the United States, and showed him fake satellite photos of Iraq troops assembled on the Saudi border. Prince Bandar bin Sultan used the photographs to convince the Saudi government that Saddam also posed a threat to Saudi Arabia and therefore their territory should be offered as support for the Americans. Further, to apply more pressure on the Saudi government, a high-level delegation consisting of Dick Cheney, Colin Powell, National Security Agency Deputy Director Robert Gates, Defense Department aide Paul Wolfowitz, and General Schwarzkopf traveled to Saudi Arabia to meet with King Fahd. Before the high-level meeting, King Fahd had sent a team to investigate the presence of Iraqi troops, but they returned without a shred of evidence. The *Times* hired two defense intelligence experts to study the photos, both of whom refuted Washington's claim about Iraqi troops on the Saudi border. Nevertheless, King Fahd finally succumbed to the pressure and agreed to allow Saudi territory to be used as the base of operations, but under the condition that it appear as if Saudi Arabia had requested American assistance.

After Iraq had invaded Kuwait, Arab nations endeavored to seek a peaceful solution to the problem. King Hussein of Jordan discussed a possible withdrawal of Iraqi troops from Kuwait with Saddam Hussein, who agreed to withdraw his troops on the condition that he would not be subject to condemnation by the Arab League. Following his meeting with Saddam, King Hussein flew to Egypt to secure a promise from President Hosni Mubarak that Egypt would not publicly condemn Iraq.

At the same time, Bush had issued an ultimatum to Saddam giving him two days to withdraw from Kuwait. King Hussein then met with Saddam Hussein on August 3, 1990, to invite him to a conference set for August 5 to negotiate a settlement with Kuwait. Saddam agreed to begin withdrawing troops on August 5 if the negotiations proved productive. However, President Bush did not want Iraq to begin withdrawing its troops from Kuwait because that would deny Bush the opportunity to declare war. As a result, the United States applied intense pressure on Egypt to introduce a resolution at the Arab League condemning Hussein. On August 3, the resolution passed just prior to the introduction of a resolution in the Security Council to impose sanctions on Iraq.

Other efforts to negotiate a peaceful settlement failed because the United States rejected every offer extended by Iraq. On August 12, Iraq offered to withdraw from Kuwait in exchange for Syrian and Israeli withdrawal from Lebanon and Israeli withdrawal from the occupied territories. The United States immediately rejected any linkage between Iraqi withdrawal and military occupations elsewhere. In another Iraqi proposal delivered to Brent Scowcroft, President Bush's National Security Advisor, Saddam offered to withdraw from Kuwait in exchange for lifting the sanctions, full Iraqi control of the Rumaila oil fields, and guaranteed access to the gulf. The White House had no interest in considering Saddam's overture and rejected it outright. President Bush's position on Iraq's solicitations was reflected in Bush's response to reporters on October 31:

> There is no compromise with this aggression...and every time somebody sends an emissary that gives Saddam Hussein a little bit of hope that there might be some way he can stop short of doing what he must do: get out of Kuwait unconditionally.

(President Bush Library)

On August 7, following King Fahd's consent, 40,000 American troops were deployed immediately to Saudi Arabia. The buildup escalated rapidly in September before there was an opportunity for sanctions, negotiations, or any other method of resolving the crisis to succeed without the use of force. By September 4, there were 100,000 American troops in the Gulf, doubling to 200,000 by mid-October. By the end of October, Bush had amassed 400,000 troops in the Gulf and by mid-January, there were 540,000 troops stationed in Saudi Arabia. Paradoxically, Congress had yet to approve United Nations Resolution 678 authorizing the use of force.

In addition to amassing troops in the Gulf, Bush was endeavoring to legitimize the war by building an international coalition of nations to join in the war effort in order to deflect criticism of American unilateralism. A number of methods were employed to win support for the war, including bribes and coercion. Egypt and Turkey were forgiven millions of dollars of debt, China was offered $114 million in aid and diplomatic normalization, and the Soviet Union was offered $4 billion in loans from Saudi Arabia, Kuwait, and the United Arab Emirates. As well, Cuba and Malaysia were subject to massive pressure and threats, and Ethiopia and Zaire were offered grants and loans. American machinations had secured the votes needed on the Security Council.

To further legitimize the declaration of war against Iraq, the United States sought a UN resolution to authorize the use of force. In effect, the United States had manufactured support for UN approval through the methods described above. The Security Council passed Resolution 678 on November 29, 1990, which stated that:

> The Security Council, noting that despite all efforts by the United Nations, Iraq refuses to comply with its obligation to implement Resolution 660 and the above mentioned subsequent resolutions, in flagrant contempt of the Security Council...Acting under Chapter VII of the Charter
>
> 1. Demands that Iraq comply fully with Resolution 660 (1990) and all subsequent relevant Resolutions, and decides while maintaining all its decisions, to allow Iraq one final opportunity to do so;
>
> 2. Authorizes Member States co-operating with the Government of Kuwait, unless Iraq on or before January 15, 1991, fully implements, as set forth in paragraph 1 above, to use all means necessary to uphold and implement resolution 660 (1990) and

all subsequent relevant Resolutions and to restore international peace and security in the area...

"All means necessary" authorized the use of force if Iraq failed to comply with the conditions set out in resolution 678. The resolution makes a mockery of the United Nations authority to "maintain international peace and security...and to bring about by peaceful mean settlement of international disputes" (United Nations Charter, Article I). In the end, the resolution passed because the United States used bribes and coercion to ensure that a majority supported the resolution. Additionally, the implementation of Resolution 678 violated the UN Charter, in particular, Articles 33, 36, and 42. For example, Article 33 requires disputing parties to "...seek a solution by negotiation, mediation, conciliation, arbitration, judicial settlement." Since the U.S. intention was to declare war on Iraq, not to resolve outstanding disputes, the UN Charter became a sham. U.S. efforts to secure passage of resolution 678 were solely for the purpose of lending the appearance of legitimacy to a war that was illegal.

Resolution 678 granted war powers to member states without any assurance that all peaceful means would be exhausted before force was used. Specifically, member states should have been required to revisit the question of force in the Security Council before going to war. This process is both the intention and spirit of the United Nations Charter with respect to avoiding war and maintaining international peace and security.

As well, President Bush sent troops to the Gulf without giving proper notification to Congress, and only after the November elections did he inform Congress that he had ordered more than 400,000 troops to Saudi Arabia.

American deployment of forces in the Persian Gulf prior to any effort to reach a peaceful settlement simply reflects Bush's absolute determination to declare war on Iraq irrespective of any possible reasonable proposal by Iraq or any call for negotiations by any other nation. On January 8, 1991, the President stated in a letter to Congressional leaders that:

The current situation in the Persian Gulf, brought about by Iraq's unprovoked invasion and subsequent brutal occupation of Kuwait, threatens U.S. vital interests. The situation also threatens the peace... Mr. Speaker, I am determined to do whatever is necessary to protect America's security.

(President Bush Library)

In sharp contrast to the words of President Bush, Arab diplomats at the United Nations said that they had received reports from Algeria, Jordan, and Yemen, all of whom were on good terms with Iraq, that Saddam Hussein would agree soon after January 15, 1991 (UN deadline) to announce his withdrawal from Kuwait. The only conditions were that Iraq would not be attacked, an international peace conference on Palestinian grievances would be convened, and disputes with Kuwait would be settled by negotiations. The United States rejected the offer as unacceptable.

Iraq was merely requesting in this final offer that serious outstanding conflicts be negotiated with no conditions attached. American intransigence clearly reveals the ferocious inflexibility of a nation determined to go to war.

On January 15, 1991, New York time, or January 16, Iraqi time, B-52s were flying towards their targets in Iraq and cruise missiles were fired from ships in the Indian Ocean. These initial attacks were the launching of an unspeakable reign of terror that would inflict massive damage and unconscionable horror on the people of Iraq.

Restricting the bombing to only military targets was not part of the U.S. war plan. The euphemism "collateral damage" refers to the destruction of civilian targets. Its sinister purpose is to use an innocuous phrase to describe the killing of innocent people and the destruction of schools, utilities, factories, or hospitals. In actual fact, during the bombing of Iraq, the whole country became collateral damage. Iraq military forces were completely incapable of defending themselves from bombers dropping bombs from 35,000 feet or ships firing cruise missiles from twenty miles out at sea. During the attack, Iraq did not offer any defense to American bombing of cities inasmuch as Iraq ground-to-air defenses and Soviet SA-6 surface-to-air missiles were incapable of reaching American bombers. Iraqis could only observe helplessly as a torrential downpour of bombs destroyed their cities and killed family, friends, and neighbors.

The bombing continued for forty-two days, dropping over eighty million tons of explosives. In the first days of the "war," the bombing destroyed Iraqi ground forces' access to military supplies, reinforcements, food, water, and medical supplies. Communication systems were severely damaged, along with tanks, armored vehicles, artillery, and other mechanized equipment, crippling their ability to fight. Moreover, the ground war was planned to occur only after Iraq itself had been demolished by bombing missions.

In addition to conventional weapons, the United States used weapons that were prohibited by international law, including fuel-air explosives, napalm, and cluster bombs. These bombs have been banned because they kill indiscriminately, unable to distinguish between military and nonmilitary targets. In fact, cluster bombs are designed to kill a large number of people, and thus dropping them in cities, towns, and villages would inevitably result in a large number of civilian deaths and injuries.

Furthermore, bombing Iraq's cities served no military purpose and was clearly aimed at the infrastructure of Iraq. Critical elements of the civilian infrastructure were destroyed, such as communication systems, oil refineries, electrical generators, water-treatment plants, dams, transportation centers, and bridges.

When the smoke had cleared, over 90 percent of Iraq's electrical capacity was destroyed, resulting in the horrific death of hundreds of thousands Iraqi children well after the war had ended. This was primarily because of the inability to boil water for purification and the inability to supply power to hospitals.

This need to boil water was a direct result of the destruction of Iraq's water-treatment plants and chlorine plants. Compounding the problem was the bombing of the sewage-treatment plants, thus causing sewage to pour out onto the streets.

As well, Iraq's capacity to produce food was severely impeded by the bombing of farmer's silos, food-processing plants, and food storage and distribution centers. Half of Iraq's agricultural output depended on irrigation systems, which had also been bombed. Food production was impeded even further by bombing a tractor-assembly plant and a fertilizer plant. Severely interfering with the feeding of babies was the destruction of a major baby milk factory. Many other factories were destroyed as well, including a vegetable oil factory, a sugar refinery, a textile mill, five engineering plants, four car-assembly plants, sixteen petrochemical plants, and a meat-storage facility.

Shockingly, the bombing included targets that are not only protected by international law but are sacrosanct according to any rational system of ethics. Twenty-eight civilian hospitals, 52 community health centers, 25 mosques, and 676 schools were struck.

Densely populated cities were hit daily, killing thousands of civilians and destroying entire neighborhoods. One of the worst horror stories of the war was the annihilation of the Amariyah bomb shelter in Baghdad, where 1,500 civilians, mostly women and children, were seeking refuge from the air assault. One bomb was dropped to penetrate the shelter's roof, which opened up a hole sufficiently large to allow a second bomb to enter the shelter and explode, incinerating most of the people inside.

In addition, civilian highway traffic was targeted, and vehicles such as buses and cars were hit on a regular basis. Among the victims were truckers transporting humanitarian shipments.

On February 21–22, 1991, the Soviet Union secured an agreement with Iraq to withdraw completely from Kuwait the day after a ceasefire went into effect. Surprisingly, President Bush refused to agree to a ceasefire, although he did promise that retreating Iraqi soldiers would not be attacked.

Iraqi forces began to withdraw from Kuwait on February 25, 1991, while coalition forces ended their campaign on February 27. Notwithstanding any agreement not to fire on retreating Iraqi soldiers, American pilots targeted Iraqi soldiers fleeing back to Iraq as well as soldiers who had already surrendered.

At the end of the war, Iraq was incapable of feeding itself, purifying water, healing the sick, or rebuilding itself. March 3, 1991, officially marked the end of the bombing but not the end of the war on Iraq. The war continued through the continued use of sanctions and further bombing in no-fly zones created by the United States and Britain.

The death and destruction resulting from the forty-two days of relentless bombing incriminates the United States in the crime of genocide in Iraq on several counts. These include "killing members of the group," "causing serious bodily or mental harm to members of the group," and "deliberately inflicting on the group conditions of life calculated to bring about its physical destruction in whole or in part."

During the "war," American bombers flew 109,000 sorties over Iraq, dropping eighty million tons of bombs indiscriminately. Approximately 150,000 helpless Iraqi soldiers and 150,000 civilians died during the bombing (*The Fire this Time*, U.S. War Crimes in the Gulf). In addition, 72,000 people were rendered homeless. The targeted group was Iraqi civilians as well as Iraqi soldiers who were victimized by the United States in the hope of overthrowing Saddam Hussein. The only U.S. criterion for ending the "war" was an offer by Saddam to withdraw from Kuwait. The argument that Saddam was responsible for the death and destruction in Iraq because he would not withdraw sooner from Kuwait is fallacious because the United States chose to bomb Iraq and is therefore responsible for the consequences. Furthermore, Bush refused all opportunities to negotiate.

The "in whole or in part" criteria is satisfied by the fact that the United States intended to continue bombing civilians and civilian targets until Saddam agreed to withdraw his troops from Kuwait. It is clear that the United States intended "to inflict on the group conditions of life calculated to bring about its physical destruction" by bombing water-treatment plants, electrical utilities, sewage-disposal facilities, silos, irrigation systems, food-processing plants, a fertilizer plant, and food-storage plants. The obvious outcome of bombing these targets was very predictable.

Although there was no deliberate intention to commit genocide, there were "acts of destruction that are not the specific goal but are predictable outcomes or by-products of a policy, which may have been avoided by a change in that policy." There is no question that the targets selected and the number of bombs dropped would cause massive damage and deprive the Iraqis of the means to provide clean water as well as the means to produce sufficient food to feed themselves. Destruction of the sewage-treatment facilities and the extreme shortage of medicine and medical equipment inevitably sentenced Iraqis to death on a massive scale by malnutrition and disease.

The outcome of the excessively mammoth bombing strategy was very well known, and therefore the U.S. "war" on Iraq clearly meets all the criteria in the Genocide Convention and therefore constitutes genocide.

The damage caused by the United States in this "war" transcends the impact on Iraq. Other victims of this assault include the American system of democracy and the effectiveness and legitimacy of the United Nations. By lying to the American people and Congress, Bush has seriously undermined the principle of accountability of the executive branch, the principal of separation of powers, and the right of the people to judge the actions of the president. His actions demonstrate flagrant disrespect both for Congress and for the people of the United States.

Respect for and effectiveness of the United Nations suffered a severe blow when one country was capable of manipulating the Security Council for its own supposed national interests. Bush's actions blatantly ignored the main purpose of the United Nations, which is to maintain international peace and security and to avoid the scourge of war. Bush was determined to fight a "war" against Iraq and bent the

United Nations to his will. When major powers can flaunt the principles of the United Nations, they undermine the only institution capable of maintaining international peace and order. American presidents are very short-sighted when they fail to recognize that the domestic law-and-order institutions that maintain internal peace and order are as essential as parallel institutions at the international level.

2

IRAQ: SANCTIONS: DEATH BY A THOUSAND CUTS.

Notwithstanding the fact that Iraq endured a gruesome, terrifying nightmare during forty-two days of relentless bombing during the American "war" with Iraq, the United States continued to inflict nefarious brutalities on the devastated people of Iraq through sanctions and ongoing bombing.

The sanctions were originally intended to force Saddam Hussein to comply with the ceasefire agreement after the 1991 war as well as to pay reparations to Kuwait. As of April 3, 1991, UN resolution 687 imposed a new condition on Iraq, which had to be met before sanctions were lifted. Saddam would have to abandon his ambitions to develop weapons of mass destruction (WMD) and to destroy all related facilities and stockpiles.

Presidents George H. Bush, Bill Clinton, and George W. Bush perverted the original purpose of the sanctions by using WMD to impose further hardships on the Iraqi people until they overthrew Saddam Hussein. There objective was to pave the way for an American-friendly leader who would not oppose American ambitions in the Middle East.

The sanctions were unmercifully harsh, thereby preventing Iraq from rebuilding basic services necessary to restore electricity, water treatment, sewage disposal, and medical facilities. Although a UN committee was in charge of screening Iraqi imports and exports, the United States had a veto on the committee and exercised it in order to foment regime change.

Death from disease, malnutrition, unclean water, and a lack of medicines all contributed to the unconscionable number of children who were dying every month, averaging 4,500.

To assess the status of Iraq's weapons of mass destruction, several inspection teams operating in Iraq gave Iraq fairly high marks both for their cooperation and their openness. The second team in 2003 reported to President George W. Bush that with one more month of investigations, they could present a complete report to the UN. However, President George W. had already decided to bomb Iraq, so even an additional month to save lives was out of the question.

Hundreds of thousands of people needlessly died due to George W.'s ostensible conviction that the threat of Saddam's WMD was so imminent that a month was too long to wait. There is no doubt that the agenda of both presidents was not the one they promulgated for public consumption. In fact, both he and his father had rigid plans to bomb Iraq with total indifference to any information that would suggest otherwise. In truth, the sanctions were more devastating than both bombings combined in terms of the death toll and were themselves an act of genocide.

After Iraq had invaded Kuwait, the UN Security Council decided to use sanctions as a method of forcing Saddam to withdraw from Kuwait. In fact, one day after Iraq's occupation of Kuwait, the UN approved the U.S.-drafted Security Council Resolution 661, which mandated sanctions against Iraq that began:

> Determined to bring the invasion and occupation of Kuwait to an end and to restore sovereignty, independence and territorial integrity to Kuwait...Mindful of its responsibilities under the Charter of the United Nations for maintenance of international peace and security...

It is clear that the original intention of the sanctions was to force Iraq to withdraw from Kuwait in order to "maintain international peace and security," not to punish the people of Iraq. The resolution continues:

> Acting under Chapter VII of the Charter of the United Nations,

1. Determines that Iraq so far has failed to comply with paragraph 2 of the resolution 660 (1990) [calling for immediate withdrawal from Kuwait] and has usurped the authority of the legitimate Government of Kuwait;

2. Decides as a consequence to take the following measures…;

3. Decides that all States shall prevent:

   a. The import into their territories of all commodities and products originating in Iraq…;

   b. Any activities by their nationals or in their territories which would promote or are calculated to promote the export or trans-shipment of any commodities or products from Iraq or Kuwait;

4. Decides that all States shall not make available to the Government of Iraq…any funds or any other financial or economic resources…except payments exclusively for strictly medical or humanitarian purposes and, in humanitarian circumstances, foodstuffs.

(UN Resolutions, from http://www.un.org/docs/scres/1990/scres90. htm)

The Security Council established a committee to monitor and report on the Iraq sanctions regime as well as to choose the items to be sanctioned. The committee was created by Resolution 661, paragraph 6:

Decides to establish…a Committee of the Security Council consisting of all members of the Council, to undertake the following tasks and to report its work to the Council with its observations and recommendations:

(a) To examine the reports on the progress of the implementation of the present resolution which will be submitted to the Secretary-General;

(b) To seek from all States further information regarding the action taken by them concerning the effective implementation of the provisions laid down in the present resolution.

Due to the decision-making process of the committee, the United States was able to implement its agenda, which was to ban all products needed to sustain life. Rules of procedure for the committee can be found in rule 28 of the provisional rules of procedure of the Security Council, which state that:

The Committee shall reach decision by consensus. If consensus cannot be reached, the Chairman should undertake such further consultations as may facilitate settlement. If after these consultations, consensus still cannot be reached, the matter may be submitted to the Security Council.

Since decisions were to be based on a consensus, the United States had the power to block any particular item under consideration. Consensus granted the United States, or any other member for that matter, a veto. Appealing to the Security Council for a ruling on an item that was not agreed upon in the committee again would also give the United States a veto as one of the five countries that have a veto.

American control over imports and exports to Iraq was greatly enhanced by Security Council Resolution 665, which enabled the United States to establish a naval blockade. Resolution 665:

Calls upon those Member States co-operating with the Government of Kuwait which are deploying maritime forces to the area to use such measures commensurate to the specific circumstances as may be necessary under

the authority of the Security Council to halt all inward
and outward maritime shipping in order to inspect and
verify their cargoes and destinations and to ensure strict
implementation of the provisions related to such shipping
laid down in Resolution 661.

Committee members were given guidelines for deciding what
constitutes a humanitarian crisis. To further stipulate the humanitarian
exceptions to the sanctions, Resolution 666 states that:

Emphasizing that it is for the Security Council, alone or
acting through the Committee, to determine whether
humanitarian circumstances have arisen...3. Requests
for the purposes of paragraphs 1 and 2 above, that the
Secretary-General seek urgently, and on a continual basis,
information from relevant United Nations and other
appropriate humanitarian agencies and all other sources on
the availability in Iraq and Kuwait, such information to be
communicated by the Secretary-General to the Committee
regularly.

Resolution 661 and Resolution 666 make it abundantly clear
that during the operation of the sanctions, any humanitarian crisis
was to be avoided by humanitarian aid. This clause must have been
invisible to the United States. In fact, by 2002, there had been over one
million deaths from the sanctions, which would indicate that there had
been a humanitarian crisis of monumental proportions. The United
States obviously used the sanctions for a purpose other than the one
intended.

One extremely debilitating requirement in the resolution was
the prohibition against the exportation of Iraqi oil. Iraq imported 70
percent of its food and needed oil revenues to pay for imported food.
With the passage of Resolution 661, foreign ports rejected Iraqi ships,
and foreign tankers ceased filling up with Iraqi oil. Iraq asked Turkey,
one of its primary sources of food, to provide emergency food assistance
for Iraqi children. As a major recipient of U.S. aid, Turkey refused the
request. Not only did the government's food assistance program for
the people of Iraq decline by 60 percent over a four-month period,

but there was no food for livestock, forcing farmers to slaughter their animals for food.

Resolution 661 had exempted food in "humanitarian circumstances," but the United States consistently blocked food and medicine from entering Iraq.

Useful in understanding the combined impact of heavy bombing and harsh sanctions that thwarted efforts to rebuild needed vital services were the reports of various organizations that visited Iraq. According to Ullrich Gottstein of the International Physicians for the Prevention of Nuclear War:

> Sanctions have prevented significant repair of the infrastructure and the combination of damaged or destroyed electrical plants, food production, water storage and sewage treatment facilities combined with profound lack of imported foods and medicine has created a medical disaster of stunning proportions.

> One of the first authoritative reports regarding the tragedy in Iraq was published in the *New England Journal of Medicine*, September 26, 1991. A group of physicians who traveled to Iraq following the Gulf War reported: "We found suffering of tragic proportions…the youngest and most vulnerable are paying the price for the actions of others. Children are dying of preventable diseases and starvation as a direct result of the Gulf crisis."

(*The Effects of Sanctions on the Civilian Population of Iraq*, International Physicians for the Prevention of Nuclear War)

The International Study Team and the Food and Agricultural Organization of the United Nations both conducted studies after the Gulf War, and Sarah Zaidi, who participated in both studies, concluded that:

> Multilateral sanctions imposed against Iraq after the invasion of Kuwait, however, made providing humanitarian assistance very difficult…The sanction policy compounded the problems of restoring the electrical system, water and

sanitation plants, and the health infrastructure to function...
let alone prewar levels.

(*War, Sanctions, and Humanitarian Assistance: The Case of Iraq 1990–1993*, Sarah Zaidi)

A UNICEF report of April 1993 reported that:

Sanctions are inhibiting the importation of spare parts,
chemicals, reagents, and the means of transportation
required to provide water and sanitation services to the
civilian population of Iraq. Huge quantities of resources
are required if Iraq is to make any real progress towards
establishing its pre-war capacity for managing water and
sewage...What has become increasingly clear is that no
significant movement toward food security can be achieved
so long as the embargo remains in place. All vital contributors
to food availability—agricultural production, importation
of foodstuffs, economic stability and income generation, are
dependent on Iraq's ability to purchase and import those
items vital to the survival of the civilian population.

(*Children, War, and Sanctions*, UNICEF report, April 1993)

Although the sanctions were ostensibly intended to be
humanitarian, in practice they became a weapon to starve the people
of Iraq and deny them access to proper medical treatment in the hope
that they would eventually overthrow Saddam Hussein. The same
strategy was implemented during the Reagan administration when the
CIA organized the Contras to conduct incursions into Nicaragua to
prosecute a war of attrition against the people of Nicaragua.

Although Security Council Resolution 661 permitted food
shipments in a humanitarian crisis, the quantity of grain imported
into Iraq under control of the UN committee was inhumane. For
example, between August 6, 1990, and April 1991, Iraq only imported
the equivalent of the daily grain requirement of the Iraqi people. The
results were devastating, as reported by a Harvard International Study
Group, which concluded that one million children were malnourished
and 120,000 suffering from acute malnutrition. A study conducted by

UNICEF concluded that 27.5 percent of children were malnourished and an estimated 500,000 children had died.

On April 8, 1991, a new condition was imposed on Iraq requiring Iraq to destroy all weapons of mass destruction, facilities for producing them, and materials related to their production. Sanctions would not be lifted until these new conditions were met as set out in Security Council Resolution 687:

> 8. Decides [UN Security Council] that Iraq shall unconditionally accept the destruction, removal, or rendering harmless, under international supervision of:
>
> (a) All chemical and biological weapons and all stocks of agents and related subsystems and components and all research, development, support, and manufacturing facilities.
>
> (b) All ballistic missiles with a range of greater than 150 kilometers and related parts, and repair and production facilities.
>
> 9. The Secretary-General...shall develop and submit for approval, a plan calling for the completion of the following acts within forty-five days of such approval:
>
> (i) The forming of a special Commission, which shall carry out immediate on-site inspection of Iraq's biological, chemical and missile capabilities...
>
> 12. Decides that Iraq shall unconditionally agree not to acquire or develop nuclear weapons...
>
> 22. Decides that upon the approval by the Security Council...that Iraq has completed all actions contemplated in paragraphs 8, 9, 10, 11, 12 and 13,

the prohibitions against the import of commodities and products originating in Iraq...shall have no further force or effect.

Resolution 687 also called for the creation of an onsite inspection team whose reports would determine whether Iraq had met the conditions set forth in the resolution. When the inspection team reported conclusively that Iraq had met the conditions of Resolution 687, then the sanctions would be lifted. This was actually a ridiculous stipulation, as inspections could take so many years to reach a sufficiently high level of confidence about Iraq's WMD programs that an inordinate number of people could die in the meantime from the sanctions.

A 1993 UNICEF report established a clear correlation between the number of casualties and the sanctions. According to the report:

> Sanctions are inhibiting the importation of spare parts, chemicals, reagents, and the means of transportation required to provide water and sanitation services to the civilian population of Iraq. Huge quantities of resources are required if Iraq is to make any real progress towards re-establishing its pre-war capacity for managing water and sewage...What has become increasingly clear is that no significant movement toward food security can be achieved so long as the embargo remains in place. All vital contributors to food availability—agricultural production, importation of foodstuffs, economic stability and income generation, are dependent on Iraq's ability to purchase and import those items vital to the survival of the civilian population.

(*Children War and Sanctions*, UNICEF Report, April 1993)

Some of the items that were banned by the committee comply with the letter and spirit of the UN Resolution because they would deprive Iraq of products that could have been used in weapons development and stockpiling. Egregiously, other prohibited imports totally unrelated to WMD were used to impose hardships on the people of Iraq. For example, the following items were banned: adhesive paper, ambulances, baking soda, bath brushes, batteries, bicycles, books, candles, chairs, chalk, children's wear, combs, desks, dolls, envelopes, eyeglasses, forks, hearing aids, ink, jackets, light bulbs, mops, napkins, pans, paper, pens, sandals, shampoo, shoes, spoons, stoves, tables, tissue paper, toilet paper, toothbrushes, wallets, and wool. There is no justification for sanctioning these products inasmuch as they only serve to deprive the Iraqi people of everyday nonmilitary items and have no relevance to WMD.

Declassified documents divulge the fact that the Americans were well aware of the humanitarian crisis caused by the sanctions. A Defense Intelligence Agency document shows U.S. awareness of the water crisis and its effects:

> Failing to secure supplies will result in a shortage of pure drinking water for much of the population. This could lead to increased incidences, if not epidemics of disease ... Unless water treatment supplies are exempted from the UN sanctions for humanitarian reasons, no adequate solution exists for Iraq's purification dilemma.

(*Iraq Water Treatment Vulnerabilities*, Defense Intelligence Agency, January 18, 1991)

The same document warns of the effects of impure water caused by the sanctions:

> Conditions are favorable to communicable disease outbreaks, particularly in major urban centres affected by coalition bombing...Current public health problems are attributable to the reduction of normal preventative medicine, waste disposal, water purification and distribution, electricity, and the decreased ability to control disease outbreaks.

(Ibid.)

Attempting to purify water was rendered impossible by the sanctioning of parts to repair water-treatment plants, chlorine plants, and electrical utilities to boil water. Furthermore, once disease struck, the sanctioning of medicine precluded treatment of these discases.

In a Capitol Hill hearing about the sanctions in Iraq in 1990, William Webster, Director of the CIA reports that:

> More than 100 countries are supporting UN resolutions that impose economic sanctions on Iraq. Coupled with the US government's increased ability to detect and follow-up attempts to circumvent the blockade, the sanctions have all but shut off Iraq's exports and reduced imports to less than 10 percent of their pre-invasion levels. All sectors of the Iraq economy are feeling the pinch of sanctions and many industries have largely shut down.

(*Persian Gulf Crisis*, Hearing of the House Armed Services Committee, December 5, 1990)

Clearly, the American government was using sanctions to impose hardship on the Iraqi people in the hope that either Saddam would capitulate or that someone in the Republican guard would assassinate him. Once Saddam was out of power, the United States could interfere in the political process in order to replace him with an American-friendly leader.

In recognition of the fact that the sanctions were starving the Iraqi people, the UN finally relented and decided to permit Iraq to sell a quantity of oil to be determined by the UN. Prior to passage of the resolution, Sadruddin Aga Khan, Consultant to the Secretary-General of the UN, was dispatched to Iraq to estimate the cost of restoring basic services to the people of Iraq. He estimated that it would cost $22 billion to achieve that goal, and he also recommended that a minimum of $6.9 billion would be needed to restore health and agriculture, half of the prewar electrical capacity, 40 percent of water and sanitation needs, and a subsistence level of food. Khan advised that for a start, Iraq should be allowed to sell $2.65 billion of oil over a four-month period, to be renewed if no further problems arose.

The United States proposed that the amount be stretched over a six-month period and reduced to $1.6 billion with a further reduction of 30 percent for a UN compensation fund. When Resolution 706 was passed on August 15, 1991, the amount of oil revenue available to the

Iraqi government was $930 million, which was a small fraction of the amount needed to have any significant impact.

UN Resolution 706 authorizing the sale of oil stated that it:

> Authorizes all States ...to permit...the import, during a period of six months from the date of adoption...of a quantity of petroleum and petroleum products originating in Iraq sufficient to produce a sum to be determined by the Council...however, not to exceed 1.6 billion United States dollars, subject to the following conditions:...

> (b) Direct payment of the full amount of each purchase of Iraqi petroleum and petroleum products by the purchaser in the State concerned into an escrow account to be established by the United Nations and administered by the Secretary-General exclusively to meet the purposes of this resolution.

Note that the money earned from the sale of oil was to be deposited into a UN account out of the reach of Saddam Hussein in order to approve and monitor expenditures. Despite this control mechanism, Saddam was able to earn some revenues other than the revenues deposited into the UN bank. His illicit revenues came mainly from unauthorized Iraqi oil sales to neighboring states.

These illicit revenues were earned by turning on huge pipelines that had been built before the sanctions were in place. The Security Council was aware of sales to Turkey and Jordan, key allies of the United States, while U.S. leaders were willing to turn a blind eye to sales of oil to allies. Saddam insisted on selecting vendors that would offer relief aid for Iraq and to states who were buying the oil through Resolution 706, otherwise known as the "food for oil" (FFO) program.

Ironically, the United States itself was responsible for the purchase of illegal oil sales from Iraq. The United States purchased oil from Iraq at below-market prices and received kickbacks from Iraq, which accounted for 52 percent of the total amount of illegal sales. In addition, the United States allowed some oil to be smuggled out and guaranteed a U.S. oil company that the oil purchased would not be confiscated.

The UN offer to allow Iraq to sell some of its oil was totally inadequate in terms of meeting the needs of the people of Iraq. Iraq refused to accept $1.6 billion as it was such an insignificant amount, and on April 14, 1995, another resolution was passed that allowed the sale of $2 billion of oil every six months. Resolution 706 stated that it:

> Authorizes States…to permit the import of petroleum and petroleum products originating in Iraq…sufficient to produce a sum not exceeding a total of one billion United States dollars every 90 days for the purposes set out in this resolution.

Resolution 706 basically allowed Iraq to earn revenues that would perpetuate a high level of starvation, malnutrition, and disease. Bearing in mind that Khan's report to the Secretary-General recommended at least $6.9 billion as an initial measure but $22 billion to restore basic services, the oil for food program was not deserving of the designation "humanitarian."

Assessing the damage of the 1991 war and the imposed sanctions uncovers a disaster of monumental proportions, exposing a severe lack of infrastructure, food, medical care, clean water, factories, healthy mothers, healthy children, and the means to correct and restore all essential services.

As a result of the sanctions, UNICEF estimates that at least one million people have died as of 1998, half of whom were children. UNICEF also reports that by 1998, between 5,000 and 6,000 children have died every month. To translate the enormity of this tragedy into terms to which people can more easily relate, more children died every month in Iraq over a ten-year period than died in the World Trade Center in one day.

UNICEF did a study in 1998 to document conditions in Iraq and found:

THE IMPACT OF SANCTIONS: A UNICEF PERSPECTIVE

DIRECT EFFECTS	HEALTH	FOOD
Decreased medicines	Increased morbidity	Higher prices for food
Decreased food imports	Low birth-rate babies	Shortages of food
Decreased agricultural imports	Infectious diseases	Decrease in household diet and caloric intake
Decreased industrial imports	Epidemics	Decreased agricultural production
Educational materials	Malnutrition	Decrease in livestock production
Water purification products	Increased mortality	
	Maternal and perinatal mortality	

(*The Impact of Sanctions*, A Study of UNICEF'S Perspective, Table 3, 1998)

A major UNICEF study, *Situation Analysis of Children and Women in Iraq*, published on April 30, 1998, reports that:

> By 1990, the Iraqi GDP per capita had risen to $US 3,508 within the framework of an oil boom, and enjoyed the largesse of a welfare state...By 1990, Iraq's Human Development Index (HDI) had far surpassed that of the countries with which it now shares inadequate social sector support....This has now changed...Economic sanctions on Iraq over the last seven years have had a devastating effect on the majority of the Iraqi people, and particularly children. These international developments affect national household levels in the form of deprivation, malnutrition and disease...Since August 1991, the effect of economic hardship on a once prosperous society has resulted in a cumulated series of setbacks, such as reduced food supply, polluted water, soaring inflation and deteriorating standards of education, posing a series of risks to child survival, a

core principle of the CRC [Convention on the Rights of Children].

(*Situation Analysis of Children and Women in Iraq*, UNICEF/IRAQ, April 30, 1998)

The same report published the following statistics:

1. Under 5 Mortality Rate (per 1000 live births) 1990/1994	52	140
2. Infant Mortality Rate (per 1000 live births) 1990/1994	31.7	111.7
3. Maternal Mortality Rate (per 100,000 live births) 1990/1994	117	310
4. Underweight (% moderate & severe)	4.5	23.4
5. Access to safe water (Total/Rural/Urban) (%) –1995		77.5/44.2/91.9
6. Gross Domestic Product per capita ($US) 1990/1993	$3508	$761

(Ibid.)

As well, the following information appeared in the study:

- The increase in mortality…for children under 5 years of age is mainly due to diarrhea, pneumonia and malnutrition.

- Malnutrition was not a public health problem in Iraq prior to the embargo. Its extent became apparent in 1991 and the prevalence has increased greatly since: 18% in 1991 to 31% in 1996 of children under 5 with chronic malnutrition. By 1997, it was estimated about one million children under 5 were chronically malnourished.

- Before the 1990 sanctions primary medical care reached about 97% of the urban population, and 78% of rural residents. Now the health system is affected by lack of even basic hospital and health centre equipment and supplies, surgical and diagnostic services.

- It is likely that the lack of safe water and sanitation has contributed greatly to the steep rise in malnutrition rates and mortality.

(Ibid.)

Humanitarian and human rights organizations became increasingly critical of the sanctions regime, which was monstrously punitive to the people of Iraq. In a letter to the Security Council, Human Rights Watch wrote:

> Human Rights Watch is writing to you concerning the humanitarian crisis in Iraq, a crisis which derives in considerable measure from the comprehensive economic sanctions imposed by the Security Council....Regarding the "infrastructural degradation" evident in the water and sanitation sector, for instance, the report states that "in the absence of key complimentary items currently on hold and adequate maintenance, spare parts and staffing, the decay rate of the entire system is accelerating." Concerning the electrical sector, the capacity and reliability of which is crucial to water treatment, refrigeration, and public health generally, the report [of the Secretary-General] states that the governorates outside the capital continue to experience outages of between twelve and eighteen hours a day.

(*His Excellency M. Moctar Ouane, President of the Security Council,* Human Rights Watch, September 20, 2000)

The Office of the High Commissioner for Human Rights at the UN called for:

> The embargo provisions affecting the humanitarian situation of the population of Iraq to be lifted and urged the international community and all Governments, including that of Iraq, to alleviate the suffering of the Iraqi population,

in particular by facilitating the delivery of food, medical supplies and the wherewithal to meet their basic needs.

(*The Human Rights Impact of Economic Sanctions on Iraq*, Office of the High Commissioner for Human Rights, September 5, 2000)

On May 22, 2003, the Security Council belatedly converted the sanction regime from one of seeping prohibitions to one of prohibitions on military products. According to UN Resolution 1483:

1. Appeals to Member States and concerned organizations to assist the people of Iraq in their efforts to reform their institutions and rebuild their country.

2. Calls upon Member States in a position to do so to respond immediately to the humanitarian appeals of the United Nations and other international organizations for Iraq and to help meet the humanitarian and other needs of the Iraqi people by providing food, medical supplies...

10. Decides that with the exception of prohibitions related to the sale or supply to Iraq of arms and related material...all prohibitions related to trade with Iraq and the provision of financial or economic resources to Iraq...shall no longer apply.

Shockingly, it took thirteen years for the nations other than the United States to apply selective sanctions prohibiting arms and military products. During that brutal thirteen years, the Iraqi people were slowly dying from a lack of clean water, food, and medical facilities. The United States masterminded the broad regime of sanctions to serve its own strategic interests and in the process committed genocide against the Iraqi people.

Apparently, the sanctions fell short of the U.S. objective to punish the Iraqi people and weaken the Iraqi state. In addition to the sanctions, the United States, Britain, and France sustained bombing operations against Iraq under the guise of a humanitarian campaign to protect the Iraqi people in the years following the Gulf War. A no-fly zone was established in Northern Iraq, north of the 36th parallel and covering 19,000 square miles, to protect the Kurdish people from attacks from Saddam Hussein. The Iraqis were prohibited from flying any aircraft including helicopters in these exclusion zones. The no-fly zones clearly violated Iraq's territorial integrity, but Washington argued that the legal basis for the establishment of no-fly zones was Security Council Resolution 688. Resolution 688 makes no reference to Chapter VII in the UN Charter.

On August 26, 1992, the U.S., Britain, and France established a southern no-fly zone south of the 32nd parallel ostensibly to protect the Shi'ite Muslims who had rebelled against Baghdad. The zone was extended northward in 1996 to include the southern third of Iraq.

There were a number of so-called violations of the no-fly zones, and on January 13, 1993, in response to one such infraction, Western forces bombed targets in Southern Iraq. Bombing missions occurred daily, presumably to protect the people of Iraq. George W. Bush exploited the ostensible humanitarian purpose of these zones to degrade Iraq's minimal capacity to defend itself from a large-scale U.S. attack.

The zones did not coincide with the regions occupied by the two groups in need of protection. General Tommy Franks, Commander of U.S. Central Command, testified before Congress in 2001 and defined the real purpose of the no-fly zones as:

1. Continued and significant troop presence to enhance deterrence and to demonstrate the American commitment to force Iraq to cooperate with the inspection process;

2. To maintain access and interaction with other Gulf governments;

3. To ensure that Iraq could not repair or improve its anti-aircraft capabilities.

The no-fly zones were established to destroy Iraqi defenses against a large-scale bombing attack as well as for training U.S. and British pilots for bombing raids in Iraq. Both of these countries were determined to destroy Iraq's weapons of mass destruction (WMD) if they existed. As well, the hypocrisy of establishing these zones for humanitarian objectives is transparent given the complete lack of concern for the suffering of the Iraqi people resulting from the sanctions.

The impact of the sanctions was far greater than the bombing. The sanctions regime "deliberately inflicted on the group conditions of life calculated to bring about its physical destruction in whole or in part." The targeted group was the Iraqi people, and the numbers clearly meet the criteria of the Genocide Convention. Preventing the group from obtaining sufficient food and water to survive along with preventing them from proper medical care unequivocally meets the criteria of "inflicting conditions of life calculated to bring about its physical destruction."

The United States may not have intended to perpetrate genocide against the people of Iraq; nevertheless, the known consequences of their actions, without any doubt, would have caused their gradual destruction. For example, President Clinton was informed by members of Congress, John Conyers and Tom Campbell, that:

> We are again writing to you to ask that you de-link economic sanctions from the military sanctions currently in place against Iraq.

> More then nine years of the most comprehensive economic embargo imposed in modern history has failed to remove Saddam Hussein…while the economy and people of Iraq continue to suffer.

> Reports from UNICEF (the United Nation's Children's Fund) and other United Nations agencies in Iraq estimate that over one million civilians, mostly children, have died from malnutrition and disease as a result of the embargo.

Earlier this year, a special United Nations Security Council
panel reported that "the gravity of the humanitarian situation
is indisputable and cannot be overstated."

(*Letter from John Conyers and Tom Campbell, Members of Congress, to
President Clinton*, Congressional Letters, November 30, 1999)

Despite the definitive evidence that the sanctions were
themselves a WMD, President Clinton refused to address the problem.
Reconstruction would have to wait.

In an attempt to begin the rebuilding process in Iraq, the UN
had passed Resolution 1483. Resolution 1483 appealed to member
states to contribute humanitarian aid to assist the people of Iraq in
rebuilding their country. The exigent entreaty for assistance was
shamefully unheeded.

Before Iraq was battered again by the United States by George
W. Bush in 2003, the infrastructure and basic services remained in
a state of disrepair. Nations other than the United States must also
share complicity in the genocide and the shame and unconscionable
indifference to the plight of the people of Iraq.

10

IRAQ—2003: BLOODIED AND BOWED.

To bomb a country that has suffered the atrocities already inflicted on the debilitated, devastated people of Iraq reflects a deep-seated ideological mindset rigidly resistant to contradictory evidence and devoid of any compassion or humanity. Contemplating another horror exacted on the Iraqi people is not only surreal but unimaginable.

Iraq had already suffered heavy bombing in the Gulf War in 1991, a cruelly harsh sanction regime, and ongoing bombing in the no-fly zones, yet it was not enough. In reality, America policymakers had still not yet achieved their true objectives. Saddam Hussein was still in power; the United States oil companies were not sharing in the oil revenues gushing out of Iraq wells; there were no military bases in Iraq; and Washington was unable to dictate policy to Saddam Hussein. The plan to bomb Iraq had a long history beginning with a Paul Wolfowitz paper in 1992 and policy papers written by a neoconservative group called the Project for a New American Century (PNAC) in 1998. A "timely" attack on the World Trade Center set the wheels in motion for implementing these long-formulated plans when Donald Rumsfield raised the issue at a meeting on September 12, 2001. Part of the planning process involved Cheney meeting with a clique of oil barons to draft a new energy policy for America, the focus of which was a map of Iraq marked with the location of all its oil wells.

All that was needed to declare another war against Iraq was a justification. With this in mind, the Bush administration jumped on 9/11 and claimed that Iraq had ties to al-Qaeda. The Bush team also cleverly exploited the now constant fear of terrorism masterfully manufactured to create fear about WMD in Iraq.

In the 1980s and early 1990s, Iraq not only possessed chemical and biological weapons but had used them against the Kurds in Northern Iraq. However, by 2003, there wasn't a legitimate weapons inspector who believed that Iraq had any WMD remaining. There had been a number of inspection teams in Iraq beginning with United Nations Special Committee (UNSCOM) who were there until 1998, followed in 2003 by the United Nations Monitoring, Verification, and Inspection Committee (UNMOVIC). The International Atomic Energy Agency (IAEA) had been inspecting Iraq for nuclear weapons development up until 2003. All three agencies presented optimistic reports to the Security Council, which should have greatly alleviated the fears of WMD, but the United States was on a deeply rooted fixed path to war.

Ignoring the reports of UN inspection teams, high-ranking Bush officials expectorated a plethora of myths about WMD, embellishing their fabrications with fear-inducing images. Falsified papers were treated as solid evidence, while the CIA's reports were mined for words supporting the inevitable decision to declare war on Iraq.

Overlooking the request from the chief weapons inspector for UNMOVIC, Hans Blix, for another month or two to complete UNMOVIC's inspection program, President Bush brazenly declared war on Iraq on March 20, 2003. The bombing met with no defense as Baghdad and other cities were bombed again with no regard for the number of people killed. When President Bush strutted out of a fighter jet that had just landed on an aircraft carrier decked out in his puerile pilot's costume, he uttered those immortal, arrogant, precipitant words: "mission accomplished." His words were, in fact, stillborn, not portending the tragic miscarriage of justice that endures to this day.

The military occupation of Iraq has since achieved the antithetical results that were expected after the initial march on Baghdad. Control over Iraq has disintegrated into a paroxysm of sectarian violence unleashing old hatreds and a reinvigorated resentment toward Americans. As well, Iraq was transformed from a nation hostile to terrorist groups to a training ground and haven for those who aspire to martyrdom.

With the death toll mounting daily and basic services in a worse state than before the war, the United States is continuing to perpetrate genocide against the people of Iraq.

In order to fully understand the lunacy of the Bushite's claims that Iraq had WMD, the UN and IAEA weapon-inspection regimes must be investigated.

One of the original purposes of the sanctions and embargo was to force Saddam Hussein to destroy all biological, chemical, or nuclear weapons and facilities for their production. The initial mechanism for discovering and eliminating any WMD was an inspection team under the auspices of the UN. Security Council Resolution 687 (see previous chapter) authorized immediate onsite inspections for chemical, biological, and nuclear weapons. The United Nations created the UN Special Committee (UNSCOM) for inspections of biological and chemical weapons and the IAEA for inspections of nuclear weapons.

From the very beginning of the inspection process, it was extremely clear that the United States had its own agenda for inspections and was not interested in fully complying with UN Resolution 687. In 1991, the Secretary of State under President George H. Bush, James Baker, said that "we are not interested in a relaxation of sanctions as long as Saddam Hussein is in power." President Clinton's Secretary of State, Warren Christopher, wrote in a *New York Times* op-ed piece in 1994 that "the U.S. does not believe that Iraq's compliance with paragraph 22 of Resolution 687 [sanctions end when Iraq meets the conditions pertaining to WMD] is enough to justify lifting the embargo." The second Secretary of State under President Clinton, Madeleine Albright, stated on March 26, 1997, that:

> We do not agree with the nations who argue that if Iraq complies with its obligations concerning weapons of mass destruction, sanctions should be lifted. Our view, which is unshakeable, is that Iraq must prove its peaceful intentions... And the evidence is overwhelming that Saddam Hussein's intentions will never be peaceful.

Further confirmation that the United States regarded the sanctions as a means to topple Saddam is evident when Robert M. Gates, U.S. Deputy National Security Advisor, claimed in May 1991 that:

Saddam is discredited and cannot be redeemed. His leadership will never be accepted by the world community. Therefore, Iraqis will pay the price while he remains in power. All possible sanctions will be maintained until he is gone…Any easing of the sanctions will be considered only when there is a new government.

(*"US Sanctions Threat Takes UN by Surprise,"* Robert M. Gates, *Los Angeles Times*, May 9, 1991)

The claim that "Hussein's intentions will never be peaceful" definitively proves that the real purpose of the sanctions was to remove Saddam Hussein from power. Despite America's claims, the UN was still acting under the terms of Resolution 687, sending UNSCOM to Iraq to assess the extent of Saddam's WMD.

Inspections for WMD in Iraq were a very complex, technical process. The cooperation of Iraq was essential to gain access to sites scheduled for inspection and to documents describing the location of WMD storage or manufacturing facilities. It was also essential to verify the alleged destruction of weapons.

Initially, Iraqi officials concealed documents and weapons, making it difficult for inspectors to gain access to sites. Iraqi soldiers sometimes held inspectors at gunpoint to prevent them from carrying out their task.

Despite these obstacles, inspection teams were able to perform their duties because of their broad powers to gain access to sites, their ability to take soil and atmospheric samples, and their access to surveillance photographs.

Iraq submitted a declaration to the United Nations detailing the location of all its WMD storage and manufacturing facilities and related documents. The first executive chairman of UNSCOM, Rolf Ekéus, sent a letter to the Iraqi government calling attention to the inaccuracies in the Iraqi declaration and advising the Iraqi government that undeclared sites would be subject to inspection.

An example of a failed attempt to foil the inspection teams occurred in 1991 when an UNSCOM team declared their intentions to inspect a nuclear site at Abu Ghraib, west of Baghdad. Despite the fact that the concealment committee (created by the Iraqi government) had ordered the nuclear materials to be moved to remote farms, the committee's effort failed because among the materials were electromagnetic isotope separators, which are easily identified by surveillance photographs.

Another example occurred in September 1991 when inspectors arrived unannounced at Iraqi nuclear headquarters, catching everyone there by surprise. The inspectors uncovered millions of pages of documentation pertaining to Iraq's nuclear weapons program.

In the spring of 1992, the work of UNSCOM was assisted by the addition of CIA operatives headed by Moe Dobbs. With Dobbs' help, UNSCOM established a functional monitoring system that no longer depended on intrusive confrontational inspections.

When Hussein Kamel, Saddam's son-in-law, defected, he revealed that there was another million pages of chemical and biological weapons documentation, which forced UNSCOM to revise its inspection methods. UNSCOM again instituted large-scale intrusive, confrontational inspections supported by a comprehensive information-gathering strategy that included inspectors on the ground, aircraft surveillance, and communication scanners to pick up Iraqi communications related to inspections.

One of the pervasive and discordant inspections took place in June 1996, when UNSCOM decided to inspect Special Republican Guard (SRG) facilities where there were possible weapons material and documentation. Iraq refused to allow inspections of the SRG facilities, leading to a standoff lasting several days as the inspectors surrounded the building. The incident triggered high-level discussions, which centered on whether the Security Council would back up the inspection team. The outcome was an agreement signed by Ekéus and Aziz that respected the sovereignty of Iraq and allowed the inspectors to do their job. The agreement defined those facilities that were sensitive and the number of inspectors allowed to enter a sensitive site. One of Iraq's issues with admitting inspectors into sensitive sites was the presence of CIA agents on inspection teams who were using the opportunity to compile a list of targets.

Early in the inspection process, Iraq obstructed the work of the inspection teams in Iraq, but by 1998, Iraqi cooperation with UNSCOM cleared the way for inspectors. In a letter to the Security Council on November 30, 1998, from the Executive Chairman of UNSCOM, Richard Butler reported that:

> We note with satisfaction that the Iraqi side is ready to cooperate with the Special Commission on several specific issues referred to in the Schedule for Work of 14 June 1998. As you are aware, the Commission has already proposed, and was ready to conduct, at the beginning of August 1998, the missions now requested by Iraq.

(*Letter from the Chairman of the Special Commission*, UN Security Council, November 30, 1998)

As well, in UNSCOM's October 11, 1996, semi-annual report to the Security Council, it noted that:

> The special commission has been in existence for more than five years. During that period it has recorded significant progress that is often overlooked...Only recently, in June 1996, over five years after the adoption of resolution 687 (1991), has Iraq provided the commission with what it states to be its formal and official declaration in full, final and complete disclosure (FFCD) in the chemical, biological, and missile fields which are called for in resolutions 687 (1991) and 707 (1991).

(*Second Report to the Security Council*, Security Council, October 11, 1996)

Despite the encouraging report, Richard Butler, who was suspected of serving as an agent for the Americans, participated in an attempt to orchestrate the end of UNSCOM. If the inspection team announced the absence of WMD, the UN would be obligated to end the sanctions, depriving the Americans of the means for inciting the overthrow of Saddam. Scott Ritter, Chief Inspector, divulged the connection between the United States and Richard Butler:

> The final straw came in the summer of 1998, when the United States pressured Richard Butler...to shut down a sensitive intelligence operation...turning the capabilities inherent in the project (which included eavesdropping on the private conversations of Saddam Hussein and his inner circle of advisors) over to the United States without any UNSCOM input or control all the while continuing to operate under UNSCOM's operational cover. In short, Richard Butler allowed the United States to use the unique access enjoyed by the UNSCOM inspectors to spy on Saddam Hussein, totally corrupting the integrity of the whole operation.

(*Frontier Justice: Weapons of Mass Destruction and the Bushwhacking of America*, Scott Ritter, p. 78)

The United States had to incite Saddam into denying the inspectors access to the sites which they had selected for inspection. According to Scott Ritter:

> Butler was instructed to organize inspection activity designed to provoke Iraq into breaking its agreement to fully cooperate with UNSCOM. Deliberately controversial sights would be selected, using intelligence provided by the United States and Great Britain.

(*Frontier Justice: Weapons of Mass Destruction and the Bushwhacking of America*, Scott Ritter, p. 102)

Over the next few days, Scott Ritter was denied access to two sites that the Iraqis defined as "sensitive-sensitive," in other words, a presidential site. Richard Butler decided that these cases should be reported to the Security Council as evidence of obstruction by the Iraqis. Following another thwarted inspection attempt where inspectors were held at gunpoint, Richard Butler delivered a censorious report to the Security Council, prompting the adoption of Resolution 1134 in October 1997, which imposed additional sanctions. In response, Iraq refused to allow further inspections on the grounds that the United States had planted spies on the inspection teams. Butler reacted by asking all inspectors to leave Iraq. Russia then negotiated a deal that would allow inspectors to continue if Russia could speak for Iraq on the Security Council. Iraq agreed to allow the inspectors to continue their work

After their return on January 12, 1998, an inspection team headed by Scott Ritter inspected seven sites. On another inspection of the Directorate for General Security (DGS), the inspectors discovered that numerous files were missing. The alarmed Iraqis threatened to end their cooperation with the inspection teams as they felt that too many inspectors on UNSCOM were either American or British intelligence agents. UN Secretary-General Kofi Annan and Tariq Aziz, Iraq's Foreign Minister, signed a memorandum of understanding that established new rules for inspecting presidential sites, specifying the number of inspectors allowed into the building. The test of the new agreement was the Ministry of Defense. Before the inspectors had an opportunity to inspect the Ministry of Defense, Albright informed Butler that Washington had formulated plans to bomb Iraq, thereby obviating the need for extending the inspection process much longer.

However, the attack would have to end on March 15, 1998, because of the pilgrimages to Mecca in Saudi Arabia. Albright asked Butler to ensure that the inspections were stopped before March 8. From March 5 to March 7, Scott Ritter and his inspection team carried out their inspections on sites in the old Ministry of Defense. Before inspecting this site, the inspection team and the Iraqis would have to negotiate the number of inspectors allowed into the building. Both sides agreed to eighteen. They found no sign of WMD, and the attack on Iraq was postponed.

As the United States was preparing for the 1998 military strike, Butler had to force the issue before Iraq cooperated on any more inspections, thus denying the justification for the war. He demanded a visit to Baath Party Headquarters, an extremely sensitive site. The sensitivity of the site resulted in delays, blockages, and evacuated buildings on the part of the Iraqis. Richard Butler, acting on the orders of Sandy Berger, National Security Advisor, ordered the inspection teams to leave Iraq. With the assistance of Sandy Berger and other U.S. government officials, Richard Butler then drafted his report to the Security Council regarding the degree of Iraqi cooperation with the inspection teams. On December 16, 1998, while Richard Butler was giving his formal presentation to the Security Council, the United States and Great Britain launched Operation Desert Fox.

Shockingly, before the Security Council had an opportunity to hear the full report and conduct a debate on the next step, U.S. and British bombing began. If the United States and Great Britain were complying with the United Nations Charter, they would have been obliged to delay all action until there was a proper debate in the Security Council. Only after a Security Council discussion on the issue of WMD could the Security Council authorize the use of force.

A second major problem with the inspection process was the close ties between Richard Butler and the Americans, who clearly had their own agenda. Butler was working for the UN and should have been obligated to adopt its agenda, which is to maintain peace, order, and security. Instead he, in fact, was promoting the interests of the United States by providing a pretext for bombing Iraq.

The rationale for the bombing of Iraq was based on Butler's contention that Iraq was not cooperating with the inspection teams. On the contrary, all the evidence suggested that the inspection teams had made remarkable progress, although there was still work to be done. In his sixth report to the Security Council since March 7, 1996, Richard Butler concluded that:

> Three central facts emerge from the present report on the Commission's work with Iraq in the last six months: the disarmament phase of the Security Council's requirements is possibly near its end in the missile and chemical weapons area but not in the biological weapons area and full disclosure by Iraq of all necessary materials and information remains the crucial ingredient for both an end to the disarmament process and future monitoring.

(Report of the Executive Chairman on the Activities of the Special Commission, UN Security Council, October 6, 1998)

In the International Atomic Energy Agency's (IAEA) report to the UN Security Council, Mohamed Elbaradei, the Director General, reported that:

> There were no indications that Iraq had achieved its programme objective, or produced or otherwise acquired any meaningful amounts of weapons-usable nuclear material. The report additionally included statements to the effect that there were no indications that Iraq had retained the physical capability (facilities and hardware) to be able to produce weapons—usable nuclear material in amounts of any practical significance.

(Report of the Director General of the International Atomic Energy Agency, UN Security Council, February 8, 1999)

Scott Ritter reached the conclusion that essentially Iraq did not pose a threat to any country when he noted that:

> This reduced capability (of WMD) reflects the effectiveness of the UNSCOM and IAEA inspection process, which despite all of Iraq's efforts to conceal, obfuscate, and distort the truth, managed to dispose of the vast majority of the prohibited weapons programs.

(Endgame: Solving the Iraq Crisis, Scott Ritter, p. 127)

According to the reports to the UN Security Council and the opinion of the Chief Weapons Inspector Scott Ritter, Iraq no longer possessed WMD with the possible exception of some biological weapons, which may or may not have existed. If UNSCOM had been allowed to complete its mission, they could have reported with 100 percent confidence that Iraq had no WMD, but due to the American agenda and Richard Butler's collusion, UNSCOM withdrew from Iraq, enabling U.S. bombers to drop more bombs on the egregiously devastated people of Iraq.

Yet, incredible as it may seem, on December 16, 1998, U.S. bombers and cruise missiles inflicted even more suffering and loss on Iraqi people. Targeting during the four days of brutal destruction was totally unrelated to WMD but was aimed at punishing the Iraqi people yet again for their failure to overthrow their leader. Destruction included a maternity hospital, a teaching hospital, the Health Ministry, the Ministry of Labor and Social Affairs, Baghdad's water system, and ten schools in Basra.

On January 30, 1999, the Security Council established three panels to "consider the parallel objectives of re-establishing an effective presence of the United Nations and the International Atomic Energy Agency in Iraq in the area of disarmament." The panel on disarmament and verification included "the participation and expertise from the United Nations Special Commission, the International Atomic Energy Agency, the United Nations Secretariat, and other relevant expertise." The panel reported to the Security Council on March 27, 1999, that:

> The Agency [IAEA] is able to state that there is no indication that Iraq possesses nuclear weapons or any meaningful amounts of weapons—usable nuclear material or that Iraq has retained any practical capability (facilities or hardware) for the production of such material...UNSCOM has supervised or been able to certify the destruction, removal, or rendering harmless of large quantities of chemical weapons (CW), their components and major weapons production equipment...the declared facilities of Iraq's BW [biological weapons] programme have been destroyed and rendered harmless.

(*Report of the UN Panel on Disarmament and Verification*, UN Security Council, March 27, 1999)

However, despite the positive reports from inspection teams in Iraq, the United States steadfastly maintained the sanctions in order to weaken Iraq as well as to convince the people to overthrow Saddam Hussein. On a previous occasion, President George H. Bush had openly called on the people of Iraq to overthrow Saddam and called on the military "to take matters into their own hands, and force Saddam

Hussein, the dictator, to step aside." The Kurds, numbering twenty-five million, are the fourth-largest ethnic group in the Middle East and live mostly in Iraq, Iran, Turkey, and Syria. Bush appealed directly to the Kurds to rebel against Saddam with the support of the United States on a CIA-funded radio station called the Voice of Free Iraq. During the Iran-Iraq war between the spring of 1987 and 1988, Iraqi chemical and conventional weapons attacks on the Kurds in Northern Iraq displaced one million Kurds. After the ceasefire in 1991, when the United States encouraged the Kurds to rebel against the Hussein regime, the Kurds captured a number of towns in Northern Iraq, including Ranya, Arbil, and Aqra. Within one week, Hussein's Republican Guard recaptured the towns and forced one million Kurds into exile in Turkey and Iran. Notwithstanding assurances of support for the Kurdish uprising, the United States did not lift a finger to assist.

This is not the first time that America offered support to a group for the purpose of overthrowing a government and then backed out at the last minute. The expatriate Cubans who invaded Cuba with the promise of American air support found themselves on Cuban shores all by themselves. In Panama, a group of officers in the Panamanian Defense Forces planning a coup against Manuel Noriega with American assistance were quickly overthrown when American support did not materialize.

In 2001, when President George W. Bush became president, Iraq was again in the crosshairs of the mighty American military machine. Plans to attack Iraq were formulated by a group called the Project for a New American Century (PNAC), a private think tank formed by a group of prominent neoconservatives including William Kristol, Elliot Abrams, Jeb Bush, Dick Cheney, Lewis Libby, Richard Perle, Donald Rumsfeld, and Paul Wolfowitz. The aims of the organization were to increase defense spending significantly in order to carry out American's global responsibilities. PNAC's focus on Iraq was an important part of their overall plan. Members of PNAC wrote a letter to President Clinton in which they argued that:

> Current American policy toward Iraq is not succeeding and
> that we may soon face a threat in the Middle East more

> serious…That strategy should aim above all at the removal
> of Saddam Hussein's regime from power.

(*Washington Post,* January 27, 1998, p. 84)

In November 2002, the White House brain trust consisting of many PNAC members formed the Committee for the Liberation of Iraq (CLI) in which the mission statement included "replacing Saddam Hussein regime with a democratic government." PNAC members hold important positions in the new Bush administration and had considerable influence in shaping foreign and defense policy. The determination to overthrow the regime of Saddam Hussein became a high priority in Washington.

The 9/11 tragedy provided the Bush Administration with the rationale to expand the American Empire under the guise of the "war on terror." Before bombing Iraq, the Bush administration had been compelled to focus on Afghanistan first, given that Osama bin Laden and his fellow terrorists were located there. However, after a token effort in Afghanistan, most American troops were hastily withdrawn from Afghanistan without capturing Osama in favor of war against Iraq, even though it was well known that Iraq had no involvement in 9/11.

The Bush administration adamantly maintained that Iraq had ties to al-Qaeda as demonstrated by Vice President Cheney when he claimed that "there's overwhelming evidence there was a connection between al-Qaeda and the Iraqi government" (January 22, 2004) and President Bush when he claimed that "There's no question that Saddam Hussein had al-Qaeda ties" (September 17, 2003).

The evidence completely contradicts the strong affirmations of administrative officials. A declassified CIA document reported that "our knowledge of Iraqi links to al-Qaeda contains many critical gaps because of limited reporting [blanked out section] and the questionable reliability of many of the sources" (*Iraq and al-Qaeda*, CIA Report, June 21, 2002). Daniel Benjamin, former terrorism adviser to the U.S. National Security Council, stated that "while there are contacts, have been contacts, there is no co-operation. There is no substantial, noteworthy relationship" (*Experts Doubt Iraq, al-Qaeda Terror Link*, CBC News, November 1, 2002). According to Jonathan Weisman of the *Washington Post*:

> A declassified report released yesterday by the Senate Select Committee on Intelligence revealed that U.S. intelligence analysts are strongly disputing the alleged links between Saddam Hussein and al-Qaeda.

("Iraq's Alleged al-Qaeda Ties Were Disputed Before War," *Washington Post*, September 9, 2006, A01)

Clearly the Bush Administration was contradicting its own intelligence agency in claiming "overwhelming evidence" that there were ties between al-Qaeda and Hussein.

President George Bush spoke to the General Assembly of the United Nations on September 12, 2002, to warn the world of the "grave and gathering danger" of Iraq's WMD. He also stated that:

> Right now, Iraq is expanding and improving facilities that are used for the production of biological weapons…Today, Iraq continues to withhold important information about its nuclear program…the conduct of the Iraqi regime is a threat to the authority of the United Nations and a threat to peace.

This speech is replete with irony. It was, in fact, the United States that was undermining the authority of the UN when it coerced and bribed members of the Security Council in order to produce favorable votes on resolutions concerning Iraq. As well, the United States used the UN when it suited their purposes and ignored it otherwise. Furthermore, the real threat to peace was the United States inasmuch as the United States resorts to aggression almost exclusively as a means of implementing foreign policy.

By 1999, UN inspection teams and panels had already established the absence of any real threat from WMD in Iraq.

Additionally, another UN inspection team was sent to Iraq to complete the work of UNSCOM, although the Bush administration was not interested in its results. As a matter of fact, the United States was nervous that the new inspection team might claim that it now had 100 percent confidence in Iraq's WMD status.

On September 16, 2002, Iraq's Foreign Minister, Naji Sabri, advised UN Secretary-General Kofi Annan that Iraq would accept the return of UN weapons inspectors "without conditions." Saddam could predict his fate based on U.S. behavior, and in an attempt to forestall it, he was willing to do whatever was necessary.

Ignoring Iraq's invitation to open Iraq for inspections, President Bush asked Congress to approve a resolution giving him absolute authority to declare war on Iraq. The resolution passed the House 296 to 133 and the Senate by 77 to 23. The President signed the resolution on October 16, 2003, one month after the Iraqi invitation, exposing the fact that Bush was 100 percent determined to attack Iraq.

While Washington was preparing for war, the United Nations was preparing to preserve the peace by resurrecting the inspection process. The UN adopted Resolution 1441 on November 8, 2002, authorizing further inspections, which Iraq accepted. The resolution granted UNMOVIC (United Nations Monitoring, Verification, and Inspection Committee) and the IAEA the right to inspect anywhere in Iraq with unconditional access. As well, Iraq had to provide an "accurate and complete" declaration of its chemical, nuclear, and biological weapons and related materials within thirty days. All violations of the resolution had to be reported to the Security Council before any further action could be undertaken. Contrary to the U.S. interpretation, there was nothing in the resolution that authorized the use of force. Paragraphs four, eleven, twelve, and fourteen specified that any assessment of Iraq's compliance and any consequences that may follow must be debated by the Security Council and no action could be undertaken by any state without the approval of the Security Council.

Dr. Hans Blix, Executive Chairman of UNMOVIC, provided an update to the Security Council on January 27, 2003, sixty days after the resumption of inspections. His report to the Security Council concluded that:

> Iraq on the whole has cooperated rather well so far with UNMOVIC in this field [cooperation]. The most important point to make is that access has been provided to all sites we have wanted to inspect and with one exception it has been prompt…These reports do not contend that weapons of mass destruction remain in Iraq, nor do they exclude the possibility. They point to no evidence and inconsistencies, which raises question marks, which must be straightened out, if weapons dossiers are to be closed and confidence is to arise…In the past two months, UNMOVIC has built up capabilities in Iraq from nothing to 260 staff members…We have now an inspection apparatus that permits us to send multiple inspection teams every day all over Iraq, by road and by air.

(*An Update on Inspection*, Report to the UN Security Council, January 27, 2003)

On the same day that Hans Blix delivered his report on Iraqi's biological and chemical weapons to the Security Council, the IAEA Program Director General, Mohamed ElBaradei, delivered his report on Iraq's nuclear program. According to his report:

> First, we have inspected all those buildings and facilities, identified through satellite imagery, as having been modified or constructed over the past four years. IAEA inspectors have been able to gain ready access and to clarify the nature of the activities currently being conducted in those buildings. No prohibited nuclear activities have been identified during these inspections…From our analysis to date it appears that the aluminum tubes would be consistent with the purpose stated by Iraq and unless modified, would not be suitable for manufacturing centrifuges.…To conclude: we have to date found no evidence that Iraq has revived its nuclear weapons programme since the elimination of the programme in the 1990s. With our verification system now in place…we should be able [with Iraq's cooperation] within the next few

months to provide credible evidence that Iraq has no nuclear weapons programme.

(*The Status of Nuclear Inspections in Iraq*, Statement to UN Security Council, January 27, 2003)

The reports from both inspection teams found that no evidence had yet been uncovered to demonstrate that Iraq had WMD, storage facilities, or manufacturing facilities. The two reports emphasized that an inspection organization had been established in Iraq to monitor further developments in Iraq's WMD programs and to identify facilities and materials that have not yet been discovered. UNSCOM and the IAEA reassured the Security Council that they were prepared to continue their work until they reach the point where the world would have 100 percent confidence that Iraq posed no threat.

Despite these reports, top members of the administration repeatedly uttered complete falsehoods when they claimed that Iraq had WMD and that America had to act quickly before "the smoking gun becomes a mushroom cloud."

For example, on January 28, 2003, President Bush delivered his State of the Union Address to Congress in which the results of the inspection teams were completely ignored. During his address he warned that:

> For the next twelve years [1991 to 2003] he [Saddam Hussein] systematically violated that agreement [UN Resolution 687]. He pursued chemical, biological and nuclear weapons, even while inspectors were in his country. Nothing to date has restrained him from his pursuit of these weapons…With nuclear arms or a full arsenal of chemical and biological weapons, Saddam Hussein could resume his ambitions of conquest in the Middle East. It has not been possible to verify Iraq's claims with respect to the nature and magnitude of its proscribed weapons programme and their current disposition…The Commission has not yet been able to conduct the substantive disarmament work…

Since the public was not privy, at the time, to the intelligence reports on which Bush and his administration were basing their conclusions, it would not have been possible to know exactly what information they had. There is one inescapable certainty, which is the fact that all the work done by various inspection teams and agencies of the UN clearly invalidated every claim of the Bush administration. These reports were readily available and should have been mandatory reading for anyone commenting on the threat of WMD in Iraq. High-ranking members of the Bush Administration obviously had no interest in these reports, which were contrary to their agenda in the Middle East.

At one point in this campaign of deception, Colin Powell, Secretary of State, brought shame to himself and every top-ranking member of the Bush government when he appeared before the Security Council on February 5, 2003. He presented the government's spurious case for fearing WMD in Iraq with CIA Director George Tenet sitting behind him, lending credibility to his case. Many veteran CIA experts cringed as Powell referred to evidence such as amateur diagrams and incompetent interpretations of satellite data that was clearly not tenable.

One of his Powell's claims was that:

> Saddam Hussein is determined to get his hands on a nuclear bomb...he has made repeated covert attempts to acquire high-specification aluminum tubes from eleven different countries, even after inspection resumed...they can be used as centrifuges for enriching uranium...Saddam Hussein recently sought significant quantities of uranium from Africa.

The Executive Director of the IAEA had reported to the Council that "from our analysis to date it appears that the aluminum tubes would be consistent with the purpose stated by Iraq." An IAEA report concluded that the size of the tubes made them unsuitable for uranium enrichment but were identical to tubes used for conventional artillery rockets.

Further, the claim that Saddam had purchased nuclear material from Niger was based on forged documents handed to the United States from Britain, whose source was the Italian intelligence service. There were spelling mistakes in the documents, days of the week did not match dates, and some of the people who had signed them were no longer involved. In addition, Joe Wilson, a former U.S. Ambassador, had been sent to Niger to investigate the claim about the purchase of uranium and concluded that the claim was false. When President Bush repeated the claim in his State of the Union Address after the White House had received Wilson's report, Joe Wilson wrote an article for the *Washington Post* in which he admonished the administration for "misrepresenting the facts on an issue that was a fundamental justification for going to war."

Paradoxically, the facts were not relevant to the decision about whether to declare war against Iraq. Once the decision had been made, the Bush administration would massage the data to prove that the war against Iraq was necessary.

On February 14, 2003, Hans Blix updated the Security Council on the results of UNMOVIC's inspection. His report contradicted President Bush and other members of his administration. Hans Blix reported that:

> Through the inspection conducted so far, we have obtained a good knowledge of the scientific and industrial landscape of Iraq, as well as its missile capability but, as before, we do not know every cave and corner. Inspections are helping to bridge the gap in knowledge that arose due to some absence of inspections between December 1998 and November 2002…The impression [cooperation on the process] remains and we do note that access to sites has so far been without problems, including those that have never been declared or inspected, as well as to Presidential sites and private residence…How much, if any, is left of Iraq's weapons of mass destruction and related proscribed items and programmes? So far, UNMOVIC has not found any such weapons, only a small number of empty chemical munitions, which should have been declared and destroyed.

(*Briefing of the Security Council*, Executive Chairman of UNMOVIC, Hans Blix, UN, February 14, 2003)

Incontestably, the Bush administration had motives other than the ones communicated to the public. Another bombing would reduce Iraq to a considerably weakened state over which the U.S. could easily gain control, so they believed. Control of Iraq would mean control over the second-largest oil reserves in the world as well as an opportunity to gain control over Iraqi oil production for the benefit of American oil multinationals who could then steal the oil through production sharing agreements. These agreements essentially meant that the American companies would own the oil and would be required to hand over only a small percentage of the revenues to Iraq.

Another motivation is related to America's fear of present and future industrial rivals and in particular China and their Asian Energy Security Grid with the threat that they might join forces with Iran and India. In order to have a competitive edge, the United States was pursuing a policy of taking control of Middle Eastern oil as a lever over competitors.

In addition, the fear of independent Shi'ite majority control over Iraq was seen as threatening because of the risk that other countries with a large Shi'ite population might join forces with Iran and Iraq to take control of Middle East oil.

Now that the preparatory groundwork for a war against Iraq was complete, British Foreign Minister Jack Straw announced a Security Council resolution supported by the United States, which would authorize the use of force against Iraq if Iraq failed to comply with other Security Council resolutions calling for the disarmament of WMD. However, both France and Russia threatened to veto any resolution authorizing the use of force.

The threat of a veto persuaded the United States to abandon any attempt to legitimize their war plans with a Security Council resolution. Instead they attempted to build a coalition to create the illusion of international approval. They had the support of, and military contributions, from Britain, Spain, and Australia. Washington was only able to create a coalition, referred to as the "Coalition of the Willing," of thirty minor nations including Albania, Dominican Republic, Marshall Islands, Micronesia, Nicaragua, and Uganda. Notwithstanding the commitment of these countries to join the coalition, the populations in these countries did not always support the war. A January 2003 poll in Britain showed that 68 percent of the people were not convinced of the need for war, and a staggering 80 percent of the population opposed it in Spain.

On Thursday, March 20, 2003, President Bush announced his intention to use force against Iraq in an address to the nation in which he said that:

> At this hour Americans and coalition forces are in the early stages of military operations to disarm Iraq, to free its people and to defend the world from a grave danger. On my orders, coalition forces have begun striking selected targets of military importance to undermine Saddam Hussein's ability to wage war.

The immediate justification was "preemptive defense." The Orwellian phrase "preemptive defense" was invented to cloak a flagrant contempt for international law with a legitimizing principle that is not recognized anywhere in international conventions and treaties. "Preemptive defense" implies that at some future unknown time, the Iraqi war machine intended to attack the United States. It has been conclusively demonstrated that Iraq did not have the capability or intention to attack the United States.

There are only two legitimate justifications in international law for using force against another country. One requires a United Nations Resolution with UN oversight of the conflict, while the other is the invocation of Article 51 of the UN Charter, which states that:

> Nothing in the present charter shall impair the inherent right of individual or collective self-defense if an armed attack occurs against a member of the United Nations, until the

Security Council has taken measures necessary to maintain
international peace and security.

In order for the war to be legal, the United States would have
had to rely on Article 51 of the UN Charter since no UN resolution
had been passed authorizing the use of force against Iraq. Resolution
687 only applied to the occupation of Kuwait. There was no Iraqi
armed attack against the United States; thus automatically the war is
deemed to be illegal. Even if there had been an act of aggression on the
part of Iraq against the United States, the United States would have
been obliged to involve the Security Council as quickly as possible.
The United States would have had to take the matter to the Security
Council immediately for debate and approval.

Furthermore, if the United States argued that the war was
preemptive and therefore necessary to protect against an imminent
act of aggression, the onus would have been on the United States
to demonstrate that such a threat existed, and even if it did, that it
meets the requirements of Article 51 of the UN Charter. Meeting the
requirements of Article 51 implies demonstrating that an armed or
missile attack is underway. These safeguards in the Charter are designed
to prevent nations from acting aggressively towards each other on
frivolous grounds. The principle of "preemptive defense" would open
Pandora's Box and would virtually give nations a blank check to attack
one another.

The United States launched the war with its "shock and awe"
strategy, which meant a massive high-tech strike against Baghdad. A
Pentagon official commenting on the strategy remarked that "there
will not be a safe place in Baghdad." It is clear that the real purpose
of "shock and awe" was to destroy as much of the Iraqi leadership and
army as possible, as well as military installations.

The strategy was to launch 300 to 400 cruise missiles on the
first day of the operation and another 300 to 400 on the second day.
That number of cruise missiles is greater than all the cruise missiles
fired in the 1991 bombing of Iraq. Numerous nonmilitary objects were
deliberately targeted, including electrical-distribution facilities, three

media facilities, government buildings, roads, and bridges. In addition, many civilians were inevitably killed, many by illegal weapons such as depleted uranium weapons and cluster bombs. Both of these weapons continue to kill many people years after the war through the effects of radiation or stepping on unexploded cluster bombs.

Following the "shock and awe" operation, a massive force of American, British, and Australian forces marched through Iraq relatively unimpeded and took control of much of the country.

Achieving its objectives in Iraq necessitated the construction of an American-style economic system while building the façade of a democracy that would be under the control of the United States. Stabilizing the country was the primary immediate priority.

Shortly after the invasion, the United States installed, without popular consent, the Coalition Provisional Authority (CPA) as a transitional government of Iraq until the U.S. could create an American-friendly façade of a democracy. On April 21, 2003, the CPA vested itself with executive, legislative, and judicial authority over the Iraqi government based on UN Security Council Resolution 1483. Jay Garner, retired U.S. Army Lieutenant General, originally headed the CPA but was quickly replaced with L. Paul Bremer, former Chairman of the National Commission on Terrorism, who remained as its head until its dissolution in July 2004. Bremer and the CPA were window dressing for a military dictatorship, charged with insuring that U.S. objectives were safe from any popular uprising. In fact, Bremer was chosen because of his nonmilitary background to obfuscate the reality of a military occupation.

The United States had carefully drafted a blueprint for Iraq under the CPA to be implemented at a time when there would be little opposition inasmuch Bremer was a military dictator. Democracy would have to wait until Americans had remade Iraq to serve U.S. interests.

To develop the blueprint for Iraq's economy, the American government hired a private contractor, Bearing Point, for $250 million to convert Iraq's economy into a free-market economy, friendly to American corporate interests. Bremer passed a number of laws under his power as head of the CPA in order to implement the above blueprint.

One of the laws called for the privatization of 200 state-owned enterprises and 100 percent foreign ownership of Iraqi-owned businesses. Forcing private businesses to sell to foreign interests ensured that all contracts handed out in Iraq, in particular for reconstruction, would go to companies such as Halliburton and Bechtel. Another law granted foreign contractors immunity from Iraq's laws. A law was also passed that dropped the tax rate on corporations from a high of 40 percent to a flat 15 percent. Furthermore, all tariffs, customs duties, import taxes, and licensing fees on imports and exports were suspended.

The result of the implementation of the American blueprint for Iraq, implemented without any input from the people of Iraq, excludes Iraqi corporations and workers from rebuilding their own country. More important to the U.S. government, it also gave the United States greater access and control over Iraqi oil.

On June 28, 2004, the CPA transferred the "sovereignty" of Iraq to a caretaker government until elections could be held on January 31, 2005. The United States was creating the illusion of progress towards democracy when, in fact, the Americans would still be in control.

Elections were held in Iraq on January 31, 2005, to choose a government in order to draft a permanent constitution. The elections were so fraught with problems that the results were meaningless. The Sunnis, who constituted 20 percent of the population and were major contributors to the insurgency, boycotted the election or were intimidated at the polling booth.

Election results are not legitimate when they are conducted under a military occupation and run by a puppet government installed by the occupying army. Primarily, the elections provided a veneer of credibility and legitimacy under which the United States was still maintaining control.

David Model

Dissent was not tolerated under Bremer, who fired 436 university professors who were members of the Baath Party. Protestors were frequently shot, as was the case when an ex-Iraqi soldier who protested against aggressive American military raids and was shot for his efforts. Demonstrations against the presence of U.S. troops near the shrine of Imam Hussein at Karbala resulted in the death of three of the protestors. Bremer's use of strong-arm tactics was rapidly alienating the Iraqi people.

Since the beginning of the occupation, Iraq has descended further and further into a violent, anarchical maelstrom. It began with attacks on American troops but quickly plunged into sectarian bloodletting. Americans had squandered the goodwill of the Iraqi people, who now overwhelmingly wanted them to leave. The UN Office for the Coordination of Humanitarian affairs describes the conditions in Iraq:

> Since the US-led invasion of 2003, Iraq has been plunged into violence and chaos. It has gone through three governments, all of which have failed to inspire the confidence of the people and improve the security situation. In 2007, the Iraq Study Group described the situation in Iraq as "grave and deteriorating." Iraqis are caught in the deadly grip of violence, fuelled on the one hand by US and Iraqi military operations and on the other by Sunni insurgents, Shia militias, death squads and criminal gangs. In late 2006–early 2007, the conflict intensified both in its voracity and the number of lives it claims every day.

(*Iraq: Humanitarian Country Profile*, UN Office for the Coordination of Humanitarian Affairs, February 2007)

The great tragedy of this war is its impact on the people of Iraq. The death toll, number of injured, destruction of the infrastructure, decline in healthcare, and monumental decrease in the standard of living bespeak a horror beyond our comprehension.

Iraq Body Count (IBC) provides the most conservative estimate of the number who died. As of February 23, 2007, IBC estimates

188

that the number of civilian deaths falls between 56,880 and 62,613. According to two John Hopkins University's Bloomberg School of Public Health studies:

> The first Hopkins study estimated that about 98,000 excess deaths (deaths above the pre-2003 mortality rate) had occurred in the 18 month period from March 2003 to September 2004. The report concluded that "violence was the primary cause of death" since the invasion and "mainly attributed [it] to coalition forces."…The second Hopkins study estimated that 655,000 excess deaths had occurred during the occupation from March 2003 through June 2006: a shockingly high number.

(*War and Occupation of Iraq*, Global Policy Forum, January 2007)

Another study by the *Lancet* Medical Journal estimates the number of dead civilians to be 650,000.

The war and violence during the occupation forced a number of people to leave their homes to seek refuge either elsewhere in Iraq or in another country. The UN Office for the Coordination of Humanitarian Affairs estimated the number of refugees:

> More than 200,000 people were displaced during the attacks on Falluja alone during 2004, while hundreds of thousands may have been uprooted in other urban attacks. The majority of the displaced have been unable to return due to insecurity, the recurrent military offenses, lack of water, electricity and health services, and because their homes were destroyed.

> Inter-communal violence, multiple military operations and human rights abuses have uprooted 3.8 million Iraqis…Iraq is today facing a displacement crisis that has seen up to 50,000 people fleeing their homes each month.

(*Iraq: Humanitarian Country Profile*, UN Office for the Coordination of Humanitarian Affairs, February 2007)

Based on the results of another study, the displacement crisis began when:

> In early November 2006, an estimated 3.4 million Iraqis had been displaced in Iraq, about 14% of the total national population. Of that number, about 1.6 million Iraqis were displaced within the country and at least 1.8 million had migrated to other countries. UNHCR, the UN Refugee Agency, has spoken of its "growing concerns over the rapidly deteriorating humanitarian situation facing hundreds of thousands of displaced Iraqis, both within and outside the country."

(*Displacement and Mortality*, Global Policy Forum, January 2007)

Many of the deaths and diseases can be attributed to lack of infrastructure, which was destroyed in 1991, not repairable during the sanctions for lack of spare parts, and destroyed even further in 2003. The result was unclean water, inadequate medical facilities, deficiency of medicines, and the inability to produce sufficient food for the people of Iraq. Anthony Arnove, in *CounterPunch* Newsletter reports that:

> The tragedy unleashed by the United States invasion and occupation of Iraq defies description. According to the most recent findings of the *Lancet* medical journal…Basic foods and necessities are beyond the reach of ordinary Iraqis because of massive inflation. "A gallon of gasoline cost as little as 4 cents in November. Now, after the International Monetary Fund persuaded the Oil Ministry to cut its subsidies, the official price is about 67 cents," the *New York Times* notes. "The spike has come as a shock to Iraqis, who make only about $150 a month on average—if they have jobs," an important proviso, since unemployment is roughly between 60% and 70% nationally.

("The US Occupation of Iraq," Anthony Arnove, *CounterPunch*, December 16/17, 2006)

The enormity of the tragedy in Iraq can be understood by contrasting conditions before the 1991 bombing and conditions today.

On February 24, 2007, a UN study described the difference:

> Saddam Hussein's 24-year rule was devastating for both the people and economy of Iraq. In 1979, Iraq was in the middle range of economic indicators. Oil made the country rich, accounting for 95 percent of foreign exchange earnings. Thus, Iraq was among the more advanced countries in the Arab world, with a rapidly growing population and economy...According to the World Bank, in the 1980s, Iraq's per capita income was $3,600, but by 2002 it had dropped to $480–$610.

(*Iraq: Humanitarian Country Profile*, UN Office for the Coordination of Humanitarian Affairs, February, 24, 2007)

The 2003 war and military occupation is an irrefutable case of genocide. More precisely, it is a continuation of the genocide begun by President George H. Bush and carried on by President Clinton. President George W. Bush stamped the ongoing genocide with his unique insignia by intensifying every crisis already plaguing Iraq and also by plunging the country into a paroxysm of violence.

The targeted group is the people of Iraq, and by 2007, there is no question that U.S. actions destroyed large numbers of Iraqis, displaced a massive number of people, and further degraded the infrastructure and the capacity of any existing facilities to operate.

Whether or not the George W. Bush administration deliberately intended to commit genocide is irrelevant, because the known and easily predictable consequences of their actions could only lead to a huge civilian toll.

The 2003 bombing, occupation, and ongoing sanctions undeniably would lead to genocide. Aside from killing more people, further bombing ensured that the people of Iraq would have even less water and electricity than before the war.

Military occupation has plunged Iraq into a hellhole of sectarian violence and subjected the people to wanton, indiscriminate killing by American forces. Therefore, President George W. Bush is guilty of genocide against the people of Iraq.

George W. Bush is not really that much different from other presidents discussed in this book in that they all have committed horrendous crimes against humanity in the name of protecting American interests. American presidents have supported brutal dictators who have slaughtered their own people, overthrown democratic governments who were serving the interests of their people, and bombed countries virtually into oblivion under the guise of spreading democracy and liberty to all oppressed peoples of the world along with defending their human rights.

These are laudable goals reflecting prevailing shibboleths domestically. These goals are an alluring mantle for the real paradigm governing foreign policy, which is the pursuit of American interests with total indifference to the consequences to people victimized by American "ideals." Underlying this paradigm is the imperative of advancing American corporate interests to the maximum extent possible.

Human rights are not a priority if they stand in the way of American imperialism, and there is always a rationalization for the crimes against humanity perpetrated by American leaders. The ultimate costs both internationally and domestically of these misplaced priorities are very destructive to the interests of the American people who have suffered economically, socially, and morally from such ancient bankrupt policies practiced in the past by all empires.

The difference in the consequences between the decay of the Roman and the American Empire is the level of cataclysmic pandemic impact concomitant with advances in technology. A collapsing Roman Empire never threatened widespread death and destruction to anywhere near the same extent as a declining American Empire. America's desperate acts to preserve some semblance of the power and prestige once accorded to the major superpower of the twentieth century has bequeathed in its wake death and destruction on a scale unknown in history with the possible exceptions of the two world wars.

Never before in history has one country perpetrated so many genocides in so many countries. Nine million victims is a highly immoral price paid by others to sustain a faltering world power.

ABOUT THE AUTHOR

David Model graduated from the University of Toronto and went on to obtain a Masters Degree from the University of Waterloo. Since 1974, David has been on faculty at Ontario's Seneca College, where he has developed and taught numerous courses in the area of political science, mass media, and global issues.

David has had three books published over the past decade, including 2005's Lying for Empire: How to Commit War Crimes with a Straight Face, published by Common Courage Press. His previous books are People before Profits: Reversing the Corporate Agenda, published by Captus Press, 1997, and Corporate Rule: Understanding and Challenging the New World Order, published by Black Rose Books, 2002.

David is an experienced lecturer who has delivered papers at many academic conferences, including "The Effectiveness of the International Judicial System" at an international criminology conference in April, 2003. He has presented a number of papers at York University including War Crimes in Iraq (April 2004), War Crimes in Serbia (April 2005) and The Applicability of Hermann's and Chomsky's Propaganda Model Today (June 2005). He will be presenting a paper based on the manuscript at the University of Glasgow in February 2008.

David's local newspaper column, "The Global Perspective" ran from 1984 to 1988 and covered such diverse topics as disarmament, arms buildup by the superpowers, and American interventions. His work has been also featured in CounterPunch, Z Magazine, and Dissident Voice.

David's unique perspective on politics has been informed by his academic, political and activist experience, as well as by his extensive travels to many hotspots such as Nicaragua, Vietnam, Guatemala and Cambodia. Touring these countries and seeing firsthand the impact of war on the people and the land inspired David to continue the journey to peace through his work and through his books.

BIBLIOGRAPHY

Aandstad, S., A. (1999). *United States Policy Towards Indonesia 1961-1965*. Retrieved from Web Site: http://aga.nvg.org/oppgaver/title.html.

Alperovitz, G. (1989). *Was Hiroshima Necessary to End the War?* Retrieved from the War Resisters League Web Site: https://www.peacewire.org/photoexibits/hiroshima/articles/hironecessary.html.

Alperovitz, G. (1995). *The Decision to Use the Atomic Bomb*. Toronto: Random House of Canada.

Amnesty International. (2002). *Guatemala's Lethal Legacy: Past Impunity and Renewed Human Rights Violations*. Retrieved from Amnesty International's Web Site: http://web.amnesty.org/library/Index/engAMR340012002?OpenDocument.

Arnove, A. (2006, December 16/17). *Act III in a Tragedy of Many Parts: The US Occupation of Iraq*. Petrolia (CA): Counterpunch. Retrieved from Web Site: http://www.counterpunch.org/arnove12162006.html.

Austin, B., S. (1996). *The Nuremburg War Crime Trials*. Retrieved from Middle Tennessee State University Web Site: http://www.mtsu.edu/~baustin/trials.htm.

Avalon Project. (n.d.). *The Moscow Conference; October 1943*. Retrieved from Yale Law School Web Site: http://www.yale.edu/lawweb/avalon/imt/moscow.htm.

Avalon Project. (1964, August 7). *The Gulf of Tonkin Resolution* (Joint Resolution of Congress: H.J. Res 1145 August 7, 1964). Retrieved from Yale Law School Web Site: http://www.yale.edu/lawweb/avalon/tonkin-g.htm.

Avalon Project. (1996). *President Johnson's Message to Congress Aug. 1964*. Retrieved from Yale Law School's Web Site: http://www.yale.edu/lawweb/avalon/tonlein-g.htm.

Ball, P., Kobrak, P., and Spirer, F. (1999). *State Violence in Guatemala, 1960-1996: A Quantitative Reflection*. Retrieved from Web Site: http://shr.aaas.org/guatemala/ciidh/qr/english/chap2.html.

Becker, B. (1992). *Iraq*. Retrieved from the Commission of Inquiry for the International War Crimes Tribunal Web Site: http://www.deoxy.org/WC/WC-consp.htm.

Bennis, P. (2004, December 20). *Iraqi Elections*. Retrieved from the Znet Web Site: http://www.zmag/content/print_article.cfm?itemID=6899&sectionID=1.

Blackburn, R. (1999, May 25). *Kosovo: The Lost Chances and Continuing Dangers*. Petrolia (CA): Counterpunch. Retrieved from Web Site: http://www.counterpunch.org/wtarchive.html.

Blix, H. (2003, January 27). *An Update on Inspection* (Report to the UN). Retrieved from the UN Web Site: http://www.un.org/Depts/unmovic/Bx27.htm.

Blix, H. (2003, February 14). *Briefings of the Security Council, 14 February 2003: An Update on Inspections*. Retrieved from the UN Web Site: http://www.un.org/Depts/unmovic/new/pages/security_council_briefings.asp.

Blix, H. (2003, April, 9). *War Planned Long in Advance*. Truthout. Retrieved from Web Site: http://www.truthout.org/docs_03.

Blum, W. (1998). *Killing Hope: Military and CIA Intervention Since World War II*. Montreal: Black Rose Books.

Blum, W. (2003). *America: Rogue States* (Extract). Monroe (ME): Common Courage Press. Retrieved from Web Site: http://www.doublestandards.org/usmurder.html.

Boyle, A., B. (2002, December 14). *International Crisis and Neutrality: US Foreign Policy Toward the Iran/Iraq war*. Petrolia (CA): Counterpunch Magazine. Retrieved from Web Site: http://www.counterpunch.org/boy/c1214.

Brière, E. (Producer). (1996). *Bitter Paradise: The Sellout of East Timor* [videotape]. Vancouver: Snapshot Productions.

Brodhead, F. (2005, August 6). *A new Look at Hiroshima and Nagasaki.* Retrieved from the Znet Website: http://www.zmag.org/content/showarticle.cfm?ItemID=8457.

Buchanan, A., R. (1964). *The United States and World War II.* New York: Harper and Row.

Bugnion, F. (n.d.). *The International Committee of the Red Cross and nuclear weapons: from Hiroshima to the dawn of the 21st century.* Retrieved from the International Committee of the Red Cross Website: http://www.icrc.org/Web/eng/siteeng0.nsf/htmlall/review-859-p511/$file/icrc_859_Bungion-eng.pdf.

Burrows, G. (2002). *The Arms Trade.* Toronto: New Internationalist Publications.

Byrne, M. (1990, January 26). *The Iran-Contra Scandal in Perspective.* The National Security Archives. Retrieved from Web Site: http://nsarchive.chadwych.com/icessay.htm.

Campbell, T., and Conyers, J. (1999, November 30). *New Congressional Letter Calls for Lifting Sanctions on Iraq.* Retrieved from the Campaign Against Sanctions on Iraq Web Site: http://www.casi.org.uk/discuss/1999/msg00771.html.

Carvin, A. (1999). *Cambodia Colonized: The Fall of Angkor to the Arrival of the French.* Retrieved from Web Site: http://wwwedwebproject.org/sideshow/history/French.html.

Center for History. (n.d.). *Quotes by U.S. Military Leaders WW II.* Retrieved from Web Site: http://hnn.us/comments/7362.html.

Central Intelligence Agency. (1962, June 13). *Report of the Meeting at the White House.* Retrieved from Web Site: http://www.foia.cia.gov/search.asp.

Central Intelligence Agency. (1983, September). *The Guatemalan Insurgency: Near-Term Prospects*. Retrieved from Web Site: http://www.foia.cia.gov/search.asp.

Chomsky, N. (1989). *Necessary Illusions: Thought Control in a Democratic Society*. Toronto: CBC.

Chomsky, N. (1991, February). *The Gulf Crisis*. Woods Hole (MA): Z Magazine. Retrieved from Web Site: http://www.zena.secureforum.com/Znet/zmag/articles/chomulfalb.

Chomsky, N. (1993). *What Uncle Sam Really Wants*. Berkeley (CA): Odonian Press.

Chomsky, N. (1993). *Year 501: The Conquest Continues*. Montreal: Black Rose Books.

Chomsky, N. (1997). *Perspectives on Power: Reflections on Human Nature and the Social Order*. Montreal: Black Rose Books.

Chomsky, N. (1999). *Profits Over People: Neoliberalism and the New World Order*. Montreal: Black Rose Books.

Chomsky, N. (1999). *The New Military Humanism: Lessons From Kosovo*. Vancouver: New Star Books.

Chomsky, N., and Albert, M. (1991, February). *Gulf War Pullout*. Woods Hole (MA): Z Magazine. Retrieved from Web Site: http://www.zena.secureforum.com/Znet/zmag/articles/chomgulfalb.

Chomsky, N., and Albert, M. (2003, April 13). *Noam Chomsky Interviewed*. Woods Hole (MA): Z Magazine. Retrieved from Web Site: http://www.zmag.org/CrisesCurEvts/Iraq/noam_chomsky.htm.

Chomsky, N. (2006, December 27). *Iraq: Yesterday, Today, and Tomorrow*. Retrieved from the Znet Website: http://www.zmag.org/content/print_article.cfm?itemID=1171&&sectionID=1.

Churchill, W. (1997). *A little Matter of Genocide: Holocaust and Denial in the Americas 1492 to the Present*. San Francisco: City Lights Books.

Civil Intelligence Association. (1973). *Results of the 1973 Church Committee Hearings on CIA Misdeeds*. Retrieved from Web Site: http://pwl.net.com/~ncoic/CIA_info.htm.

Clark, R. (Producer). (1991, March 5). *Nowhere to Hide: Ramsey Clark in Iraq* [videotape]. San Francisco: International Action Center.

Clark, R. (1996, January 29). *Letter to the UN Security Council*. Retrieved from Web Site: http://www.iacenter.org/rcsan.htm.

Clark, R. (2002). *The Fire This Time: War Crimes in the Gulf*. New York: International Action Center.

Cornell Law School. (2002). *International Court of Justice*. Retrieved from Cornell Law School Web Site: www.lawschool.cornell.edu/librar.Commission for Historical Clarification. (1994, June 23). *Report of the Commission for Historical Clarification for Guatemala*. Retrieved from Web Site: http://shr.aaas.org/guatemala/ceh/english/toc.html.

Committee on the Judiciary, United States Senate. (1971, April 21, 22). *War-Related Civilian Problems in Indochina, Part II: Laos and Cambodia*. Washington: U.S. Government Printing Office.

Costello, P. (1997). *Accord: Guatemala Project*. Retrieved from Web Site: http://www.c-r.org/our-work/accord/guatemala/historical-background.php.

Council on Hemispheric Affairs. (1988). *Guatemala Worst Human Rights Violator in Latin America for 1988*. Retrieved from Web Site: http://www.coha.org/press%20release%20Archives/1988/88.5%pdf.

Council on Hemispheric Affairs. (2006, September 22). *COHA Open Letter to the Financial Times*. Retrieved from Web Site: http://www.coha.org/2006/09/22/coha-open-letter-to-the-financial-times/.

Crime Prevention Group. (n.d.). *Early Efforts to Prevent Genocide, Act Against Mass Killing, and Maintain Peace on an International Basis*. Retrieved from Web Site: http://medicolegal.tripod.com/earlyintlaw.htm.

Cronin, R., P. (1984). *The Kissinger Commission*. Retrieved from Web Site: http://www.uscubacommission.org/kisscom.htm.

Derek, M. (2003). *History of US Interventions: Laos 1958-1953*. Retrieved from the Cooperative Research website: http://www. cooperativeresearch.org/timeline_pf.jsp?timeline=laos.

Dwyer, K. (2001, November-December). *Rogue State: A History of U.S. Terror*. Retrieved from the International Socialist Review Website: http://www.isreview.org/issues/20/rouge_state.shtml.

EuropaWorld. (2001, June). *The Convention on the Prevention and Punishment of the Crime of Genocide*. Retrieved from the EuropaWorld Web Site: http://www.europaworld.org/issue40/the_conventionthepr evention22601.htm.

Farrel, J. (n.d.). *To Start a War: The Tonkin Gulf Incident*. Retrieved from the Cold War Web Site: http://www.audfaz.com/coldwar/ tonkin.htm.

Fein, H. (1995, October 24). *Genocide and Other State Murders in the Twentieth Century*. Retrieved from Web Site: http://www.ushmm.org/ Conscience/analysis/details.php?content=1995-10-24-02&menupa ge=History%20%26&20Concept.

Ferrel, R., H. (Ed.). (1966). *Truman and the Bomb, a Documentary History*. Boulder: High Plains Publishing Co. Retrieved from the Truman Presidential Museum and Library Web Site: http://www.trumanlibrary. org/whistlestop/study_collections/bomb/large/ferrell.htm.

Fisk, R. (2003, September 9). *Meet the New Iraqi Strongman: Paul Bremer*. Petrolia (CA): Counterpunch Magazine. Retrieved from Web Site: http://www.counterpunch.org/fisk09092003.html.

Fisk, R. (2007, February 9). *Iraqi insurgents offer peace in return for US concessions.* Retrieved from The Independent Website: http://news. independent.co.uk/world/fisk/artical2251354.ece.

Flounders, S. (2003, August 18). *Another War Crime? Iraqi Cities "Hot" with Depleted Uranium.* Retrieved from the International Action Center Web Site: http://www.iacenter.org/du-warcrime.htm.

Gates, R., M. (1991, May 9). *US Sanctions Threat Takes UN by Surprise.* Los Angeles : Los Angeles Times.

Gellately, R., and Kiernan, B. (Eds.). (2003). *The Specter of Genocide: Mass Murder in Historical Perspective.* New York: Cambridge University Press.

Gill, N., S. (1987, December). *Ancient Iran-Persia, the Medes and the Persians.* Retrieved from Web Site: www.ancienthistory.about.com/cs/persiaempirl/a/persiaintro.htm.

Global Issues Website. (2005, October 2). *Iraq-Post 1991 Persian Gulf War/Sanctions.* Retrieved from Web Site: http://www.globalissues. org/Geopolitics/MiddleEast/Iraq/Sanctions.asp.

Global Policy Forum. (2000, September 21). *Human Rights Watch Criticizes SC on Sanctions.* Retrieved from Web Site: http://www. globalpolicy.org/sanction/Iraq1/ngo/hrw0009.htm.

Global Policy Forum. (2007, January). *Report: War and Occupation in Iraq.* Retrieved from Web Site: http://www.globalpolicy.org/security/ issues/iraq/occupation/report/humanitarian.htm.

Goose, S. (2003, April 1). *U.S. Using Cluster Munitions in Iraq.* Retrieved from Human Rights Watch Web Site: http://www.hrw.org/ press/2003/04/us040103.htm.

Gordon, B. (2000, May). *Reflections on Hiroshima.* Retrieved from the Wesleyan University Web Site: http://www.wgordon.web.wesleyan. edu/papers/author.htm.

Gottstein, U. (n.d.). *The Effects of Sanctions on the Civilian Community of Iraq*. Retrieved from the International Physicians for the Prevention of Nuclear War Web Site: http://www.mapw.org.au/congress/p4.htm.

Graham, D. (2000, January 26). *The Holocaust*. Retrieved from the Holocaust Ring Web Site: www.datasync.com/~davidg59/genocide.html.

Grant, J., S., Moss, L., A., G., and Unger, J. (Eds.). (1971). *Cambodia: The Widening War in Indochina*. New York: Washington Square Press.

Grimm, N. (2003, April 25). *Pressure on US to Remove Depleted Uranium from Iraq*. Retrieved from ABC Radio Australia Web Site: www.abc.net.au/am/content/2003/s840116.htm.

Griswold, D. (1998). *Indonesia 1965*. From the Workers' World Website: http://www.workers.org/indonesia/chapt1.html.

Hamilton-Merritt, J. (1999). *Tragic Mountains: The Hmong, the Americans, and the Secret Wars of Laos, 1942 – 1992*. Bloomington: Indiana University Press.

Harry S. Truman Library. (1945). *Hiroshima*. (Harry Truman's Diaries and Papers). Retrieved from Web Site: https://www.doug-long.con/hst.htm.

Hartung, W. (1995, May). *A World Policy Institute Issue Brief*. Retrieved from the World Policy Website: http://www.worldpolicy.org/projects/arms/reports/wawrep.html.

Head, M. (1999, July 19). *US orchestrated Suharto's slaughter in Indonesia*. Retrieved from the World Socialist Web Site: http://www.wsws.org/articles/1999/indo1-j19_prn.shtml.

Heidhues, M. (2001). *The Limits of Intervention: U.S. Involvement in Indonesia*. Retrieved from Web Site: http://72.14.203.104/search?q=cache:Kajb1dbSRh0J:www.student-online.net/Publokationen/729/HS_USA.doc+peter+dale+sukarno+1955+election&hl=en&ct=clnk&cd=15.

Herman, E. (1992). *Beyond Hypocrisy: Decoding the News in an Age of Propaganda*. Montreal: Black Rose Books.

Herman, H., S. (1997, September). *Pol Pot and Kissinger: On War Criminality and impunity*. Retrieved from Z Magazine Web Site: http://www.zmag.org/zmag/articles/hermansept97.htm.

Herman, E., S., and Chomsky, N. (1988). *Manufacturing Consent: The Political Economy of the Mass Media*. New York: Pantheon Books.

Herman, E. (2001, November 9). *Genocide as Collateral Damage, But With Sincere Regrets*. Retrieved from the Znet Website: http://www.Zmag.org/Sustainers/content/2001-11/09herman.cfm.

Hersh, M. (1983). *The Price of Power: Kissinger in the Nixon Whitehouse*. New York: Simon & Shuster, Inc.

History of the U.N. (2000). *Basic Facts About the United Nations*. Retrieved from Web Site: http://www.un.org/aboutun/history.htm.

Holland, J. (2005, October 5). *Iraq and Oil-for-food: The Real Story*. Retrieved from Global Policy Forum Website: http://www.globalpolicy.org/security/sanction/iraq1/oilforfood/2005/1005realstory.htm.

Huck, J. (2003, January, issue #50). *Covert War in Guatemala*. Press for Conversion, pp. 14-15. Retrieved from Web Site: www.coat.ncf.ca/our_magazine/links/issue50/files/50_14-15.pdf.

Human Rights Watch. (2001). *Human Rights Developments in Guatemala*. Retrieved from Web Site: https://www.hrw.org/wr2k1/americas/guatemala.html.

Human Rights Watch. (2001, October). *Cluster Bombs in Afghanistan*. Retrieved from Web Site: http://www.hrw.org/backgrounder/arms/cluster-bck1031.htm.

Human Rights Watch. (2002, January). *Background Paper on Geneva Conventions and Persons Held by U.S. Forces*. Retrieved from Web Site: http://www.hrw.org/backgrounder/usa/pow-bck.htm.

Human Rights Watch. (2002, August). *Guatemala: Political Violence Unchecked.* Retrieved from Web Site: http://hrw.org/press/2002/08/guatemission.htm.

Human Rights Watch. (2003). *U.S. Using Cluster Munitions in Iraq.* Retrieved from Web Site: http://www.hrw.org/press/04/us040103.htm.

Humphrey, H,. H. (1975, March 21). *Senate Committee on Foreign Relations Report on Supplemental Assistance for Cambodia.* Retrieved from Web Site: http://www.vietnam.ttu.edu/star/images/239/2390214003.pdf.

Immerman, R., H. (1982). *The CIA in Guatemala: The Foreign Policy of Intervention.* Austin: University of Texas Press.

Indira, R. (2006, February 17). *Indonesia: The Crimes against Humanity of 1965 and their Impact on Today's Indonesia.* Retrieved from Web Site: http://www.hrsolidarity.net/mainfile.php/2005vol15no06/2464/?print=yes.

International Action Center. (n.d.). *Sanctions Violate International Law.* Retrieved from Web Site: http://www.iacenter.org/sanction.htm.

International Action Center. (2003, April 2). *The World Stands Together Against War.* Retrieved from Web Site: http://www.iacenter.org/iraq_watch.htm.

International Atomic Energy Agency: Iraq Nuclear Verification Office. (2002, November 27). *IAEA's Mandate in Iraq.* Retrieved from Web Site: http://www.iaea.org/worldatom/Programmes/ActionTeam/.

International Court of Justice. (1997, February 28). *Advisory Opinion in the Nuclear Weapons Cases: A First Appraisal.* Retrieved from Web Site: http://www.icrc.org/Web/Eng/siteeng0.nsf/html/57jNFT.

International Law Commission. (1950). *Principles of the Nuremberg Tribunal.* Retrieved from Web Site: http://deoxy.org/wc/wc-nurem.htm.

International Red Cross. (n.d.). *International Humanitarian Law.* Retrieved from Web Site: http://www.redcross.lv/en/conventions.htm.

Iraq Body Count Project. (2003, November). *How Many Civilians were Killed by Cluster Bombs*. Retrieved from Web Site: http://www.iraqbodycount.net/bodycount.htm.

Iraq Body Count Project. (2007, February). *Iraq Body Count*. Retrieved from Web Site: http://www.iraqbodycount.net/bodycount.htm.

Jardine, M. (1995). *East Timor: Genocide in Paradise*. Tucson (AZ): Odonian Press.

Jayaprakash, N., D. (2001, October 25). *Hiroshima to New York*. Retrieved from the Counterpunch Website: http://www.counterpunch.org/jayaprakash1.html.

Johnson, D. (1976). *Gestapu: The CIA's "Track Two" in Indonesia*. Retrieved from Web Site: http://wwwhartfoed-hwp.com/archives/54b/033.html.

Joint Resolution of Both Houses of Congress. (1973, November 7). *War Powers Resolution* (Public Law 93-148). Retrieved from Web Site: http://www.usconstitution.com/WarPowersResolution.htm.

Kiernan, B. (2002). *The Pol Pot Regime: Race, Power, and Genocide in Cambodia under the Khmer Rouge, 1975 – 79*. New Haven (CT): Yale University Press.

Kiljunen, K. (ed.). (1982). *The Report of the Kampuchea Inquiry Commission*. London: Zed Books.

Kobrak, P. (1999). *Organizing and Repression in the University of San Carlos, 1944 to 1996*. Retrieved from the American Association for the Advancement of Sciences' Website: http://shr.aaas.org/guatemala/ciidh/org_rep/english/part2_5.html.

Kolko, G. (1988). *Confronting the Third World: United States Foreign Policy 1945-1980*. Toronto: Random House of Canada Limited.

Kutz, C. (2000). *Complicity: Ethics and Law for a Collective Age*. Cambridge: Cambridge University Press.

Lee, R., A. (2000). *Warfare and Conflict Between Kosovar Albanians and Serbs since 1912.* Retrieved from the History Guy's Web Site: www.historyguy.com/kosovar_serb_warfare.html.

Lee, G., Y. (n.d.). *Refugees from Laos: Historical Background and Causes.* Retrieved from website: http://wwwhmongnet.org/hmong-au/refugee.htm.

Levich, J. (2003, May 13). *Democracy Comes to Iraq.* Petrolia (CA): Counterpunch Magazine. Retrieved from Web Site: http://www.counterpunch.org/levich05132003.html.

Linder, D. (n.d.). *Charter of the International Military Tribunal.* Retrieved from the University of Missouri-Kansas City Law School Web Site: http://www.law.umkc/faculty/projects/ftrials/nuremberg/nuremberg.htm.

Linder, D. (n.d.). *The Nuremberg Trials: A Chronology.* Retrieved from the University of Missouri-Kansas City Law School Web Site: http://www.law.umkc.edu/faculty/projects/ftrials/nuremberg/nuremberg.htm.

Long, D. (1995). *Hiroshima. Was it Necessary?* Retrieved from Web Site: http://www.douglong/hiroshima.htm.

Lyons, M., J. (1999). *World War II: A Short History.* Upper Saddle River (NJ). Prentice-Hall Inc.

Macarthur, J., R. (1992). *Second Front: Censorship and Propaganda in the Gulf War.* New York: Hill and Wang.

Mahajan, R. (2003). *Full Spectrum Dominance: U.S. Power in Iraq and Beyond.* Toronto: Hudson House.

Masri, R. (1998). Sanctions are Criminal. In B. Becker and Sara Flounders (Eds.), *Challenge to Genocide: Let Iraq Live.* (pp. 33-37). New York: International Action Center.

McPherson, A. (1996). *Guatemala, United States Assistance, and the Logic of Cold War Dependency*. Retrieved from Web Site: http://userwww. sfsu.edu/~epf/1996/guat.html.

Mitchel, P., R., and Schoeffel, J. (Eds.). (2002). *Understanding Power: The Indispensable Chomsky.* New York: The New Press.

Model, D. (2005). *Lying for Empire: How to Commit War Crimes with a Straight Face.* Monroe (ME): Common Courage Press.

Möise, E., E. (1998, November 4). *The First Indochina War.* Retrieved from Clemson University Law School Web Site: http://hubcap. clemson.edu/~eemoise/viet3.htm.

National Security Archives. (1970, December 9). *Taped conversation between Kissinger and Nixon on the bombing of Cambodia 8:50p. m.* Retrieved from Web Site: www.gwu.edu/~nsarchiv/NSAEBB/ NSAEBB123/Box%2029,%20File%202,%20Kissinger%20%96%.

National Security Archive. (1970, December 9). *Taped conversation between Kissinger and General Haig about bombing of Cambodia.* Retrieved from Web Site: http://www.gwu.edu/~nsarchiv/NSAEEB/ NSAEEB123/Box%2029,%20File%202,% 20Kissinger%20%96% 20Haig,%201970%208,50%20pm%20106-10pd.

National Security Council. (1963, October 29). *Memorandum of Conference with the President. Retrieved from* http://www.gwu.edu/ `nsarchiv/NSAEBB101/un19.pdf.

Office of the United Nations High Commissioner for Human Rights. (2002). *Geneva Conventions Relative to the Protection of Civilian Persons in the Time of War.* Retrieved from the United Nations Web Site: http://www.unhchr.ch/htm/menu3/b/92.htm.

Owen, T. and Kiernan, B. (2006, December 7). *Bombs Over Cambodia.* Retrieved from Z Magazine Web Site: http://www.zmag.org/content/ showarticle.cfm?ItemID=11571.

Oziewicz, E. (2004, January 9). *U.S. Exaggerated Iraqi Threat.* Toronto: The Globe and Mail.

Parenti, M. (1996). *Dirty Truths: Reflections on Politics, Media, Ideology, Conspiracy, Ethnic Life and Class Power.* San Francisco: City Light Books.

Parry, R. (1999, May 27). *Reagan & Guatemala's death files.* Retrieved from Consortiumnews Web Site: http://www.hartford-hwp.com/archives/45/272.html.

Parry, R. (2003, November 13). *Iraq: Quicksand & Blood.* Retrieved from Consortiumnews Web Site: http://consortiumnews.com/Print/2004/100604.html.

Parry, R. (2005). *History of Guatemala's Death Squads.* Retrieved from Consortiumnews Website: http://consortiumnews.com/2005/011005.html.

Paul, J., Rempel, J., Patterson, J., Megally, H., Moavero, T., and Miller, C. (2000, March 22). *Open Letter to the Security Council Concerning the Humanitarian Situation in Iraq.* Retrieved from Web Site: http://www.globalpolicy.org/security/sanction/iraq1/ngolettr.htm.

PBS Television Network. (1987, March 4). *President Reagan's Speech About Iran Contra.* Retrieved from Web Site: http://pbs.org/wgbh/amex/reagan/filmmore/reference/primary/irancontra.html.

Pease, L. (1996, Sept-Oct). *JFK, Indonesia, CIA and Freeport Sulphur.* Retrieved from the Probe website: http://www.webcam.com/~lpease/collections/hidden/freeport-indonesia.htm.

Perkins, J. (2004). *Confessions of an Economic Hit Man.* New York: Plume.

Peurifoy, J., E. (1954). *Communist Aggression in Guatemala, 1954.* Report to the Subcommittee on Latin America of the Select Committee on Communist Aggression (U.S. House of Representatives). Retrieved from Web Site: http://www.wadsworth.com/history_features/ext/ap/chapter28/chapter28.3.html.

Pilger, J. (2003, September 23). *Lies and More Lies*. Znet Commentaries. Retrieved from Web Site: http://www.zmag.org/sustainers/content/2003-23/01pilger.cfm.

Plesch, D. (2003, February 5). *U.S. Claims Dismissed by Blix*. London: The Guardian. Retrieved from Web Site: http://www.guardian.co.uk/Iraq/story/0,2763,889135,00.html.

Prevent Genocide International. (n.d.) *The Legal Definition of Genocide*. Retrieved from Website: http://www.preventgenocide.org/genocide/officialtext-printerfriendly.htm.

Public Papers of the Presidents. (August 9, 1945). *Radio Report to the American People on the Potsdam Conference – August 9, 1945*. Retrieved from Web Site: http://www.presidency.ucsb.edu/site/docs/index_ppus.php.

Rampton, S., and Stauber, J. (2003). *Weapons of Mass Deception: The Use of Propaganda in Bush's War on Iraq*. New York: Penguin.

Ransom, D. (1975). *Ford Country: Building an Elite for Indonesia*. Retrieved from Website: http://www.cia-on-campus.org/internat/indo.html.

Revolution Online. (2005, December 19). *The Vietnam War: Destroying the Village in Order to Save It*. Retrieved from Web Site: http://rwor.org/a/027/vietnam-destroy-village.htm.

Risen, J. (2006). *State of War: The Secret History of the CIA and the Bush Administration*. New York: Free Press.

Ritter, S. (1999). *Endgame: Solving the Iraq Crisis*. Toronto: Simon & Shuster.

Ritter, S. (2003). *Frontier Justice: Weapons of Mass Destruction and the Bushwacking of America*. New York: Context Books.

Robinson, J., P., and Goldblat, J. (1984, May). *Chemical Warfare in the Iran-Iraq War*. Retrieved from Stockholm International Peace Research Web Site: http://projects.sipri.se/cbw/research/factsheet-1984.html.

Rogers, J. (1975, June 3). *Cambodians are Starving, Refugees Say*. Washington (DC): Washington Post.

Ronayne, P. (2001). *Never Again: The United States and the Prevention and Punishment of Genocide since the Holocaust*. Lanham (MD): Rowman & Littlefield Publishers, INC.

Rummel, R., J. (1997). *Statistics of Democide:Statistics of Vietnamese Democide*. Retrieved from Web Site: http://www.hawaii.edu/powerkills/SOD.CHAP6.HTM.

Salinger, P., and Laurent, E. (1991). *Secret Dossier: The Hidden Agenda Behind the Gulf War*. New York: Penguin Books.

Sartre, J. (1996, November 15). *On Genocide*. Retrieved from Russell Vietnam War Crimes Tribunal Website: http://www.tc.umn.edu/~awalzer/Rhet1381/1381VietNam/1381OnGenocideText.html.

Scott, D. (1985). *The United States and the Overthrow of Sukarno, 1965-1967*. Retrieved from Web Site: http://www.namebase.org/scott.html.

Shafer, E., J. (2005, August). *Nuclear Risks: Necessity and Illegality*. Retrieved from the Lawyers' Committee on Nuclear Policy INC Website: http://www.lcnp.org/disarmament/necessity-illegality.htm.

Shawcross, W. (2002). *Sideshow: Kissinger, Nixon, and the Destruction of Cambodia* (2nd ed.). New York: First Cooper Square Press.

Small, D. (2002, March). *Ghosts of Genocide: The CIA, Suharto and Terrorist Culture*. Retrieved from Web Site: http://www.converge.org.nz/abc/prsp25.htm.

Smith, G. (2002, October 9). *The Silence of Bombs*. San Francisco: AlterNet. Retrieved from Web Site: http://www.alternet.org/module/printversion/14263.

Spector, R., H. (1984). *Eagles Against the Sun: The American War with Japan*. Toronto: Random House.

St. Clair, J. (2003, July 16). *Back to the Future in Guatemala*. Petrolia (CA): Counterpunch Magazine. Retrieved from Web Site: http://www.counterpunch.org/stclair07162003.html.

Streeter, S., M. (2000, November). *Interpreting the 1954 U.S. Intervention in Guatemala: Realist, Revisionist, and Postrevisionist Perspectives*. Retrieved from McMaster University History Cooperative Web Site: http://www.historycooperative.org/journals/ht/34.1/streeter.htm.

Tanter, R. (1998, July-September). *Suharto, war criminal*. Retrieved from "Inside Indonesia" Web Site: http://www.insideindonesia.org/edit55/genoc.htm.

The American War Library. (1988). *Gulf of Tonkin Notebook*. Retrieved from Web Site: http://members.aol.com/warlibrary/vwton3.htm.

The American War Library. (1988). *Notes on the Gulf of Tonkin Incident*. Retrieved from Web Site: http://members.aol.com/warlibrary/vwton2.htm.

The Odyssey: World Trek for Service and Education. (1999, February 27). *U.S. Responsibility for Guatemalan Genocide*. Retrieved from Web Site: http://www.worldtrek.org/odyssey/latin_america/022799/022799dumbnina.html.

The Pentagon. (1971). *The Pentagon Papers*. Boston: Beacon Press. Retrieved from Web Site: http://www.mthdyoke.edu/acad/intrel.htm.

Truman Presidential Library. (1945, June 18). *Minutes of Meeting Held at the White House on Monday, 18 June 1945*. Retrieved from Web

Site: http://www.trumanlibrary.org/whistlestop/study_collections/bomb/large/meeting-minutes/bmil13-5.htm.

Truman Presidential Library. (1945, August 9). *Truman's Diary Entries August 1945*. Retrieved from Web Site: http://www.trumanlibrary.org/whistlestop/study_collections/bomb/large/truman_diaries/bma3-5.htm.

UNICEF Website. (1998, April 30). *Situation Analysis of Children and Women in Iraq*. Retrieved from Web Site: http://www.unicef.org/index.php.

United Nations Human Rights Website. (2002). *Charter of the United Nations*. Retrieved from Web Site: http://193.194.138.1   90/html/menu3/b/ch-chpl.htm.

United Nations Security Council. (1990, August 6). *Resolution 661*. retrieved from Web Site: http://www.fas.org/news/un/sres/sres0661.htm.

United Nations Security Council. (1991). *All Resolutions for 1991*. Retrieved from Web Site: http://www.un.org/Docs/scres/1991/sceas91.htm.

United Nations Security Council. (1995, August 14). *Resolution 986*. Retrieved from Web Site: http://www.ibiblio.org/obl/reg.burma/archives/199607/msg00394.html.

United Nations Security Council. (2003). *Resolution 1483*. Retrieved from Web Site: http://daccessdds.un.org/doc/UNDOC/GEN/N03/368/53/PDF/N0336853.pdf?.

United Nations Security Council. (n.d.). *Security Council Resolutions*. Retrieved April 29, 2003, from Web Site: http://www.un.org/documents/scres.htm

United Nations Website. (2003, January 27). *An Update on Inspection*. Retrieved from Web Site: http://www.un.org/Depts/unmovic/Bx27.htm.

United Nations Website. (1990, September 13). *Resolution 666.* Retrieved from Web Site: http://www.un.org/documents/scres.htm.

United Nations Website. (1991, April 8). *Resolution 687.* Retrieved from Web Site: http://www.un.org/documents/scres/htm.

United Nations Website. (1998, October 6). *Report of Executive Chairmen on the activities of the Special Commission to the Security Council.* Retrieved from Web Site: http://www.un.org/Depts/unscom/sres98-920.htm.

United Overseas Chinese of Greater New York. (n.d.). *Open letter to Mr. Maurice Glele Ahanhanso (UN Special Rapporteur on Racial Discrimination).* Retrieved from Web Site: http://www.geocities.com/capitolhill/4120/unletter.html20074.

U.S. Central Intelligence Agency. (1972, February 18). *National Intelligence Estimates: Taking Stock in Cambodia.* Retrieved from Web Site: http://www.Vietnam.ttu.edu/star/images/041/04113173005.pdf.

U.S. Central Intelligence Agency. (1974, April, 11). *National Intelligence Estimates: The Short Term Prospects for Cambodia Through August 1974 (document: 0001166469).* Retrieved from the CIA Web Site: http://www.foia.cia.gov/.

U.S. Central Intelligence Agency. (1975, February 13). *Prospects for Cambodia through August 1975.* Retrieved from the CIA Web Site: http://www.foia.cia.gov/browse_docs.asp?.

U.S. Department of State. (1964, July 26). *Telegram from the State Department to the Embassy in Laos Regarding Proposed Bombing of Laos.* Retrieved from Web Site: http://www.mtholyoke.edu/intrel/pentagon3/doc163.htm.

U.S. Department of State. (1964, July 27). *Telegram from the Embassy in Laos to the State Department Regarding Proposed Bombing in Laos.* Retrieved from Web Site: http://www.mtholyoke.edu/acad/intrel/pentagon3/doc164.htm.

U.S. Department of State. (1964, August 17). *Cable from the U.S. Embassy in Laos to the State Department on Proposal to Initiate Bombing in Laos.* Retrieved from Web Site: http://www.mtholyoke.edu/acad/intrel/pentagon3/doc178.htm.

U.S. Department of State. (1964-1968). *CIA Memorandum for State Department.* Retrieved from Web Site: http://www.state.gov/r/pa/ho/frus/johnson1b/xxvi/4442.htm.

U.S. Department of State. (1964-1968). *State Memorandum for CIA.* Retrieved from Web Site: http://www.state.gov/pa/ho/frus/johnson1b/xxvi/4446.htm.

U.S. Department of State. (1964-1968). *Sukarno's Confrontation With the United States.* Retrieved from Web Site: http://www.state.gov/r/pa/ho/frus/johnson1b/xxvi/4443.htm.

U.S. Department of State. (1964-1968). *Foreign Relations 1964-1968, Volume XXVI, Indonesia.* Retrieved from Web Site: http://www.state.gov/r/pa/ho/frus/johnson1b/xxvi/4435.htm.

U.S. Department of State. (1967, October 23). *Guatemala: A Counter-Insurgency Running Wild?* Retrieved from Web Site: http://www2.gwu.edu/~nsarchiv/NSAEBB32/05-01.htm.

U.S. Department of State. (1964-1968). *Foreign Relations, Volume XXVI, Indonesia; Philippines.* Retrieved from Web Site: http://www.state.gov/r/pa//ho/frus/johnson/xxvi/4445.htm.

U.S. Department of State. (1964-1968). *The United States and Suharto.* Retrieved from Web Site: http://www.state.gov/r/pa/ho/frus/johnson1b/xxvi/4422.htm.

U.S. Department of State. (1968) *Guatemala and Counter-terror.* Retrieved from Web Site: http://www2.gwu.edu/~nsarchiv/NSAEBB/NSAEBB32/08-01.htm.

U.S. Vientiane Embassy. (1974, April 26). *Telegram from U.S. Embassy to State Department*. Retrieved from Web Site: http://vientiane. usembassy.gov/.

Vltchek, A. (2006, November 14). *"Secret War" Still Killing Thousands*. Retrieved from the Worldpress Web Site: http://www.worldpress.org/ print_article.cfm?article_id=2682&dont=yes.

Weisman, J. (2006, September 9). *Iraq's Alleged Al-Qaeda Ties Were Disputed Before the War*. Washington: Washington Post.

Wells-Dang, A. (2002, August). *Agent Orange in Laos: Documentary Evidence*. Retrieved from Web Site: http://www.ffrd.org/Agent_ Orange/laosao.htm.

Zaidi, S. (1994). *War, Sanctions, and Humanitarian Assistance: The Case of Iraq 1990-1993*. Retrieved from Web Site: http://www.ippnw.org/ MGS/VIN3Zaidi.html.

Zeese, K. (2006, May 10). *The Corporate Takeover of Iraq's Economy*. Petrolia (CA): Counterpunch Magazine. Retrieved from Web Site: http://www.counterpunch.org/zeese05102006.html.

Zobecki, D., T. (Ed.). (2002). *Vietnam: A Reader*. New York: I Books Inc.

Printed in the United States
120618LV00003B/224/P

9 781434 375162